INTERNATIONAL HUMAN RIGHTS

IN A NUTSHELL

SECOND EDITION

By

THOMAS BUERGENTHAL

Lobingier Professor of Comparative and International Law
The George Washington University Law School
Member, United Nations Human Rights Committee
Judge, Inter-American Court of Human Rights (1979–91)

ST. PAUL, MINN.
WEST PUBLISHING CO.
1995

 TEXT IS PRINTED ON 10% POST CONSUMER RECYCLED PAPER

 PRINTED WITH SOY INK™

To the memory of my mother,
Gerda Bürgenthal

*

PREFACE

The second edition of this book follows the basic format of the first. The purpose of the book remains the same: it is designed to serve both as a self-contained introduction to the international law of human rights and to complement other course materials by providing the reader with a concise overview of human rights norms and the institutional context within which they evolve. The book has grown significantly in size, however, to take account of many new developments in the field.

The first edition was published in 1988. The world has changed quite dramatically in the seven years that have elapsed since then. The Cold War and the Soviet empire came to an end during that period and with it the ideological conflict between East and West which had divided the international community for almost five decades. Apartheid was abolished in South Africa and replaced with a multi-racial government. The geopolitical map of Europe underwent a dramatic transformation comparable to that which followed the First World War and democratically-elected governments consolidated their hold over Latin America.

Although these events have neither significantly depoliticized the manner in which the international community deals with human rights issues nor dramatically improved the human rights climate in many other parts of the world, they have contributed to an international dialogue on the subject that is more serious than in the past and devoid of the ideological posturing and sloganeering so characteristic of the pre-1990 period. With the demise of the ideological blocs that tended to provide cover for human rights violators, some of these states are now more responsive to international pressure to improve their human rights record and less likely to prevent international action to promote human rights. Of course, there are still many states which violate human rights with impunity and reject international measures to strengthen the ability of the international community to deal with violations. Their numbers, influence and ability to block major human rights initiatives have decreased significantly however since the end of the Cold War. All of these factors have permitted the international community in recent years to strengthen the normative and institutional framework for dealing with human rights problems.

The increased size of this book is attributable to the expansion of international human rights norms and institutions that the above developments have produced. Some chapters had to be extensively revised and whole new sections added. This is true in particular of the chapters on the United Nations and Europe. The chapters dealing with the United States and the inter-American system also had to be substantially expanded. In short, the revisions take account of many developments and institutions that are new or that have gained greater importance since the publication of the first edition. Readers needing additional information on specific topics will here also find more extensive references to scholarly writings and primary sources than were provided before.

This book is dedicated to the memory of my mother, Gerda Bürgenthal, whose courage and resilience enabled her to survive the Nazi concentration camps of Auschwitz and Ravensbrück with her humanity, dignity and sense of humor unimpaired. She inspired me by her example to believe that the bonds which unite the human family compel all of us to oppose oppression whosoever might be its victims.

THOMAS BUERGENTHAL

Washington, D.C.
May 1995.

*

ACKNOWLEDGMENT

Many individuals contributed to making this edition possible, but no one deserves as much credit as Lynn Haaland and Shehernaz Joshi. Ms. Haaland's work as my research assistant, critic, and sounding board greatly improved the quality of this book. Her enthusiasm, commitment and high professional standards made my task so much easier and saved me from many a mistake. Despite her principal position as Executive Coordinator of the International Legal Studies Program I direct at the George Washington Law School, Ms. Joshi not only transcribed the different versions of the manuscript and made numerous valuable suggestions, but also assumed many additional obligations in the office to give me more time to work on the book. She is a truly outstanding collaborator. I am profoundly grateful to both Lynn and Shehernaz.

My special thanks go to Dr. Jean-Marie Henckaerts and Ms. Lauren Ambinder for their research assistance and many insightful suggestions. I am also grateful to the students in my human rights classes who have over the years been subjected to different versions of this book. Their perceptive questions and comments have helped to improve its quality and utility.

Mr. Paul Zarins, our International and Comparative Law Librarian, has my profound appreciation

IX

for his invaluable contributions to this book and my research activities in general. I feel truly blessed to be able to count on the services of this outstanding professional. My special thanks also go to Ms. Jahna Hartwig for putting her computer skills at my disposal and for the numerous ways in which she helped me while this book was being written.

I should also like to express my appreciation to the George Washington University Law School and, in particular, to Dean Jack Friedenthal for facilitating my research and for providing me with an academic environment that encourages scholarly activities.

My wife, Peggy Buergenthal, contributed to this and the first edition of this book in many important ways. She has a wonderful gift of spotting obfuscation and sentences that are confusing or misleading, and her editing skills are truly admirable. I have shamelessly exploited these attributes as well as her patience and understanding. She knows how much I appreciate her and her unique contributions to this book.

OUTLINE

CHAPTER 2. THE UNITED NATIONS HUMAN RIGHTS SYSTEM

OUTLINE

CHAPTER 3. THE EUROPEAN SYSTEM FOR THE PROTECTION OF HUMAN RIGHTS

CHAPTER 4. THE INTER–AMERICAN HUMAN RIGHTS SYSTEM

CHAPTER 7. THE U.S. AND INTERNATIONAL HUMAN RIGHTS

CHAPTER 8. NON–GOVERNMENTAL HUMAN RIGHTS ORGANIZATIONS

TABLE OF CASES

References are to Pages

A

TABLE OF CASES

B

C

D

E

F

N

P

R

T

U

V

W

*

INTERNATIONAL HUMAN RIGHTS

IN A NUTSHELL

SECOND EDITION

*

CHAPTER 1

HISTORICAL ANTECEDENTS OF INTERNATIONAL HUMAN RIGHTS LAW

I. INTRODUCTION

This chapter describes the principal historical antecedents of the modern international law of human rights. As used in this book, the international law of human rights is defined as the law that deals with the protection of individuals and groups against violations by governments of their internationally guaranteed rights, and with the promotion of these rights. This branch of the law is sometimes also referred to as international protection of human rights or international human rights law. Although scholars might disagree over whether one or the other of these labels is more appropriate, here they are used interchangeably.

II. PRE–WORLD WAR II LAW

§ 1–1. Introduction

International human rights law has its historical antecedents in a number of international legal doctrines and institutions. *See generally* L. Henkin, *The Age of Rights* 13 (1990). The most important of these are humanitarian intervention, state responsibility for injuries to aliens, protection of minorities, the Mandates and Minorities Systems of the League of Nations, and international humanitarian law. To the extent that these doctrines and institutions survive today, they may be said to form an integral part of contemporary international human rights law. We deal with them in this chapter principally for the purpose of exploring the role they played in the development of that law.

§ 1–2. Human Rights and Traditional International Law

Traditional international law was defined as the law governing relations between nation-states exclusively. This meant that only states were subjects of and had legal rights under international law. The traditional definition was expanded somewhat after World War I to include various newly-created intergovernmental organizations which were acknowledged to have some very limited rights under international law. Individual human beings were not deemed to have international legal rights as such; they were said to be objects rather than subjects of international law. To the extent that states had any international legal obligations relating to individuals, they were deemed to be obligations owed to the states whose nationality the individuals possessed. *See, e.g.*, L. Oppenheim, *International Law: A Treatise*, vol. 1, at 362 (2d ed. 1912).

These theories about the nature of international law compelled the conclusion that the manner in which a state treated its own nationals was not regulated by international law and, consequently, did not affect the rights of other states. Because international law did not apply to human rights violations committed by a state against individuals having its nationality, that entire subject matter was deemed to fall within the exclusive domestic jurisdiction of each state, barring other states from interceding or intervening on behalf of the nationals of any state which maltreated them. There were exceptions to this rule of non-intervention. They are dealt with in the sections that follow.

§ 1–3. Humanitarian Intervention

The doctrine of humanitarian intervention, as expounded by Hugo Grotius in the 17th century and other early international lawyers, recognized as lawful the use of force by one or more states to stop the maltreatment by a state of its own nationals when that conduct was so brutal and large-scale as to shock the conscience of the community of nations. *See* E.C. Stowell, *Intervention in International Law* 53 (1921); L. Sohn & T. Buergenthal, *International Protection of Human Rights* 137 (1973). This doctrine was greatly misused in the past and frequently served as a pretext for the occupation or invasion of weaker countries. Brownlie, "Humanitarian Intervention," *in* J.N. Moore (ed.), *Law and Civil War in the Modern World* 217 (1974). Nevertheless, the doctrine of humanitarian intervention was the first to give expression to the proposition that there were some limits to the freedom states enjoyed under international law in dealing with their own nationals. *See generally* F. Teson, *Humanitarian Intervention: An Inquiry Into Law and Morality* (1988). Contemporary arguments about the rights of international organizations or groups of states to use force, if necessary, to put an end to massive violations of human rights have been justified at times by reference to this doctrine. *See, e.g.,* Lillich, "Intervention to Protect Human Rights," 15 McGill L.J. 205 (1969). *But see* Franck & Rodley, "After Bangladesh: The Law of Humanitarian Intervention by Military Force," 67 Am. J. Int'l L.275 (1973), who question the soundness of this argument as far as unilateral military action by individual states is concerned.

The United Nations Security Council is today increasingly taking action to deal with large-scale violations of human rights by authorizing enforcement measures under the powers that Chapter VII of the UN Charter confers on it. This charter applies to situations involving a "threat to the peace, breach of the peace, or act of aggression." *UN Charter*, art. 39. Such action has been taken by the Security Council in decisions relating to the Kurds in Iraq, the former Yugoslavia and Haiti. Because the resolutions authorizing these measures are ambiguous in terms of the legal norms and factual considerations giving rise to them, it is premature to assert that the Security Council has adopted a modern version of the doctrine of collective humanitarian intervention. Considering, however, that its recent decisions contain important characteristics traditionally associated with this doctrine, it appears that the Council is moving in that direction. *See* Delbrück, "A more Effective International Law or a New World Law?—Some Aspects of the Development of International Law in a Changing International System," 68 Ind. L. J. 705, 707 (1993). *See also* Hutchinson, "Restoring Hope: U.N. Security Council Resolutions for Somalia and an Expanded Doctrine of Humanitarian Intervention," 34 Harv. Int'l L.J. 624 (1993). *But see* Farer, "Human Rights in Law's Empire: The Jurisprudence War," 85 Am. J. Int'l L. 117 (1991); Higgins, "International Law and the Avoidance, Containment and Resolution of Disputes," 230 Recueil des Cours 324–28 (1991). The establishment by the Security Council of the International Tribunal for the Former Yugoslavia to punish those responsible for crimes against humanity, genocide and war crimes in the armed conflict in that region may also be seen as a modern form of collective humanitarian intervention for dealing with the massive human rights violations that have been and continue to be committed there. *See* Meron, "War Crimes in Yugoslavia and the Development of International Law," 88 Am. J. Int'l L. 78, 79 (1994).

§ 1–4. Early Human Rights Treaties

It is a well established principle of international law that a state may limit its sovereignty by treaty

and thus internationalize a subject that is otherwise
not regulated by international law. For example, if
one state concludes a treaty with another state in
which they agree to treat their nationals in a humane manner and to accord them certain human
rights, they have to the extent of that agreement
internationalized that particular subject. *See* Henkin, "Human Rights and 'Domestic Jurisdiction',"
in T. Buergenthal (ed.), *Human Rights, International Law and the Helsinki Accord* 21 (1977). As
between these two states, neither can henceforth
lawfully assert that how it treats its own nationals
is a subject that falls exclusively within its domestic
jurisdiction. Advisory Opinion on Nationality Decrees Issued in Tunis and Morocco, P.C.I.J., Ser. B,
No. 4 (1923).

This principle has been extremely important in
the development of international human rights law
and the gradual internationalization of human
rights. Buergenthal, "Domestic Jurisdiction, Intervention and Human Rights," *in* P. Brown & D.
MacLean (eds.), *Human Rights and U.S. Foreign
Policy* 111 (1979). Although the internationalization process continues to this day every time a
human rights treaty enters into force, it began in
the 19th century with the conclusion of treaties to
ban the slave trade and international agreements to
protect Christian minorities in the Ottoman (Turkish) Empire. *See, e.g.,* Treaty of Paris of 30 March
1856; Treaty of Berlin of 13 July 1878. These
treaties were relied upon by the states comprising
the Concert of Europe to intercede diplomatically

and at times even to intervene militarily on behalf of the Christian populations in the Turkish Empire. *See* Sohn & Buergenthal, *supra*, at 143–92. The Treaty of Berlin of 1878 is of particular interest because of the special legal status it accorded to some religious groups; it also served as a model for the Minorities System that was subsequently established within the framework of the League of Nations.

§ 1–5. The League of Nations

The Covenant of the League of Nations, the treaty which in 1920 established the League and served as its constitution, contained no general provisions dealing with human rights. The notion that human rights should be internationally protected had not yet gained acceptance by the community of nations, nor was it seriously contemplated by those who drafted that treaty. The Covenant did, however, contain two provisions (Articles 22 and 23) that bear on the development of international human rights law. The League also played an important role in helping with the implementation of post-World War I treaties for the protection of minorities.

1. The Mandates System

Article 22 of the Covenant established the Mandates System of the League. This provision applied only to the former colonies of the states that had lost the First World War. It transformed these colonies into League Mandates to be administered as such by the victorious powers. The latter agreed with the League to administer these territories pursuant to "the principle that the well-being and development of [the native] peoples form a sacred trust of civilisation...." The Mandatory Powers also undertook to provide the League with annual reports bearing on the discharge of their responsibilities. These reports were reviewed by the Mandates Commission of the League.

The Mandates Commission gradually acquired more power in supervising the administration of the Mandates and the manner in which the native populations were treated. *See generally,* Sohn & Buergenthal, *supra,* at 337–73. The dissolution of the League ended this development. In its stead, the United Nations established the UN Trusteeship System, which was entrusted with supervisory power over the remaining Mandates and other non-self-governing territories. Among the last of these territories to gain independence (in 1990) was Namibia. It had been administered by South Africa under the South–West Africa Mandate. South Africa had for many years refused to comply with U.N. General Assembly and Security Council resolutions calling on it to relinquish control over Namibia. The bitter dispute between the U.N. and South Africa concerning Namibia generated considerable litigation before the International Court of Justice. *See* Advisory Opinion on the International Status of South–West Africa, 1950 I.C.J. Rep. 128; Advisory Opinion on Voting Procedure, 1955 I.C.J. Rep. 67; Advisory Opinion on Hearings of Petitioners, 1956

I.C.J. Rep. 23; Ethiopia and Liberia v. South Africa (Preliminary Objections), 1962 I.C.J. Rep. 319; Ethiopia and Liberia v. South Africa (Judgment), 1966 I.C.J. Rep. 6; Advisory Opinion on the Legal Consequences for States of the Continued Presence of South Africa in Namibia, 1971 I.C.J. Rep. 16. For an analysis of these cases and the relevant resolution, *see* L.B. Sohn, *Rights in Conflict: The United Nations and South Africa* 24–31 and 148–49 (1994). *See also* Schwelb, "The International Court of Justice and the Human Rights Clauses of the Charter," 66 Am. J. Int'l L. 337 (1972).

2. International Labor Standards

Article 23 of the League of Nations Covenant concerned human rights in that it dealt, *inter alia*, with questions relating to the "fair and humane conditions of labour for men, women, and children." It also envisaged the establishment of international organizations to promote this objective. That function was assumed by the International Labor Organization, which came into being at about the same time as the League. The ILO survived the League and is now one of the Specialized Agencies of the United Nations. *See* § 2–25, *infra*. The legislative activities and the supervisory machinery established by the ILO to promote and monitor compliance with international labor standards have over the years made important contributions to the improvement of the conditions of work and the development of international human rights law. *See* C.W. Jenks, *Human Rights and International Labour Standards*

(1960); E.A. Landy, *The Effectiveness of International Supervision: Thirty Years of I.L.O. Experience* (1966); V. Leary, *International Labour Conventions and National Law* (1981). *But see* Cordova, "Some Reflections on the Overproduction of International Labor Standards," 14 Comp. Labor L. 138 (1993).

3.   *The Minorities System*

The League of Nations also played a very important role in developing an international system for the protection of minorities. *See generally,* Sohn & Buergenthal, *supra,* at 213. This subject was not regulated by the Covenant. Instead, the League derived its powers in this field from a series of treaties concluded after World War I. One consequence of that war was a substantial redrawing of the political map of Europe and of the Middle East. A number of new states came into being and others regained their independence. Some of these countries, notably Poland, Czechoslovakia, Hungary, Yugoslavia, Bulgaria, Albania and Rumania, included pockets of ethnic, linguistic and religious minorities. These minorities had good historical reasons for fearing that the new political order would threaten their cultural survival. The governments of the victor nations—the so-called Principal Allied and Associated Powers—insisted therefore that the new states conclude special treaties for the protection of their ethnic, linguistic and religious minorities. *See generally* H. Hannum, *Autonomy, Sovereignty and Self–Determination* 51 (1990).

The first treaty to establish this protective regime was the Treaty between the Principal Allied and Associated Powers and Poland, signed at Versailles on June 29, 1919. It served as a model for the other treaties. In them, the states to which the minorities system applied undertook not to discriminate against members of the protected minorities and to grant them special rights necessary for the preservation of their ethnic, religious or linguistic integrity, including the right to the official use of their languages, the right to maintain their schools, and the right to practice their religions. To ensure compliance, the treaties contained provisions similar to Article 12 of the Polish treaty, which declared that "Poland agrees that the stipulations in the foregoing Articles, so far as they affect persons belonging to racial, religious or linguistic minorities, constitute obligations of international concern and shall be placed under the guarantee of the League of Nations."

The League of Nations agreed to serve as guarantor of the obligations that the parties assumed in these treaties. It exercised that function by developing a system for dealing with petitions by minorities charging violations of their rights. That system was relatively effective and quite advanced for its time. The petitions were reviewed by a Committee of Three of the League Council, the states concerned were given an opportunity to present their views and, when appropriate, the Permanent Court of International Justice was asked to render advisory opinions on disputed questions of law. *See generally* J. Stone, *International Guarantees of Minority Rights* (1934). *See also* Advisory Opinion on Minority Schools in Albania, P.C.I.J., Ser. A/B, No. 64 (1935); Advisory Opinion on Access to German Minority Schools in Upper Silesia, P.C.I.J., Ser. A/B, No. 40 (1931); Advisory Opinion on Greco–Bulgarian "Communities," P.C.I.J., Ser. B, No. 17 (1930). In addition, the League served as guarantor for certain special political arrangements in which the rights of minorities were also protected. *See, e.g.,* Advisory Opinion on the Consistency of Certain Danzig Legislative Decrees with the Constitution of the Free City, P.C.I.J., Ser. A/B, No. 65 (1935), a fascinating case that examines the meaning of "law" in the context of the Nazi takeover of Danzig.

Although some isolated minorities arrangements of the League era survive to this day, the League's minorities system as such died with it. *See generally* T. Modeen, *The International Protection of National Minorities in Europe* (1969); I.L. Claude, *National Minorities: An International Problem* (1955). It is important to recognize nevertheless that some modern international human rights institutions bear considerable resemblance to the institutions that were first developed by the League for the administration of the minorities system.

For many years after their establishment, the United Nations and other international organizations showed very little interest in the protection of minorities, focusing instead on individual rights, non-discrimination and equal protection. With the end of the Cold War and the rise of nationalism in various parts of the world, the international community has again begun to focus on the development of international norms and institutions designed to protect the rights of minorities. Some of the actions taken in this regard within the framework of the United Nations, the Council of Europe, and the Organization of Security and Cooperation in Europe are discussed in § 3–28, *infra*.

§ 1–6. State Responsibility for Injury to Aliens

Traditional international law recognized very early in its development that states had an obligation to treat foreign nationals in a manner that conformed to certain minimum standards of civilization or justice. This obligation was deemed to be owed to the state of the individual's nationality because human beings as such did not have rights under international law. Hence, when individuals were subjected by a foreign government to treatment that violated international law, only the state of their nationality was considered to have a cause of action under international law against the offending state. Mavrommatis Palestine Concessions (Jurisdiction), P.C.I.J., Ser. A, No. 2 (1934). When damages were awarded, however, the successful state usually compensated its nationals for the damages they had sustained, although international law did not require such payment.

Disputes involving claims under the law of state responsibility for injuries to aliens were commonly resolved through diplomatic negotiations between the governments concerned. Sometimes the failure of the offending state to comply with demands for satisfaction, usually the payment of compensation, led to the use of force. *See, e.g.,* Finlay, Pacifico and Other British Claims against Greece, Sohn & Buergenthal, *supra,* at 40. More often than not, however, the disputes were resolved by diplomatic means, international arbitration or adjudication. For the relevant legal doctrines, *see* E.M. Borchard, *The Diplomatic Protection of Citizens Abroad or the Law of International Claims* (1915); C.F. Amerasinghe, *State Responsibility for Injuries to Aliens* (1967).

The legal fiction that the injury suffered by the alien abroad was an injury to the state of the alien's nationality preserved the notion that only states were subjects of international law. It also had the negative consequence of leaving stateless persons and those who possessed the nationality of the offending state without protection. No state had standing to espouse their claims because no state could validly claim that its rights were affected when these human beings were injured.

The substantive law applicable to claims by states on behalf of their nationals was derived for the most part from so-called "general principles of law recognized by civilized nations." *See* I.C.J. Statute, art. 38 (1)(c). These principles had their source in natural law and various domestic legal doctrines applicable to the treatment of individuals. International arbitrators and tribunals drew on this body of law and doctrine to give substance to concepts such as "denial of justice," "minimum standards of justice," etc. When modern international law came to recognize that individuals, irrespective of their nationality, should enjoy certain basic human rights, the substantive principles of the law of state responsibility provided a reservoir of norms that could be drawn upon in codifying international human rights law. Today, because of the dramatic evolution and extensive codification of human rights law, human rights law nourishes the law of state responsibility. Here it is important to remember, as the *Restatement of the Foreign Relations Law of the United States (Third)* (1987) [hereinafter cited as *Restatement (Third)*] aptly notes, that "the difference in history and in jurisprudential origins between the older law of responsibility for injury to aliens and the newer law of human rights should not conceal their essential affinity and their convergence." Introductory Note to Part VII, *id.*, vol. 2, at 145. The *Restatement* goes on to point out that "as the law of human rights developed, the law of responsibility for injury to aliens, as applied to natural persons, began to refer to violations of their 'fundamental human rights,' and states began to invoke contemporary norms of human rights as the basis for claims for injury to their nationals." *Id.*, at 1058. *See generally* F.V. Garcia–Amador, L. Sohn & R. Baxter, *Recent Codification of the Law of State Responsibility for Injuries to Aliens* (1974).

Notwithstanding the growth of human rights law, the law of state responsibility for injuries to aliens continues to play an important role in contemporary diplomatic relations. States still espouse the claims of their nationals, be they natural persons or corporations. Today these actions tend to be based more often than not on rights and obligations spelled out in the growing number of bilateral and multilateral investment treaties and in so-called treaties of friendship, commerce and navigation. These treaties frequently confer jurisdiction on existing or *ad hoc* international tribunals to resolve disputes relating to the application or interpretation of these agreements and thus provide an international remedy which may in some cases be more effective than available human rights procedures. For a recent case involving a bilateral treaty between the United States and Italy, *see* Case Concerning Elettronica Sicula S.p.A. (Elsi), 1989 I.C.J. Rep. 15. Sometimes special *ad hoc* tribunals are created to deal with similar disputes. One interesting example is the Iran–United States Claims Tribunal, which was established in 1981. *See* Stewart & Sherman, "Developments at the Iran–United States Claims Tribunal: 1981–83," 24 Va. J. Int'l L. 1 (1984); Caron, "The Nature of the Iran–United States Claims Tribunal and the Evolving Structure of International Dispute Resolution," 84 Am. J. Int'l L. 104 (1990). More recently, the United Nations Security Council established the United Nations Compensation Commission to deal with individual and corporate claims against Iraq arising from its invasion of Kuwait. On this subject, see Lillich, Brower, *et al.*, "Claims against Iraq: The

UN Compensation Commission and Other Remedies," 86 Am. Soc. Int'l L. Proc. 477 (1992).

§ 1–7. Humanitarian Law

This branch of international law can today be defined as "the human rights component of the law of war." T. Buergenthal & H. Maier, *Public International Law in a Nutshell* 140 (1985). Humanitarian law is much older, however, than international human rights law. Its modern development is usually traced to a series of initiatives undertaken in the 19th century by the Swiss, who advocated the conclusion of international agreements making certain humanitarian rules applicable in the conduct of war. *See* P. Boissier, *History of the International Committee of the Red Cross: From Solferino to Tsushima* (1985). These initiatives produced the Geneva Convention of 1864, which was designed to protect medical personnel and hospital installations. It also provided that "wounded or sick combatants, to whatever nation they may belong, shall be collected and cared for." (Article 6(1).) For the text of this and other relevant instruments, see International Red Cross Handbook, published and periodically updated by the International Committee of the Red Cross. The Geneva Convention of 1864 was followed by the Hague Convention No. III of 1899, which established comparable humanitarian rules applicable to naval warfare. These treaties have been revised, amplified and modernized from time to time and now comprise a vast body of law dealing with almost all aspects of modern armed conflict.

Much of that law is today codified in the four Geneva Conventions of 1949 and the two Protocols Additional to these Conventions. *See* Dinstein, "Human Rights in Armed Conflict: International Humanitarian Law," *in* T. Meron, *Human Rights in International Law: Legal and Policy Issues* 345 (1984); M. Bothe, K.J. Partsch & W. Solf, *New Rules for Victims of Armed Conflicts: A Commentary on the Two 1977 Protocols Additional to the Geneva Conventions of 1949* (1982).

Although modern humanitarian law predates the development of international human rights law and had some influence on it, *see, e.g.,* common Article 3 of the Geneva Conventions of 1949, various provisions of the most recent Protocols mirror the principles underlying modern international human rights instruments. *See generally* T. Meron, *Human Rights and Humanitarian Norms as Customary Law* (1989). It is also worth noting that the derogation clauses of the principal international human rights treaties incorporate by reference the humanitarian law treaties and obligations of the state parties thereto. *See* International Covenant on Civil and Political Rights, art. 4; European Convention of Human Rights, art. 15; American Convention on Human Rights, art. 27; T. Meron, *Human Rights in Internal Strife: Their International Protection* 23 (1987). Modern international human rights law thus embraces humanitarian law, attempting to provide at least some protection in peacetime as in war. On this entire subject, see Chapter 6 (Humanitarian Law), *infra.*

§ 1–8. The Past and Modern International Human Rights Law

Traditional international law developed various doctrines and institutions that were designed to protect different groups of human beings: slaves, minorities, certain native populations, foreign nationals, victims of massive violations, combatants, etc. That law and practice provided the conceptual and institutional underpinnings for the development of contemporary international human rights law. Moreover, many of the older institutions and doctrines continue to exist side-by-side, with or form an inherent part of, the modern international law of human rights. In certain areas, that law has been profoundly influenced by its antecedents. An awareness of the historical roots of modern international law of human rights will consequently give the reader a deeper understanding of that law.

As we shall see in the chapters that follow, modern international human rights law differs most significantly from its historical antecedents in that today individual human beings are deemed to have internationally guaranteed rights as individuals and not as nationals of a particular state. There now also exist a growing number of international institutions with jurisdiction to protect individuals against human rights violations committed by states of their own nationality as well as by any other states. Although these remedies are often still quite inadequate or ineffective, the vast body of international human rights law now in existence—as well as the mushrooming of international institutions designed to implement that law—have internationalized the subject of human rights beyond all expectations. This development has in turn produced a political climate in which the protection of human rights has become one of the most important items on the agenda of the contemporary international political discourse involving governments, inter-governmental organizations, and a vast international network of non-governmental organizations.

As a result, human beings around the world have increasingly been led to believe that states and the international community have an obligation to protect their human rights. The expectations that this phenomenon creates makes it politically ever more difficult for growing numbers of states to deny that they have such an obligation which, of course, facilitates the efforts of those who promote the international protection of human rights. In other words, what we are witnessing at this moment is a human rights revolution in progress. The gains are many, but they remain to be consolidated. Much of the needed law is already on the books. Unfortunately, however, the institutions to enforce the law are still quite weak. *See* Buergenthal, "The Human Rights Revolution," 23 St. Mary's L.J. 3 (1991). The task that remains is to give "teeth" to the law by strengthening international mechanisms which protect human rights and to extend their jurisdiction to all parts of the world.

CHAPTER 2

THE UNITED NATIONS HUMAN RIGHTS SYSTEM

I. INTRODUCTION

This chapter deals with the human rights provisions of the Charter of the United Nations and provides an overview of the law and institutions that have been developed within the UN framework. These legal norms and institutions derive either from the Charter itself or the human rights treaties adopted under the auspices of the UN.

II. THE UN CHARTER

§ 2–1. Introduction

Modern international human rights law is a post-World War II phenomenon. Its development can be attributed to the monstrous violations of human rights of the Hitler era and to the belief that these violations and possibly the war itself might have been prevented had an effective international system for the protection of human rights existed in the days of the League of Nations.

The international human rights cause was eloquently espoused as early as 1941 by President Franklin D. Roosevelt. In his famous "Four Freedoms" speech, he called for "a world founded upon four essential human freedoms." These he identified as "freedom of speech and expression," "freedom of every person to worship God in his own way," "freedom from want," and "freedom from fear." Roosevelt's vision of "the moral order," as he characterized it, became the clarion call of the nations that fought the Axis in the Second World War and founded the United Nations. *See* A. Holcombe, *Human Rights in the Modern World* 4–5 (1948).

§ 2–2. The San Francisco Conference and Human Rights

The human rights provisions which ultimately found their way into the Charter of the United Nations fell far short of the expectations created by Roosevelt's vision and the wartime rhetoric. § 2–1, *supra. See generally* J. Robinson, *Human Rights and Fundamental Freedoms in the Charter of the United Nations: A Commentary* (1946). That was to be expected, for each of the principal victorious powers had troublesome human rights problems of its own. The Soviet Union had its *Gulag*, the United States its *de jure* racial discrimination, France and Great Britain their colonial empires. Given their own vulnerability as far as human rights were concerned, it was not in the political interest of these countries to draft a Charter that established an effective international system for the protection of human rights, which is what some smaller democratic nations advocated. Although the big powers prevailed to the extent that the San Francisco Conference produced no protective system as such, the UN Charter did nevertheless lay the legal and conceptual foundation for the development of contemporary international human rights law. Sohn, "The New International Law: Protection of the Rights of Individuals Rather than States," 32 Am. U. L. Rev. 1 (1982).

§ 2–3. Human Rights in the UN Charter

Article 1(3) of the Charter of the United Nations proclaims the following goal as one of the "purposes" of the UN:

> To achieve international co-operation in solving international problems of an economic, social, cultural, or humanitarian character, and in promoting and encouraging respect for human rights and for fundamental freedoms for all without distinction as to race, sex, language, or religion.

The basic obligations of the Organization and its Member States in achieving these purposes are set out in Articles 55 and 56 of the Charter. These provisions read as follows:

Article 55

With a view to the creation of conditions of stability and well-being which are necessary for peaceful and friendly relations among nations based on respect for the principle of equal rights and self-determination of peoples, the United Nations shall promote:

(a) higher standards of living, full employment, and conditions of economic and social progress and development;

(b) solutions of international economic, social, health, and related problems; and international cultural and educational cooperation; and

(c) universal respect for, and observance of, human rights and fundamental freedoms for all without distinction as to race, sex, language, or religion.

Article 56

All Members pledge themselves to take joint and separate action in co-operation with the Organization for the achievement of the purposes set forth in Article 55.

Although the subject matter mandate spelled out in Article 55 is broad, it confers very limited powers on the Organization. The charge is to "promote," and that responsibility is assigned to the UN General Assembly and the Economic and Social Council, both organs whose resolutions on this subject are not legally binding. The "pledge" of the Member States under Article 56 is limited to the promotion of the "achievement of the purposes set forth in Article 55," that is, "to promote ... universal respect for, and observance of, human rights and fundamental freedoms...." (Art. 55(c).) Moreover, the UN Charter does not define what is meant by "human rights and fundamental freedoms." Article 55(c) does, however, contain a very unambiguous non-discrimination clause which, when read together with Article 56, makes clear that the Member States and the Organization have an obligation to promote human rights and fundamental freedoms "without distinction as to race, sex, language, or religion."

Article 56 requires Member States "to take joint and separate action in co-operation with the Organization" to accomplish the objectives spelled out in Article 55. To facilitate this cooperation, Article 13(1) of the Charter provides that the General Assembly "shall initiate studies and make recommendations for the purpose of: ... (b) ... assisting in the realization of human rights and fundamental freedoms for all without distinction as to race, sex, language, or religion." The Charter confers similar power on the UN Economic and Social Council (ECOSOC). It authorizes the ECOSOC to "make recommendations for the purpose of promoting respect for, and observance of, human rights and fundamental freedoms for all" and requires it to "set up commissions in economic and social fields and for the promotion of human rights...." (Arts. 62(2) and 68.)

Despite their vagueness, the human rights provisions of the UN Charter have had a number of important consequences. First, the UN Charter "internationalized" human rights. That is to say, by adhering to the Charter, which is a multilateral treaty, the States Parties recognized that the "human rights" referred to in it are a subject of international concern and, to that extent, no longer within their exclusive domestic jurisdiction. *See* § 1–4, *supra*. Although the validity of this proposition was frequently challenged by some states in the early years of the United Nations, the issue is today no longer open to doubt. *See* L. Henkin, *The Age of Rights* 51 (1990). The fact that a state which has ratified the Charter cannot assert that human rights as a subject falls within its exclusive domestic jurisdiction does not mean, however, that every violation of human rights by a Member State of the UN is a matter of international concern. What it does mean is that even in the absence of any other treaty obligations, a state today can no longer assert that the maltreatment of its own nationals, regardless of how massive or systematic, is a matter within its exclusive domestic jurisdiction. For the practice of the UN on this subject, see R. Higgins, *The Development of International Law through the Political Organs of the United Nations* 58 (1963); L. Sohn & T. Buergenthal, *International Protection of Human Rights* 556 (1973); L. Sohn, *Rights in Conflict: The United Nations and South Africa* 48 and 63 (1994). *See also* Cassese, "The General Assembly: Historical Perspective 1945–1989," *in* P. Alston (ed.), *The United Nations and Human Rights: A Critical Appraisal* 25 (1992).

Second, the obligation of the Member States of the UN to cooperate with the Organization in the promotion of human rights and fundamental freedoms has provided the UN with the requisite legal authority to undertake a massive effort to define and codify these rights. That effort is reflected in the adoption of the International Bill of Human Rights, § 2–4, *infra*, and the numerous other human rights instruments in existence today. These texts are reproduced in the two-volume United Nations publication, entitled *Human Rights: A Compilation of International Instruments* (1993). The result is a vast body of legal norms, a veritable human rights code, that gives meaning to the phrase "human rights and fundamental freedoms" and clarifies the obligations imposed by Articles 55 and 56 of the Charter. Buergenthal, "International Human Rights Law and Institutions: Accomplishments and Prospects," 63 Wash. L. Rev. 1 (1988). *See also* Simma & Alston, "The Sources of Human Rights Law: Custom, Jus Cogens and General Principles," 12 Australian Y.B. Int'l L. 82 (1992), for more far-reaching conclusions.

Third, the Organization has over the years succeeded in clarifying the scope of the Member States' obligation to "promote" human rights, expanding it and creating UN Charter-based institutions designed to ensure compliance by governments. Today it is generally recognized, for example, that a UN Member State which engages in practices amounting to a "consistent pattern of gross violations" of internationally guaranteed human rights is not in compliance with its obligation to "promote . . . universal respect for, and observance of . . ." these rights and that, consequently, it violates the UN Charter. *See* § 2–20 and § 2–22, *infra*. *See also Restatement (Third)* § 701 and § 702, and the accompanying notes. The UN has sought to enforce this obligation with resolutions calling on specific states to stop such violations and by empowering the UN Commission on Human Rights and its subsidiary bodies to establish procedures to review allegations of violations. *See* Sohn, "Human Rights: Their Implementation and Supervision by the United Nations," *in* T. Meron (ed.), *Human Rights in International Law: Legal and Policy Issues* 368, 384–89 (1984); Rodley, "United Nations Non–Treaty Procedures for Dealing with Human Rights," *in* H. Hannum (ed.), *Guide to International Human Rights Practice* 60 (2d. ed. 1992).

III. THE INTERNATIONAL BILL OF HUMAN RIGHTS

§ 2–4. Introduction

The International Bill of Human Rights consists, in addition to the human rights provisions of the UN Charter, of the Universal Declaration of Human Rights, the two International Covenants on Human Rights and the Optional Protocol to the Covenant on Civil and Political Rights. See generally, Henkin, "The International Bill of Rights: The Universal Declaration and the Covenants," in R. Bernhardt & J.A. Jolowicz (eds.), International Enforcement of Human Rights 1 (1987). These instruments will be analyzed in the sections that follow.

Proposals that a "Bill of Rights" or "Declaration of the Essential Rights of Man" be appended to the Charter were made but not acted upon at the San Francisco Conference. These efforts were revived at the very first meeting of the United Nations. Shortly thereafter, its newly-created Commission on Human Rights was charged with drafting "an international bill of human rights." The Commission soon recognized that it would be relatively easy to adopt the text of a hortatory declaration, but that it would prove much more difficult to reach agreement on the wording of a legally binding treaty. The Commission decided, therefore, to work first on a declaration and to take up immediately afterwards the preparation of one or more draft treaties. This approach produced the Universal Declaration of Human Rights, which was adopted by the UN General Assembly in December, 1948. UN Gen. Ass.Res. 217A (III). *See generally* N. Robinson, *The Universal Declaration of Human Rights: Its Origin, Significance, and Interpretation* (1958). It took 18 more years before the treaties—the two Covenants and the Optional Protocol—were adopted by the Assembly and opened for signature. For the drafting history of these documents, *see* Sohn, "A Short History of United Nations Documents on Human Rights," *in The United Nations and Human Rights* 101 (18th Report of the Commission to Study the Organization of Peace, 1968). Another ten years elapsed before the two Covenants entered into force in 1976.

§ 2–5. The Universal Declaration of Human Rights

The Universal Declaration is the first comprehensive human rights instrument to be proclaimed by a

universal international organization. *See generally*
A. Eide *et al.* (eds.), *The Universal Declaration of
Human Rights: A Commentary* (1992). Because of
its moral status and the legal and political importance it has acquired over the years, the Declaration
ranks with the Magna Carta, the French Declaration of the Rights of Man and the American Declaration of Independence as a milestone in mankind's
struggle for freedom and human dignity. Its debt
to these great historic documents is unmistakable.
"All human beings are born free and equal in
dignity and rights," proclaims Article 1 of the Universal Declaration, and Article 28 adds "everyone is
entitled to a social and international order in which
the rights and freedoms set forth in this Declaration
can be fully realized."

1. *The Rights and Freedoms*

The Universal Declaration proclaims two broad
categories of rights: civil and political rights, on the
one hand, and economic, social and cultural rights
on the other. Its catalog of civil and political rights
includes the right to life, liberty, and security of
person; the prohibition of slavery, of torture and
cruel, inhuman or degrading treatment; the right
not to be subjected to arbitrary arrest, detention or
exile; the right to a fair trial in both civil and
criminal matters, the presumption of innocence and
the prohibition against the application of *ex post
facto* laws and penalties. The Declaration recognizes the right to privacy and the right to own
property. It proclaims freedom of speech, religion,

assembly and freedom of movement. The latter embraces the right of everyone "to leave any country, including his own, and to return to his country." Also guaranteed are the right "to seek and to enjoy in other countries asylum from persecution" and the right to a nationality. Important political rights are proclaimed in Article 21 of the Declaration, including the individual's right "to take part in the government of his country, directly or through freely chosen representatives." That provision also declares that the "will of the people shall be the basis of the authority of government" and requires "periodic and genuine elections" by universal suffrage.

The catalog of economic, social and cultural rights proclaimed in the Declaration starts with the proposition, expressed in Article 22, that

> Everyone, as a member of society ... is entitled to realization, through national effort and international co-operation and in accordance with the organization and resources of each State, of the economic, social and cultural rights indispensable for his dignity and the free development of his personality.

The Declaration then proclaims the individual's right to social security, to work, and to "protection against unemployment," to "equal pay for equal work," and to "just and favourable remuneration ensuring for himself and his family an existence worthy of human dignity, and supplemented, if necessary, by other means of social protection." The right "to rest and leisure, including reasonable limitation of working hours and periodic holidays with pay" is recognized in Article 24. Article 25 of the Declaration states that everyone has the right "to a standard of living adequate for the health and well-being of himself and of his family." It also recognizes the individual's right "to security in the event of unemployment, sickness, disability, widowhood, old age or other lack of livelihood in circumstances beyond his control."

The right to education is dealt with in Article 26 of the Declaration which provides, among other things, that education shall be free "at least in the elementary and fundamental stages." Article 26 also declares that

Education shall be directed to the full development of the human personality and to the strengthening of respect for human rights and fundamental freedoms. It shall promote understanding, tolerance, and friendship among all nations, racial or religious groups, and shall further the activities of the United Nations for the maintenance of peace.

Article 27 of the Declaration deals with cultural rights and states, *inter alia,* that every human being has "the right freely to participate in the cultural life of the community, to enjoy the arts and to share in scientific advancement and its benefits."

The Declaration recognizes that the rights it proclaims are not absolute. It permits a state to enact laws limiting the exercise of these rights, provided their sole purpose is to secure "due recognition and respect for the rights and freedoms of others and of meeting the just requirements of morality, public order and the general welfare in a democratic society." (Art. 29(2).) A government's authority to impose such restrictions is further limited by Article 30, which provides that "nothing in this Declaration may be interpreted as implying for any State, group or person any right to engage in any activity or to perform any act aimed at the destruction of any of the rights and freedoms" proclaimed in the Declaration. In other words, a government would violate the Declaration if its reliance on the power to impose lawful restrictions or limitations on the exercise of certain human rights was a mere pretext for denying these rights.

2. *Legal Effect and Political Importance*

The Universal Declaration is not a treaty. It was adopted by the UN General Assembly as a resolution having no force of law. Its purpose, according to its preamble, is to provide "a common understanding" of the human rights and fundamental freedoms referred to in the UN Charter and to serve "as a common standard of achievement for all peoples and all nations...."

In the decades that have elapsed since its adoption in 1948, the Declaration has undergone a dramatic transformation. Today few international lawyers would deny that the Declaration is a normative instrument that creates at least some legal obligations for the Member States of the UN. The dispute about its legal character concerns not so much claims that it lacks all legal force. The disagreement focuses instead on questions about whether all the rights it proclaims are binding and under what circumstances, and on whether its obligatory character derives either from its status as an authoritative interpretation of the human rights obligations contained in the UN Charter, its status as customary international law, or its status as a general principle of law. *See Restatement (Third)* § 701, Reporters' Notes 4–6; Sohn, "The New International Law: Protection of the Rights of Individuals Rather than States," 32 Am. U. L. Rev. 1, 16–17 (1982); L. Henkin, *The Age of Rights* 19 (1990); Simma & Alston, "The Source of Human Rights Law: Custom, Jus Cogens, and General Principles," 12 Australian Y.B. Int'l L. 82 (1992).

The process leading to the transformation of the Universal Declaration from a non-binding recommendation to an instrument having a normative character was set in motion, in part at least, because the effort to draft and adopt the Covenants remained stalled in the UN for almost two decades. During that time the need for authoritative standards defining the human rights obligations of UN Member States became ever more urgent. As time went on, the Declaration came to be utilized with ever greater frequency for that purpose. Whenever governments, the UN or other international organizations wished to invoke human rights norms or condemn their violations, they would refer to and draw on the Declaration as the applicable standard.

Thus the Declaration came to symbolize what the international community means by "human rights," reinforcing the conviction that all governments have an "obligation" to ensure the enjoyment of the rights the Declaration proclaims. *See* Humphrey, "The Universal Declaration of Human Rights: Its History, Impact and Juridical Character," *in* B. Ramcharan (ed.), *Human Rights: Thirty Years After the Universal Declaration* 21, at 28–37 (1979).

The legal significance of this process has been analyzed in at least three ways. Some international lawyers and governments have contended that the UN's consistent reliance on the Universal Declaration when applying the human rights provisions of the UN Charter compels the conclusion that the Declaration has come to be accepted as an authoritative interpretation of these provisions. According to this view, the Member States of the UN have agreed that they have an obligation under the Charter to promote "universal respect for, and observance of" the rights which the Declaration proclaims. Waldock, "Human Rights in Contemporary International Law and the Significance of the European Convention," *in The European Convention of Human Rights* 1, at 14 (Int'l & Comp. L. Supp. Publ. No. 11, 1965); Buergenthal, "International Human Rights Law and Institutions: Accomplishments and Prospects," 63 Wash. L. Rev. 1, at 9 (1988). Whether a state can be deemed to violate this obligation when it denies all, some or even only one of these rights will then depend upon the interpretation given to the undertaking contained in Article 55(c) of the Charter read together with Article 56.

Another view that is gaining increasing support sees in the repeated reliance on and resort to the Universal Declaration by governments and intergovernmental organizations the requisite state practice which is capable of giving rise to customary international law. This theory leads to the conclusion that the Declaration or, at the very least, some of its provisions, have become customary international law. A careful analysis of the relevant state practice suggests, however, that not all the rights proclaimed in the Declaration have to date acquired this status. That is why the _Restatement (Third)_ characterizes only some rights proclaimed in the Universal Declaration as customary international law. Without claiming to be exhaustive, it lists the following governmental practices as violating international law: genocide, slavery, murder or causing the disappearance of individuals, torture or other cruel, inhuman or degrading treatment or punishment, prolonged arbitrary detention, systematic racial discrimination, and consistent patterns of gross violations of internationally recognized human rights. _Restatement (Third)_ § 702. _See also_ T. Meron, _Human Rights and Humanitarian Norms as Customary Law_ 92–95 (1989) (containing a useful analysis of the process for reaching conclusions of this type).

One distinguished commentator has combined the two aforementioned theories by advancing the following view:

The Declaration ... is now considered to be an authoritative interpretation of the U.N. Charter, spelling out in considerable detail the meaning of the phrase "human rights and fundamental freedoms," which Member States agreed in the Charter to promote and observe. The Universal Declaration has joined the Charter ... as part of the constitutional structure of the world community. The Declaration, as an authoritative listing of human rights, has become a basic component of international customary law, binding all states, not only members of the United Nations.

Sohn, "The New International Law: Protection of the Rights of Individuals Rather than States," 32 Am. U. L. Rev. 1, at 16–17 (1982). It remains to be seen whether this characterization of the Universal Declaration will gain general acceptance, particularly if it is understood as imposing on all states an immediate obligation to conform to its every provision. Some commentators are now putting forth a third theory, which characterizes various international human rights norms, including the Universal Declaration, as being reflective of a dynamic modern aspect of general principles of law. Simma & Alston, "The Source of Human Rights Law: Custom, Jus Cogens, and General Principles," 12 Australian Y.B. Int'l L. 82 (1992). *See also* Charney, "Universal International Law," 87 Am. J. Int'l L. 529, 549 (1993). Whatever the theory, it is today clear that the international community attributes a very special moral and normative status to the Universal Declaration that no other instrument of its kind has acquired. *See, e.g.,* Vienna Declaration, Preamble, adopted at the World Conference on Human Rights, June, 1993.

§ 2–6. The International Covenants on Human Rights: Introduction

The Covenant on Economic, Social and Cultural Rights and the Covenant on Civil and Political Rights were adopted by the UN General Assembly and opened for signature in December 1966. Another decade passed before thirty-five states—the number required to bring the Covenants into force—ratified both instruments. This number has increased significantly in recent years and by the end of 1994 grew to some 130 States Parties. The United States ratified the Covenant in 1992. Being treaties, the Covenants create binding legal obligations for the States Parties. Therefore, as between them, issues relating to compliance with and the enjoyment of the rights guaranteed by the Covenants are matters of international concern and thus are no longer within their domestic jurisdiction. For a debate on the full implications of this conclusion, see Henkin, "Human Rights and 'Domestic Jurisdiction'," in T. Buergenthal, *Human Rights, International Law and the Helsinki Accord* 21, at 29–33 (1977), and Frowein, "The Interrelationship Between the Helsinki Final Act, the International Covenants on Human Rights, and the European Convention on Human Rights," *id.*, 71, at 77–80.

The Covenants have a number of common substantive provisions. Two of these deal with what might be described as "peoples" or "collective" rights. Article 1(1) of both Covenants proclaims that "all peoples have the right of self-determination." *See* Hannum, "Rethinking Self–Determination," 34 Va. J. Int'l L. 1, 17–18 (1993). Both instruments recognize in Article 1(2) that "all peoples" have the right to freely dispose of their natural resources and that "in no case may a people be deprived of its own means of subsistence." *See generally* Morphet, "The Development of Article 1 of the Human Rights Covenants," *in* D.M. Hill (ed.), *Human Rights and Foreign Policy—Principles and Practice* 67 (1989). They also bar discrimination based on race, color, sex, language, religion, political or other opinion, national or social origin, property or birth. *See* C.P. Covenant, art. 2(1); E.S.C. Covenant, art. 2(2). *See generally* Ramcharan, "Equality and Nondiscrimination," *in* L. Henkin (ed.), *The International Bill of Human Rights* 246 (1981).

As will be seen below, each Covenant establishes a distinct international enforcement system designed to ensure that the States Parties comply with their obligations. These so-called measures of implementation are amplified in the case of the C.P. Covenant by the Optional Protocol. It permits individuals to file petitions charging violations of their rights under that Covenant.

§ 2–7. Covenant on Civil and Political Rights

The catalog of civil and political rights enumerated in this Covenant is drafted with greater juridical specificity and lists more rights than the Universal Declaration. For the drafting history of the Covenant, *see* M.J. Bossuyt, *Guide to the "Travaux Préparatoires" of the International Covenant on Civil and Political Rights* (1987). One important addition is the undertaking by states not to deny members of ethnic, religious or linguistic minorities the right, "in community with other members of their group, to enjoy their own culture, to profess and practice their own religion, or to use their own language." C.P. Covenant, art. 27. For a thorough analysis of this provision, *see* P. Thornberry, *International Law and the Rights of Minorities* 141 (1991). Article 27 inspired the Declaration on the Rights of Persons Belonging to National or Ethnic Religious and Linguistic Minorities, adopted by the United Nations in 1992. *See* A. Philips & A. Rosas (eds.), The UN Minority Rights Declaration (1993). *See also* Human Rights Committee (hereafter HRC), General Comment No. 23(50) (art. 27), Doc. CCPR/C/21/Rev. 1/Add. 5 (1994). Among other rights guaranteed in the C.P. Covenant that are not expressly mentioned in the Universal Declaration are freedom from imprisonment for debt, the right of all persons deprived of their liberty to be treated with humanity and with respect for the inherent dignity of the human person, and the right of every child "to acquire a nationality" and to be accorded "such measures of protection as are required by his status as a minor."

The Universal Declaration proclaims some important rights which do not appear in the C.P. Covenant, including the right to own property, to seek and enjoy asylum and the right to a nationality. The right to own property was not included in the Covenant because the various ideological and political blocs represented in the UN at the time could not agree on its scope and definition. For an overall analysis of the rights and their legislative history, see L. Henkin (ed.), *The International Bill of Human Rights: The Covenant on Civil and Political Rights* (1981); Lillich, "Civil Rights," *in* T. Meron (ed.), *Human Rights in International Law: Legal and Policy Issues* 115 (1984); M. Nowak, *U.N. Covenant on Civil and Political Rights: CCPR Commentary* (1993).

The C.P. Covenant contains a "derogation clause," which permits the States Parties "in time of public emergency that threatens the life of the nation" to suspend all but seven of the most fundamental rights. C.P. Covenant, art. 4. *See* Buergenthal, "To Respect and to Ensure: State Obligations and Permissible Derogations," *in* Henkin, *supra,* at 72, 78–86. *See also*, J. Fitzpatrick, *The International System for Protecting Rights During States of Emergency* 82 (1994) (containing a thorough analysis of the practice of the Human Rights Committee relating to Article 4). The Covenant also permits the states to limit and restrict the exercise of the rights it proclaims. A good example of this approach is Article 18, which guarantees freedom of religion and declares in paragraph 3 that "freedom to manifest one's religion or beliefs may be subject only to such limitations as are prescribed by law and are necessary to protect public safety, order, health, or morals or the fundamental rights and freedoms of others." For an interpretation of this provision by the Human Rights Committee, see HRC General Comment No. 22 (48), Doc. A/48/40, Annex IV (1993). *See also* Higgins, "Derogations under Human Rights Treaties," 48 Brit. Y. B. Int'l L. 281, 283–86 (1975–76); Kiss, "Permissible Limitations on Rights," *in* Henkin, *supra,* at 290. These types of provisions are partially balanced by Article 5(1), which prohibits the imposition of restrictions or limitations aimed at the destruction of the rights or "their limitation to a greater extent than is provided for in the present Covenant." In practice, particularly in states that lack a strong and independent judiciary, the provisions which permit derogations and other restrictions are frequently invoked to justify non-compliance by governments violating their human rights obligations. *See generally* D. McGoldrick, *The Human Rights Committee: Its Role in the Development of the International Covenant on Civil and Political Rights* 300 (1994).

The obligations which the States Parties assume by ratifying the C.P. Covenant are set out in Article 2. Paragraph 1 of that provision reads as follows:

Each State Party to the present Covenant undertakes to respect and to ensure to all individuals within its territory and subject to its jurisdiction the rights recognized in the present Covenant, without distinction of any kind, such as race, colour, sex, language, religion, political or other opinion, national or social origin, property, birth or other status.

This provision is supplemented by Article 2(2), which requires the States Parties "to adopt such legislative or other measures as may be necessary to give effect to the rights" guaranteed in the Covenant whenever such provisions do not already exist in its domestic law. Unlike the Covenant on Economic, Social and Cultural Rights, which calls for progressive implementation tied to available resources, the C.P. Covenant imposes an immediate obligation "to respect and to ensure" the rights it proclaims and to take whatever other measures are necessary to bring about that result. HRC, General Comment Nos. 2(13) and 3(13), Doc. A/36/40, at 108–109 (1981). *Cf.* Schachter, "The Obligation to Implement the Covenant in Domestic Law," *in* Henkin, *supra* at 311. *But see* Buergenthal, "To Respect and to Ensure: State Obligations and Permissible Derogations," *id.,* at 72–78. For a discussion of the extraterritorial reach of the Covenant, see Meron, "Extraterritoriality of Human Rights Treaties," 89 Am. J. Int'l 78 (1995).

The C.P. Covenant established a Human Rights Committee (hereinafter the HRC or Committee) and confers on it various functions designed to ensure that the States Parties comply with the obligations they assumed by ratifying the treaty. These functions consist of the administration of the reporting system and the inter-state complaint mechanism provided for in the Covenant. Additional functions are exercised by the HRC under the

Optional Protocol to the C.P. Covenant, which established a right of individual petition. *See* § 2–8, *infra*. The Committee consists of 18 members. They are nominated and elected by the States Parties, but serve in their individual capacities and not as government representatives. C.P. Covenant, art. 28. The practice of the HRC is extensively analyzed in McGoldrick, *supra*.

The Committee's principal function is to examine the reports all States Parties are required to submit "on the measures they have adopted which give effect to the rights recognized ... [in the Covenant] and on the progress made in the enjoyment of these rights." C.P. Covenant, art. 40(1). Over the years, the Committee has developed a comprehensive set of reporting guidelines and procedures for dealing with these reports. Opsahl, "The Human Rights Committee," *in* P. Alston, *The United Nations and Human Rights: A Critical Appraisal* 369, 397–419 (1991); Pocar, "Current Developments and Approaches in the Practice of the Human Rights Committee in Consideration of State Reports," *in* A. Eide & J. Helgesen (eds.), *The Future of Human Rights Protection in a Changing World* 51 (1991). These guidelines are designed to prod the States Parties into compliance with their treaty obligations and to assist them in overcoming difficulties in doing so. The Covenant does not expressly confer on the Committee the power to verify the state reports by undertaking its own *in loco* investigations although it could seek permission from the states concerned to do so. Committee members may, however, draw on their own knowledge as human rights experts and on information provided them by non-governmental human rights organizations in questioning the representatives of the states who, under the Committee's rules of procedure, are to be present when their reports are examined. By requiring the representatives to explain the contents of the reports and by asking for supplemental information, the Committee is able to pinpoint serious compliance problems and to call them to the attention of the UN General Assembly in its annual report. C.P. Covenant, art. 40(4). *See* T. Meron, *Human Rights Law–Making in the United Nations* 123 (1986).

The evolution of the reporting system has accelerated in recent years, transforming it into an increasingly more effective instrument for the implementation of the Covenant. For example, while it was once disputed within the Committee whether its members could draw on information provided them by non-governmental organizations in examining state reports, such information is now officially circulated to the members. The Committee today also includes its conclusions about individual state reports, together with additional views of any of its members, in the Committee's annual report, which is transmitted to the States Parties and the UN General Assembly. Moreover, the Committee recently began to require states to report what action they have taken to give effect to the Committee's recommendation addressed to them in an individual case considered by it under the Optional

Protocol. It has also decided to bring to the attention of the UN Secretary General and through him to appropriate UN bodies information concerning grave violations of human rights revealed in the course of the examination of a state report. Furthermore, building on its practice in dealing with individual petitions and in examining state reports, the Committee has adopted an increasing number of so-called General Comments that spell out the meaning of various provisions of the Covenant. The General Comments resemble advisory opinions which interpret the Covenant.

The Covenant also provides for an inter-state complaint machinery that enables one State Party to charge another with a violation of the treaty. C.P. Covenant, arts. 41 and 42. *See generally* M. Nowak, *U.N. Covenant on Civil and Political Rights: CCPR Commentary* 580 and 604 (1993). This remedy is optional, however, and can be resorted to only by and against States Parties that have made separate declarations recognizing the Committee's jurisdiction to receive such complaints. C.P. Covenant, art. 41(2). Although the provision of the Covenant permitting this action entered into force after ten states accepted the requisite jurisdiction, the inter-state complaint mechanism has not as yet been resorted to.

The system for dealing with inter-state complaints provides neither for adjudication nor quasi-adjudication. Instead, it establishes little more than a formal conciliation machinery. *See generally,* Robertson, "The Implementation System: Inter-

national Measures," *in* Henkin, *supra,* at 332, 351–
56. The system is designed to function as follows.
Let us assume that a State Party (X) believes that
another State Party (Y) is violating the Covenant.
State X makes this allegation in a formal statement
addressed to Y which must answer to charges within a period of three months. If X and Y do not
resolve their differences within a period of six
months, each of them has the right to submit the
matter to the Human Rights Committee. It will
then invite the parties to present their case and to
submit whatever evidence they have. The Committee must also offer "its good offices to the States
Parties concerned with a view to a friendly solution
of the matter on the basis of respect for human
rights and fundamental freedoms as recognized in
the present Covenant." C.P. Covenant, art.
41(1)(e). If a friendly solution is reached, the Committee reports the terms of the settlement. If there
is no such agreement within a period of twelve
months, the Committee must prepare a report, containing a brief statement of the facts as well as the
written and oral submissions of the parties. Normally the proceedings end here, although the Committee may, with the consent of States X and Y,
appoint a so-called *ad hoc* Conciliation Commission.
This body consists of five members acceptable to the
parties who serve in their individual capacities.
The Commission has the power, after examining
the charges and if it fails to negotiate a friendly
settlement, to make its own findings of all the
relevant facts and to suggest how the dispute

should be settled. The parties are not formally required to accept the proposed solution, although their failure to do so may be called to the attention of the UN General Assembly by the Human Rights Committee in its annual report.

§ 2–8. The Optional Protocol to the Covenant on Civil and Political Rights

This treaty, adopted as a separate instrument, supplements the measures of implementation of the C.P. Covenant. It enables private parties, claiming to be victims of a violation of the Covenant, to file so-called "individual" communications or complaints with the Human Rights Committee. The complaints may only be filed against States Parties to the Covenant that have ratified the Protocol. Protocol, arts. 1 and 2. *See* A.H. Robertson & J.G. Merrills, *Human Rights in the World* 54 (3d ed. 1989); Ophsal, "The Human Rights Committee," in Alston, *supra,* at 420. The Committee deals with these complaints in two stages. It must first pass on the admissibility of the communication, which is governed by the provisions of Articles 2, 3 and 5 of the Protocol. *See* Higgins, "Admissibility under the *Optional Protocol to the Covenant on Civil and Political Rights,*" Can. Hum. Rts. Y. B. 57 (1991–92). Only if a communication has been ruled admissible does it move to the second stage of the proceedings, which deals with the merits of the complaint. *See* Rules of Procedure of the Human Rights Committee, Rules 93 and 94, Doc. CCPR/C/3/ Rev. 3 (1994). After it has passed on the admissibility of the complaint, the Committee brings the matter to the attention of the state involved, which has six months within which to respond to the charges. Protocol, art. 4. The written communications of the States Party and the individual complainant are then reviewed by the Committee and its findings communicated to the parties. Protocol, art. 5. A summary of these findings is reproduced in the Committee's annual report to the UN General Assembly. Protocol, art. 6 and C.P. Covenant, art. 45.

Since the entry into force of the Protocol in 1976, the Human Rights Committee has dealt with an ever-increasing number of individual communications. Many of these have been ruled inadmissible, in large part because domestic remedies had not been exhausted or because they involved "the same matter" that was "being examined under another procedure of international investigation or settlement." Protocol, art. 5(2). In recent years, the number of admissible communications has grown significantly. In dealing with communications, the Committee has been able to develop a valuable body of caselaw interpreting and applying the Covenant and Protocol. *See* Human Rights Committee, *Selected Decisions Under the Optional Protocol: Second to Sixteenth Sessions,* UN Publ. No. E.84.XIV.2 (1984); *Id., Seventeenth to Thirty–Second Sessions (October 1982–April 1988)* UN Publ. No. E.89.XIV.1 (1990). The dramatic increase in the number of States Parties that have ratified the Optional Protocol in recent years and the resultant increase in the caselaw under it has compelled the Committee to issue its annual report to the General Assembly in two volumes, with the second volume consisting of its practice under the Protocol.

The Committee has also been able to gradually strengthen the effectiveness of the human rights mechanism established by the Protocol. *See* De Zayas, "The Follow-up Procedure of the UN Human Rights Committee," 47 ICJ Rev. 28 (1991). Thus, for example, it now has the power to propose interim measures "to avoid irreparable damage to the victim" of an alleged violation of the Covenant. Rules of Procedure of the Human Rights Committee, Rule 86. The Committee now also requires the States Parties to indicate in their periodic reports what measures they have taken to give effect to the Committee's recommendations in those individual cases in which they were held to have violated the Covenant. "In particular, the State Party should indicate what remedy it has afforded the author of the communication whose rights the Committee found to have been violated." HRC, Revised Guidelines for the Preparation of State Party Reports, *Report of the Human Rights Committee*, UN Doc. 40 (A/46/40), Annex VIII, 206, 208 (1991). *See also* Pocar, "Legal Value of the Committee's Views," Can. Hum. Rts. Y.B. 119 (1991–92).

§ 2–9. Second Optional Protocol to the International Covenant on Civil and Political Rights

This Protocol was opened for signature on December 15, 1989 and entered into force on July 11,

1991. Pursuant to its terms, it is deemed to be an additional provision of the C.P. Covenant. The Protocol's objective is the abolition of the death penalty. To this end it provides, first, that once a state has ratified the Protocol, "no one within [its] jurisdiction ... shall be executed," and, second, that each State Party must take whatever measures are necessary to abolish the death penalty within its jurisdiction. Second Optional Protocol, art. 1. The only reservation that may be made to the Protocol would allow "for the application of the death penalty in time of war pursuant to a conviction for a most serious crime of a military nature committed during wartime." *Id.,* art. 2. The Protocol also makes the right it guarantees non-derogable under Article 4 of the Covenant. *Id.,* art. 6(2).

The Protocol extends the jurisdiction of the Human Rights Committee under Article 40 of the Covenant. It does so also for inter-state complaints with regard to states that have recognized the Committee's jurisdiction under Article 41 of the Covenant and for individual complaints in cases involving States Parties to the [First] Optional Protocol. Second Optional Protocol, arts. 3–5.

§ 2–10 Covenant on Economic, Social and Cultural Rights

This Covenant contains a longer and much more comprehensive catalog of economic, social and cultural rights than the Universal Declaration. It recognizes the following rights: the right to work; the right to the enjoyment of just and favorable conditions of work; the right to form and join trade unions; the right to social security, including social insurance; the right to the protection of the family; the right to an adequate standard of living; the right to the enjoyment of the highest attainable standard of physical and mental health; the right of everyone to education; and the right to take part in cultural life.

The Covenant does not merely list these rights; it describes and defines them in considerable detail and frequently sets out the steps that should be taken to achieve their realization. Typical of this approach is Article 7, which reads as follows:

The States Parties to the present Covenant recognize the right of everyone to the enjoyment of just and favourable conditions of work, which ensure, in particular:

(a) Remuneration which provides all workers as a minimum with:

(i) Fair wages and equal remuneration for work of equal value without distinction of any kind, in particular women being guaranteed conditions of work not inferior to those enjoyed by men, with equal pay for equal work;

(ii) A decent living for themselves and their families in accordance with the provisions of the present Covenant;

(b) Safe and healthy working conditions;

(c) Equal opportunity for everyone to be promoted in his employment to an appropriate higher level, subject to no considerations other than those of seniority and competence;

(d) Rest, leisure and reasonable limitation of working hours and periodic holidays with pay, as well as remuneration for public holidays.

By ratifying this Covenant, a State Party does not assume the obligation of immediate implementation found in the Civil and Political Covenant. The E.S.C. Covenant adopts a very different approach, which finds expression in Article 2(1).

Each State Party to the present Covenant undertakes to take steps, individually and through international assistance and co-operation, especially economic and technical, to the maximum of its available resources, with a view to achieving progressively the full realization of the rights recognized in the present Covenant by all appropriate means, including particularly the adoption of legislative measures.

As this language indicates, by ratifying this Covenant a state does not undertake to give immediate effect to all rights it enumerates. Instead, the state obligates itself merely to take steps "to the maximum of its available resources" in order to achieve "progressively the full realization" of these rights.

What accounts for the differences in the methods of implementation adopted in the two Covenants? As a general proposition, the protection of most civil and political rights requires few, if any, economic resources. With minor exceptions, little more is required of a government than legislation and a

decision not to engage in certain illegal practices—
not to torture people, not to imprison them arbi-
trarily, etc. The burden tends to be heavier and
the task more complicated when economic, social or
cultural rights are involved. In general, their enjoyment cannot be fully ensured without economic
and technical resources, education and planning,
the gradual reordering of social priorities and, in
many cases, international cooperation. These considerations are reflected in the "progressive" or
"programmatic" obligations which the States Parties to the E.S.C. Covenant have assumed. It would
be unrealistic to require immediate compliance with
all rights, given the nature of these rights and the
specific problems each state must deal with to ensure their full enjoyment. *See* Trubek, "Economic,
Social and Cultural Rights in the Third World:
Human Rights and Human Needs," *in* T. Meron,
Human Rights in International Law, 205, 213–22
(1984); A.G. Mower, *International Cooperation for
Social Justice: Global and Regional Protection of
Economic/Social Rights* (1985).

These realities also explain why, as a practical
matter, the standards by which to measure compliance under the E.S.C. Covenant will differ from
those that apply to treaties dealing with civil and
political rights. Since each state will invariably
face different problems and since no two states are
likely to have the same "available resources," different criteria will have to be applied to different
states in determining whether they are living up to
their treaty obligations. This is not to say, howev-

er, that no rights guaranteed in this Covenant can
be enforced by legislation or that judicial remedies
will always be inappropriate.

The assumption that the E.S.C. Covenant creates
no immediate obligations for the States Parties was
put to rest by the Committee on Economic, Social
and Cultural Rights—the body established to supervise the implementation of this treaty—in its General Comment No. 3 (1990). Report of the Committee on Economic, Social and Cultural Rights, Fifth
Session, U.N. Doc. E/199/23. E/C.12/1990/8, at 83
(1991). In its thorough analysis of Article 2(1), the
Committee points out that "while the Covenant
provides for progressive realization and acknowl-
edges the constraints due to limits of available
resources, it also imposes various obligations which
are of immediate effect." Among these, the Committee singles out two in particular: the undertaking of the States Parties to guarantee that the
rights set out in the Covenant will be exercised
without discrimination; and the undertaking in Article 2(1) "to take steps." As for the undertaking
of non-discrimination, the Committee notes that
legislation and the provision of judicial remedies
can often appropriately promote compliance with
this obligation. Regarding the undertaking to take
steps, the Committee notes that although "the full
realization of the relevant rights may be achieved
progressively, steps towards that goal must be tak-
en within a reasonably short time after the Covenant's entry into force for the States concerned."
The Committee also emphasizes "that a minimum

core obligation to ensure the satisfaction of, at the very least, minimum essential levels of each of the rights is incumbent upon every State party." *Id.*, at 86. *See generally* Andreassen *et al.*, "Compliance with Economic and Social Human Rights: Realistic Evaluations and Monitoring in the Light of Immediate Obligations," *in* A. Eide & B. Hagtret (eds.), *Human Rights in Perspective: A Global Assessment* 252 (1992).

The E.S.C. Covenant does not establish any interstate or individual complaints system. It only requires the States Parties to submit "reports on the measures which they have adopted and the progress made in achieving the observance of the rights recognized herein." E.S.C. Covenant, art. 16(1). The E.S.C. Covenant itself does not, moreover, establish a special committee to review the reports; it stipulates merely that they are to be submitted to the UN Economic and Social Council. Starting in 1976, ECOSOC adopted a series of resolutions that culminated in the establishment of a "Committee on Economic, Social and Cultural Rights," composed of 18 experts elected in their personal capacities. ECOSOC Resolution 1985/17 of May 22, 1985. The Committee held its first meeting in March 1987. Alston & Simma, "First Session of the UN Committee on Economic, Social and Cultural Rights," 81 Am. J. Int'l L. 747 (1987). Prior thereto ECOSOC had delegated the task of reviewing the state reports to a working group of its members, known as the Sessional Working Group on the Implementation of the International Covenant on

Economic, Social and Cultural Rights. That body reported its general findings to ECOSOC, the UN Commission on Human Rights and to the Specialized Agencies of the UN concerned with economic, social and cultural rights. *See* Alston, "The United Nations Specialized Agencies and Implementation of the International Covenant on Economic, Social and Cultural Rights," 18 Colum. J. Transn. L. 79 (1979). These early efforts to promote the implementation of the ESC Covenant were not very effective. The situation changed with the establishment of the permanent Committee. Despite numerous obstacles, some bureaucratic and others inherent in the nature of the E.S.C. Covenant, this body has gradually devised a sound and creative approach for getting states to live up to their treaty obligations. It has also used its General Comments and analyses of state reports to clarify the meaning of the many ambiguous provisions of the Covenant, thus providing the international community with an analytically helpful interpretative gloss on the normative character of economic, social and cultural rights. *See* Alston, "The Committee on Economic, Social and Cultural Rights," *in* P. Alston (ed.), *The United Nations and Human Rights* 473 (1992). *See also* Craven, "Towards an Unofficial Petition Procedure: A Review on the Role of the UN Committee on Economic, Social and Cultural Rights," *in* K. Drzewicki, C. Krause & A. Rosas (eds.), *Social Rights as Human Rights* 91 (1994).

IV. OTHER MAJOR UN HUMAN RIGHTS TREATIES

§ 2–11. Introduction

In addition to the International Bill of Human Rights, the UN has over the years promulgated a large number of treaties dealing with specific types of human rights violations, including genocide, racial discrimination, apartheid, discrimination against women, torture, etc. *See* U.N. Center for Human Rights, *Human Rights: A Compilation of International Instruments,* vol. 1, (1993). Some of these instruments will be discussed in the sections that follow.

§ 2–12. The Convention on the Prevention and Punishment of the Crime of Genocide

The Genocide Convention was adopted by the UN General Assembly on December 9, 1948 and entered into force on January 12, 1951. The extermination of millions of Jews and members of other national, ethnic and religious groups during the Nazi Holocaust prompted the adoption of the Genocide Convention, which outlaws this crime. *See* Lemkin, "Genocide as a Crime under International Law," 41 Am. J. Int'l L. 145 (1947).

The Convention declares that genocide, whether committed in time of peace or time of war, is a crime under international law. A "crime under international law" is a grave offense against the law of nations for which the individual perpetrator is punishable. It differs from a mere violation of international law, which makes a government liable for the resulting damages without imposing criminal responsibility on individuals. Article IV of the Genocide Convention accordingly provides that "persons committing genocide ... shall be punished, whether they are constitutionally responsible rulers, public officials or private individuals." The Convention defines "genocide" as the commission of certain enumerated acts "with intent to destroy, in whole or in part, a national, ethnic, racial or religious group, as such." (Art. II.) The acts constituting genocide are: (a) killing members of the group; (b) causing serious bodily or mental harm to members of the group; (c) deliberately inflicting on the group conditions of life calculated to bring about its physical destruction in whole or in part; (d) imposing measures intended to prevent births within the group; (e) forcibly transferring children of the group to another group. To be guilty of the crime of genocide, an individual must have committed one of the foregoing acts with the specific intent of destroying, in whole or in part, a national, ethnic, racial or religious group. The killing of some members of a group could consequently amount to genocide if carried out with the intent of destroying the group or a substantial part thereof.

It is worth noting that by outlawing the destruction of national, ethnic, racial and religious groups, the Genocide Convention formally recognizes the right of these groups to exist as groups. Viewed in this light, the Convention must be considered the centerpiece of the international law that applies to the protection of the rights of groups, be they minorities or majorities. Dinstein, "Collective Human Rights of Peoples and Minorities," 25 Int'l & Comp. L. Q. 102, 105 (1976).

The Genocide Convention takes account of the possibility that those charged with genocide might be tried by an international criminal court, but it does not establish such a tribunal. Although a permanent international criminal court has yet to be established—the UN Security Council created an *ad hoc* tribunal for the former Yugoslavia in 1993 and expanded its jurisdiction in 1994 to deal with the Rwandan genocide. *See* Chapter 6, *infra*. Dispute between two or more States Parties relating to the interpretation of the Convention may be appealed by either of them to the International Court of Justice. Genocide Convention, art. IX. The ICJ does not, however, have jurisdiction to try individuals for genocide. Hence, until a permanent international criminal court is established for that purpose or where no competent *ad hoc* tribunal exists, the punishment of the offenders is left to national courts. In dealing with this subject, Article VI of the Genocide Convention speaks only of "a competent tribunal of the State in the territory of which the act [of genocide] was committed." It is clear, nevertheless, that the courts of other states, particularly those of the perpetrator's nationality, would also have jurisdiction under international law generally. Also, there is considerable authority for the proposition that the universality principle of jurisdiction applies to the crime of genocide, thus giving the courts of all nations jurisdiction over the offense. *See* Attorney General of Israel v. Eichmann, 36 Int'l L.Rep. 5 (1968); *Restatement (Third)* § 404; M.C. Bassiouni, *Crimes Against Humanity in International Law* 519–20 (1992). On the drafting history of the Convention, see N. Robinson, *The Genocide Convention: A Commentary* (1960); Lippman, "The Drafting of the 1948 Convention on the Prevention and Punishment of the Crime of Genocide," 3 Boston U. Int'l L. J. 1 (1984).

§ 2–13. International Convention on the Elimination of All Forms of Racial Discrimination

This treaty was adopted by the UN General Assembly in 1965 and entered into force in 1969. The Convention has been described as "the most comprehensive and unambiguous codification in treaty form of the idea of the equality of races." Schwelb, "The International Convention on the Elimination of Racial Discrimination," 15 Int'l & Comp. L.Q. 996, at 1057 (1966). The Convention prohibits "racial discrimination," which it defines as "any distinction, exclusion, restriction or preference based on race, colour, descent, or national or ethnic origin" having the purpose or effect of "nullifying or impairing the recognition, enjoyment or exercise, on an equal footing, of human rights and fundamental freedoms in the political, economic, social, cultural or any other field of public life." (Art. 1(1).) The International Court of Justice has accepted this definition of racial discrimination as an authoritative interpretation of the meaning and scope of the non-discrimination clause of the UN Charter. Advisory Opinion on Legal Consequences for States of the Continued Presence of South Africa in Namibia, 1971 I.C.J. Rep. 16, at 57 (1971); Schwelb, "The International Court of Justice and the Human Rights Clauses of the Charter," 66 Am. J. Int'l L. 337, 350–51 (1972).

The States Parties to the Convention have the legal obligation to eliminate racial discrimination in their territory and to enact whatever laws are necessary to ensure non-discrimination in the exercise and enjoyment of various human rights. The Convention enumerates a long list of basic civil, political, economic, social and cultural rights to which this obligation applies. The list includes the rights set out in the Universal Declaration and the two Covenants. *See* Racial Convention, art. 5.

Besides outlawing racial discrimination by governmental authorities, the Convention requires each State Party to "prohibit and bring to an end, by all appropriate means, including legislation as required by circumstances, racial discrimination by any person, group or organization." Racial Convention, art. 2(1)(d). The Convention also declares that

Special measures ... for the sole purpose of securing adequate advancement of certain racial or ethnic groups or individuals requiring such protection as may be necessary in order to ensure such groups or individuals equal enjoyment or exercise of human rights and fundamental freedoms shall not be deemed racial discrimination, provided, however, that such measures do not, as a consequence, lead to the maintenance of separate rights for different racial groups and that they shall not be continued after the objectives for which they were taken have been achieved. Racial Convention, art. 1(4).

This language suggests that temporary affirmative action programs and preferential quota systems for minority groups are lawful, provided they are designed to remedy the consequences of past racial discrimination and do not in fact foster other forms of racial discrimination. For an analysis of the Convention, *see* T. Meron, *Human Rights Law–Making in the United Nations* 7 (1986); N. Lerner, *The UN Convention on the Elimination of All Forms of Racial Discrimination* (1980). *See also* N. Lerner, *Group Rights and Discrimination in International Law* (1990).

The enforcement machinery of the Convention consists of a Committee on the Elimination of Racial Discrimination (CERD) that is composed of 18 members. *See generally* UN Centre for Human Rights, *The First Twenty Years: Progress Report of the Committee on the Elimination of Racial Discrimination* (1991); Partsch, "The Committee on the Elimination of Racial Discrimination," *in* P. Alston, *The United Nations and Human Rights* 339 (1992). The CERD members are elected by the States Parties but serve in their individual capacities. The Convention confers a number of functions on the CERD. These include the review of the periodic reports the States Parties have an obligation to prepare "on the legislative, judicial, administrative or other measures which they have adopted to give effect to the provisions" of the Convention. Racial Convention, art. 9. The CERD also has the power to deal with inter-state and individual communications. *Id.*, arts. 11 and 14.

The CERD was the first UN treaty organ to develop a number of promising approaches designed to transform the review of state reports into a dynamic implementation technique. Its practice served as the model for other bodies, such as the Human Rights Committee. *See* Buergenthal, "Implementing the UN Racial Convention," 12 Tex. Int'l L.J. 187 (1977); Gomez del Prado, "United Nations Conventions on Human Rights: The Practice of the Human Rights Committee and the Committee on the Elimination of Racial Discrimination in Dealing with Reporting Obligations of States Parties," 7 Hum. Rts. Q. 492 (1985); Fischer, "Reporting Under the Covenant on Civil and Political Rights: The First Five Years of the Human Rights Committee," 76 Am. J. Int'l L. 142, 145 (1982). Over time, however, some UN treaty bodies, particularly the Human Rights Committee, appear to have made greater progress than the CERD in strengthening the reporting system and in devising creative methods to prod the States Parties into complying with their treaty obligations. *Compare* Partsch, "The Committee on the Elimination of

Racial Discrimination," *in* Alston, *supra*, at 339, *with* Opsahl, "The Human Rights Committee," *id.*, at 369.

By ratifying the Racial Convention, a state automatically submits itself to the jurisdiction of the CERD to deal with inter-state communications directed against it by any other State Party. Thus, unlike in the case of the CP Covenant, the inter-state complaint system under the Racial Convention is not optional. Racial Convention, art. 11. The procedure for dealing with these communications envisages a two-stage process. Here the CERD first passes on the admissibility of the complaint and gathers all relevant information thereon. Thereafter an *ad hoc* Conciliation Commission is established and charged with the task of preparing a report on the dispute and making appropriate recommendations to the states concerned. Racial Convention, arts. 12 and 13. The inter-state complaint mechanism has not as yet been utilized.

The individual petition system established by the Racial Convention is optional and thus requires a separate declaration recognizing the jurisdiction of the CERD to receive such communications. Racial Convention, art. 14. *See generally* Lerner, "Individual Petitions Under the International Convention on the Elimination of all Forms of Racial Discrimination," *in* I. Cotler & F.P. Eliadis (eds.), *International Human Rights Law: Theory and Practice* 435 (1992). Unlike in the case of inter-state complaints, CERD deals with individual communications without the aid of an *ad hoc* conciliation commission. After studying the information received from the state concerned and the petitioner, the CERD summarizes its findings and makes appropriate recommendations, which are published in its annual report to the UN General Assembly. Although the Racial Convention entered into force in 1969, the number of ten states necessary to bring the individual petition system into effect was not reached until 1982. Moreover, despite the fact that close to 140 states have ratified the Convention, less than 20 have thus far accepted the right of individual petition. To date the CERD has dealt with only a handful of individual petitions. *See* Report of the Committee on the Elimination of Racial Discrimination, U.N. Doc. A/48/18, at 105 (1994).

The Racial Convention also confers jurisdiction on the International Court of Justice to deal with disputes between the States Parties. The relevant provision is Article 22, which reads as follows:

> Any dispute between two or more States Parties with respect to the interpretation or application of this Convention, which is not settled by negotiation or by the procedures expressly provided for in this Convention, shall, at the request of any of the parties to the dispute, be referred to the International Court of Justice for decision, unless the disputants agree to another mode of settlement.

Thus, by ratifying the Convention a state is deemed to have accepted the jurisdiction of the Court to decide disputes arising under the treaty. However, many States Parties, including the United States, have ratified the Convention with a reservation to Article 22, requiring the consent of both parties to the dispute before it may be referred to the Court. They have thus effectively opted out of the provisions of Article 22.

§ 2–14. International Convention on the Suppression and the Punishment of the Crime of Apartheid

This Convention was adopted and opened for signature by the UN General Assembly on November 30, 1973. It entered into force on July 18, 1976 and has been ratified by more than 70 states.

As its name indicates, the purpose of this treaty is to suppress and punish apartheid. The Convention proclaims apartheid "a crime against humanity" and declares all inhuman acts attributable to the policies and practices of apartheid "crimes violating the principles of international law." (Art. I.) Although Article II of the Convention defines "the crime of *apartheid* "by reference to the policies of racial segregation and discrimination being practised in "southern Africa," the language of that provision is broad enough to cover similar policies, were they to be adopted in other regions of the world. Liability for the commission of the crime of apartheid extends not only to those "individuals, members of organizations and institutions and representatives of the State" who commit the offense, but also to all those who "directly abet, encourage or co-operate" in its commission regardless where such individuals may be at the time. (Art. III.) A person charged with the offense may be tried by any State Party and by any "international penal tribunal having jurisdiction with respect to those States Parties which shall have accepted its jurisdiction." (Art. V.) The Convention does not establish such a tribunal.

The measures of implementation provided for by the Convention consist of a periodic reporting requirement by the States Parties and the establishment of a Group of Three to review the reports. This body is designated by the chairman of the UN Commission of Human Rights from among those States Parties to the Convention that are members of the Commission. (Arts. VII and IX.) The Convention also empowers the UN Human Rights Commission to prepare various studies and reports relating to the crime of apartheid, including a list of individuals, organizations, institutions and representatives of states that are alleged to be guilty of the offense. (Art. X(1)(b).)

§ 2–15. Convention on the Elimination of All Forms of Discrimination Against Women

The UN General Assembly adopted this treaty on December 18, 1979; it entered into force on September 3, 1981. The CEDAW seeks to do away with discrimination against women, which it defines as "any distinction, exclusion, or restriction made on the basis of sex" that impairs the enjoyment by women of "human rights and fundamental freedoms in the political, economic, social, cultural, civil or any other field." (Art. 1.) In addition to the obligation to condemn discrimination against women, the States Parties undertake, *inter alia,* "to embody the principle of equality of men and women in their national constitutions or other appropriate legislation" and to adopt laws or other measures "including sanctions where appropriate, prohibiting all discrimination against women." (Art. 2.) The Convention also requires the States Parties to take a series of measures in the political, social, economic and cultural realm to advance the enjoyment of equal rights by women in all walks of life. Thus, for example, Article 5 of the Convention provides that

States Parties shall take all appropriate measures:

(a) To modify the social and cultural patterns of conduct of men and women, with a view to achieving the elimination of prejudices and customary and all other practices which are based on the idea of the inferiority or the superiority of either of the sexes or on stereotyped roles for men and women.

In like manner, the CEDAW addresses a wide range of problems encountered by women in their struggle for equality. *See generally* N. Hevener, *International Law and the Status of Women* (1983); T. Meron, *Human Rights Law–Making in the United Nations* 53 (1986); Cook, "State Accountability Under the Convention on the Elimination of All Forms of

Discrimination Against Women," *in* R.J. Cook (ed.), *Human Rights of Women* 228 (1994).

The effectiveness of the CEDAW in promoting the protection of the rights it guarantees has been undermined to a significant extent by the many reservations made by states in ratifying this treaty. These reservations seek to preserve various national or religious institutions that are in conflict with the Convention. Some of them, moreover, are clearly incompatible with the object and purpose of the Convention, despite the fact that its Article 28(2) declares that "a reservation incompatible with the object and purpose of the present Convention shall not be permitted." *See* Clark, "The Vienna Convention Reservations Regime and the Convention on Discrimination Against Women," 85 Am. J. Int'l L. 281 (1991). The effort to get states to withdraw their reservations, which has as yet not had much success, received a boost from the 1993 Vienna World Conference on Human Rights, which called on the CEDAW Committee to "continue its review of reservations to the Convention" and urged the states "to withdraw reservations that are contrary to the object and purpose of the Convention or which are otherwise incompatible with international treaty law." Vienna Declaration and Programme of Action, U.N. Doc. A/Conf. 157/23, Art. II, para. 39 (1993). *See* Sullivan, "Women's Human Rights and the 1993 World Conference on Human Rights," 88 Am. J. Int'l L. 152 (1994). It remains to be seen what effect this appeal will have on the States Parties.

The measures of implementation provided for by the Convention consist of periodic reports by the States Parties relating to "the legislative, judicial, administrative or other measures they have adopted to give effect to the provisions of the Convention." (Art. 18(1).) These reports are reviewed by the Committee on the Elimination of Discrimination against Women. (Art. 17.) The CEDAW Committee consists of 23 experts elected by the States Parties but serving in their personal capacities. It reports on its activities to the States Parties, the UN Commission on the Status of Women, and the General Assembly. The CEDAW Committee has been something of a step-child among UN human rights treaty organs when compared, for example, to the UN Human Rights Committee or to CERD. This is due in part to the fact that Article 20 (1) of the Convention provides that "the Committee shall normally meet for a period of not more than two weeks annually," which is not enough time to discharge its responsibilities to review state reports and interpret the Convention. Moreover, the CEDAW does not set up an inter-state or individual complaint mechanism whose existence would strengthen the Committee's authority. *See generally* Byrnes, "The Other Human Rights Treaty Body: The Work of the Committee on the Elimination of Discrimination against Women," 14 Yale J. Int'l L. 1 (1989); Jacobson, "The Committee on the Elimination of Discrimination against Women," *in* Alston, *supra*, at 444. *See also* Meron, "Enhancing the Effectiveness of the Prohibition of Discrimination against Women," 84 Am. J. Int'l L. 213 (1990), who addresses some of these issues and recommends the adoption of an additional protocol to the CEDAW establishing an individual communications mechanism. *Id.*, at 216. This recommendation received the support of the World Conference on Human Rights. *See* Vienna Declaration and Programme of Action, *supra*, para. 40.

Under Article 29(1) of the CEDAW disputes between the States Parties relating to the interpretation or application of the Convention may be submitted to the International Court of Justice by any of the parties to the dispute. Although this provision could be invoked to challenge reservations incompatible with the object and purpose of the treaty, many states that have made these reservations or that otherwise violate the CEDAW have also availed themselves of the right, expressly spelled in Article 29(2), to decline to accept the Court's jurisdiction under Article 29(1). No State Party has to date invoked Article 29(1).

§ 2–16. Convention Against Torture and Other Cruel, Inhuman or Degrading Treatment

This treaty was adopted by the UN General Assembly on December 10, 1984 and entered into force on June 28, 1987 after the 20th instrument of ratification necessary to bring it into force was deposited. *See generally* Lerner, "The U.N. Convention on Torture," 16 Israel Y.B. Hum. Rts. 126 (1986); J.H. Burgers & H. Danelius, *The United*

Nations Convention against Torture: A Handbook on the Convention against Torture and Other Cruel, Inhuman or Degrading Treatment or Punishment (1988). The Convention is designed to prevent and punish torture committed "by or at the instigation of or with the consent or acquiescence of a public official or other person acting in an official capacity." (Art. 1(1).) In other words, it covers not only torture inflicted by government officials but also by private individuals or groups whose conduct such officials encourage or tolerate. The Convention defines torture as "any act by which severe pain or suffering, whether physical or mental, is intentionally inflicted on a person" for the purpose, *inter alia,* of "obtaining from him or a third person information or a confession." (Art. 1(1).) The States Parties undertake to adopt "effective legislative, administrative, judicial or other measures to prevent" torture in any territory under their jurisdiction. (Art. 2(1).) They must also "ensure that all acts of torture are offenses under [their] criminal law." (Art. 49(1).) The States Parties are required to treat torture as an extraditable offense (Art. 8) and not to extradite a person to a country where he/she "would be in danger of being subjected to torture." Art. 3(1). On this latter point, see Mutomba v. Switzerland, Communication No. 13/993, UN Committee on Torture (CAT), Decision of April 27, 1994, 15 Hum. Rts. L. J. 164 (1994), holding that Switzerland would violate Article 3 of the Convention were it to expel or return Mr.

Mutomba to Zaire, where he was in danger of being tortured.

It is important to note that the Torture Convention declares that there are "no exceptional circumstances whatsoever" to justify torture and that no orders from superior officers or a public authority may be validly invoked as a justification. (Arts. 2(2) and 2(3).) The Convention also contains a number of provisions designed to ensure that the formal prohibition of torture becomes a reality on the domestic plane. Article 11, for example, reads as follows:

Each State Party shall keep under systematic review interrogation rules, instructions, methods and practices as well as arrangements for the custody and treatment of persons subjected to any form of arrest, detention or imprisonment in any territory under its jurisdiction, with a view to preventing any cases of torture.

The measures of implementation provided for in the Torture Convention are administered by the Committee on Torture (CAT). *See generally* N. Rodley, *The Treatment of Prisoners Under International Law* 128 (1987); Dormenval, "UN Committee Against Torture: Practice and Perspectives," 8 Neth. Q. Hum. Rts. 26 (1990); Byrnes, "The Committee against Torture," *in* Alston, *supra*, at 509. The CAT is composed of ten independent experts elected by the States Parties to the Convention. The only other UN human rights treaty body that is as small is the Committee of the Rights of the

Child. *See* § 2–17, *infra*. The measures of implementation consist of an obligatory reporting system
(Art. 19) as well as optional inter-state (Art. 21) and
individual complaint (art. 22) mechanisms. These
two mechanisms are patterned on those provided
for under the Covenant on Civil and Political Rights
and its Optional Protocol. In addition to these
measures of implementation, the Torture Convention empowers the CAT to undertake certain inves-
tigatory action on its own initiative. Thus, Article
20, authorizes the Committee to initiate an inquiry
when it receives "reliable information" suggesting
"well-founded indications that torture is being systematically practised in the territory of a State
Party." Although the inquiry is to be confidential
and requires the Committee to seek the cooperation
of the State Party concerned, the language of Article 20 indicates that the state's failure to cooperate
does not deprive the Committee *ipso facto* of the
right to proceed with the investigation. However,
the Committee does need the state's consent to
investigate the charges in its territory. (Art. 20(3).)
When the proceedings have been concluded, the
Committee may decide to prepare a summary of its
findings for inclusion in its annual report. That
report is submitted to the States Parties and the
UN General Assembly. (Arts. 24 and 20(5).) For
action taken by CAT under Article 20, *see* "Activities of the Committee against Torture pursuant to
Article 20 of the Convention against Torture and
Other Cruel, Inhuman or Degrading Treatment or
Punishment," UN Doc. A/48/44/Add.1 (Nov. 9,

1993), 14 Hum. Rts. L.J. 426 (1993), describing an inquiry involving torture in Turkey.

The States Parties may, however, avoid the application of the powers that Article 20 confers on the CAT. They are permitted to do so by Article 28, which provides that "each State may, at the time of signature or ratification of this Convention or accession thereto, declare that it does not recognize the competence of the Committee provided for in article 20." This possibility "to contract out" of Article 20 has been utilized by the States Parties much less frequently than one might have expected, despite the fact that Article 20 confers on the CAT an enforcement weapon that is potentially very powerful. The Torture Convention also permits disputes between the States Parties relating to the interpretation or application of the treaty to be appealed by any one of them to the International Court of Justice. (Art. 30(1)). However, Article 30(2) permits states to opt out of the application of paragraph 1, and many states have done so.

§ 2–17. Convention on the Rights of the Child

This treaty was adopted by the UN General Assembly on November 20, 1989 and entered into force on September 2, 1990. By 1994, more than 150 states had ratified the Convention. For useful analyses of the most important aspects of the Convention, *see* "The Rights of the Child," UN Bulletin of Human Rights, No. 91/2, 1–82 (1992). By ratifying the Convention, the States Parties assume the obligation to accord children within their jurisdiction an extensive catalog of civil, political, economic, social and cultural rights "irrespective of the child's or his or her parent's or legal guardian's race, colour, sex, language, religion, political or other opinion, national, ethnic or social origin, property, disability, birth or other status." (Art. 2(1)). The Convention defines a child as "every human being below the age of eighteen unless under the law applicable to the child, majority is attained earlier." (Art. 1.) The guiding principle of the Convention is spelled out in Article 3(1), which declares that "in all actions concerning children, whether undertaken by public or private social welfare institutions, courts of law, administrative authorities or legislative bodies, the best interests of the child shall be a primary consideration." *See* Alston, "The Legal Framework of the Convention on the Rights of the Child," Bulletin of Human Rights, No. 91/2, at 1 (UN, 1992).

Although many of the rights the Convention proclaims are set out in one form or another in existing international human rights treaties, this is the first time that children have been singled out as exclusive subjects of international rights and protection. The Convention seeks to protect children against a large number of practices of special danger to their welfare, among them economic exploitation, illicit use of drugs, all forms of sexual exploitation and abuse, and traffic in children. It also bars the recruitment of children under the age of fifteen into the armed forces of the States Parties. *See generally* Lopatka, "The Importance of the Convention on the Rights of the Child," Bulletin of Human Rights, No. 91/2 *supra*, at 56. *See also* Price Cohen & Miljeteig–Olssen, "Status Report: United Nations Convention on the Rights of the Child," 7 N.Y.L. Sch. J. Hum. Rts. 367 (1991).

The Convention establishes a Committee on the Rights of the Child (CRC Committee), which is charged with the tasks of "examining the progress made by the States Parties in achieving the realization of the obligations undertaken in the present Convention." Art. 43(1). The Committee is composed of ten members who serve in their personal capacities. Its principal task is to review the reports which the States Parties are required to submit to the Committee on the measures they have taken in implementing the Convention. (Art. 44.) It has no power to receive individual or inter-state complaints. For an overview of the work of the CRC Committee, see Report of the Committee on the Rights of the Child, UN Doc. A/49/41 (1994).

V. UN CHARTER–BASED INSTITUTIONS

§ 2–18. Introduction

In addition to the supervisory bodies that have been established under UN human rights treaties, there also exist within the UN framework various institutions and procedures which have their constitutional basis in the Charter of the United Nations itself. This is true of such major human rights organs as the UN Commission on Human Rights, the Sub–Commission on Prevention of Discrimination and Protection of Minorities, the Commission on the Status of Women, and the newly created office of High Commissioner of Human Rights. The same is true of the procedures the UN has developed to deal with especially serious violations of human rights. This chapter describes only the four institutions just referred to and the procedures for dealing with so-called gross violations of human rights. For a more comprehensive overview, *see* P. Alston (ed.), *The United Nations and Human Rights: A Critical Appraisal* (1992).

§ 2–19. Commission on Human Rights

Article 68 of the UN Charter mandates the Economic and Social Council (ECOSOC) to establish "commissions in economic and social fields and for the promotion of human rights." ECOSOC complied with this mandate in 1946 by creating the Commission on Human Rights. Initially composed of 18 members, the size of the Commission has been expanded over the years; today it consists of 53 states. The states name their own Commission representatives, who serve as instructed government delegates and not in their personal capacities. The 53 Member States are designated by ECOSOC according to a formula designed to ensure equitable geographical distribution between different regions of the world. *See generally* H. Tolley, *The U.N. Commission on Human Rights (1987);* Alston, *"The Commission on Human Rights," in* Alston, *supra,* at 126.

The Commission's terms of reference require it to submit to ECOSOC proposals, recommendations and reports dealing with international human rights instruments, the protection of minorities and prevention of discrimination, and related human rights matters. Its charge also includes assisting ECOSOC with the coordination of the human rights activities of the UN system. In the first decades of its fifty-year existence, the Commission devoted itself principally to purely promotional activities and the preparation of draft international human rights instruments. The Universal Declaration and the Covenants, for example, were drafted by the Commission. In those years, the Commission was barred from taking any action on specific situations or charges that a UN Member State engaged in human rights violations. *See* § 2–22, *infra.* Its role began to change in the late 1960's as human rights concerns increasingly intruded on, and became an integral part of, the political agenda of the United Nations. The past two decades have seen a dramatic expansion of the number of human rights issues brought to the attention of the UN and an increasing willingness of its membership to have the UN address them. Although today all UN organs, including the Security Council, deal with some human rights matters, the Human Rights Commission's jurisdiction and agenda have vastly expanded over time as far as promotion and protection are concerned. There are now few human rights and related subjects that are not brought to the attention of the Commission. *See, e.g.,* Commission on Human Rights, Report on the Fiftieth

Session, UN Doc. E/1994/24, E/CN.4/1994/132 (1994). The Commission has therefore become, together with the UN Human Rights Centre which serves as the human rights secretariat of the UN, the nerve center of the UN human rights apparatus. It acts as coordinator of the many existing UN human rights institutions and programs as well as the principal UN forum for addressing charges of human rights violations.

Although the Commission deserves credit for establishing many useful programs to promote human rights (*e.g.*, UN human rights advisory services), today it focuses principally on efforts to deal with human rights violations. It discharges the latter function through an ever expanding network of working groups and rapporteurs with thematic or country mandates. *See* "List of Special Procedures of the UN Commission on Human Rights," 14 Hum. Rts. L.J. 131 (1993). *See also* T. Meron, *Human Rights Law–Making in the United Nations* 272 (1986); Weissbrodt, "The Three 'Theme' Special Rapporteurs of the UN Commission on Human Rights," 80 Am. J. Int'l L. 685 (1986); Rodley, "United Nations Non–Treaty Procedures for Dealing with Human Rights Violations," *in* H. Hannum (ed.), *Guide to International Human Rights Practice* 60, 70 (2d ed. 1992). Although some have criticized the operation of these institutions, see Van Dongen, "System Overload of the U.N. Special Procedures," 14 Hum. Rts. L.J. 130 (1993), it cannot be doubted that these techniques call the world's attention to massive violations of human rights which might otherwise go unnoticed outside the countries where they are being committed. The rapporteur system grew out of and is the logical consequence of special procedures established under ECOSOC Resolutions 1503 and 1235, which empower the Commission to deal with gross violations of human Rights. These procedures are discussed in § 2–22, *infra.*

The Commission has frequently been criticized for its ineffectiveness, for its politically motivated or selective approach in dealing with charges of human rights violations. Although much of this criticism is justified, it overlooks the fact that the Commission can do no more than the states comprising it want it to do. *See* Tolley, *supra,* at 187. Moreover, since the Commission is a political body, it should surprise no one, regrettable as this may be, that it tends to politicize the issues before it. Yet it would be a mistake not to recognize that the Commission has played an important role in broadening the human rights agenda of the UN and in pioneering the use of new international techniques for dealing with human rights violations. It deserves much of the credit for transforming human rights into a major item on the agenda of the international community and for broadening the legal scope and application of the human rights provisions of the UN Charter.

§ 2–20. Sub–Commission on Prevention of Discrimination and Protection of Minorities.

The Sub–Commission, a subsidiary organ of the Commission on Human Rights, was established in

1947. It has traditionally been the UN institution most sympathetic to the cause of human rights. This is due in large part to the fact that its members, unlike those of the Commission, serve in their personal capacities. Although this fact does not always guarantee that each member will be a free agent—here much depends upon the form of government of the representative's home state—many independent-minded individuals have in the past served and continue to serve on this body. *See generally* Tolley, *supra*, at 163; Eide, "The Sub–Commission on Prevention of Discrimination and Protection of Minorities," *in* Alston, *supra,* at 211.

The Sub–Commission consists of 26 members, elected by the Commission from a list of nominees designated by the Member States of the UN. They serve for a period of four years and may be reelected. The terms of reference of the Sub–Commission require it to undertake studies and to make recommendations to the Human Rights Commission "concerning the prevention of discrimination of any kind relating to human rights and fundamental freedoms and the protection of racial, national, religious and linguistic minorities." It is also empowered "to perform any other functions which may be entrusted to it by the Economic and Social Council or the Commission on Human Rights." ECOSOC Res. 9 (II) of June 21, 1946. In practice, these terms of reference have been interpreted broadly enough to permit the Sub–Commission to deal with the whole range of human rights issues that arise in the UN context. *See generally* Humphrey, "The

United Nations Sub–Commission on the Prevention of Discrimination and the Protection of Minorities," 62 Am. J. Int'l L. 869 (1968); Haver, "The Mandate of the UN Sub–Commission on the Prevention of Discrimination and Protection of Minorities," 21 Colum. J. Transnat'l L. 103 (1982); Eide, "The Sub–Commission . . .," *in* Alston, *supra*, at 213. As a result, the Sub–Commission has prepared a variety of studies and reports; it has participated in the drafting of human rights instruments; and it has devoted much time in recent years to the examination of charges of human rights violations. In fact, the Sub–Commission is largely responsible for stimulating the development of various UN procedures for dealing with such violations and for pushing the UN's political human rights organs to strengthen these institutions. It has played a particularly important role in the implementation of the 1503 procedures, *see* § 2–22, *infra*, and in focusing the UN's attention on human rights issues relating, *inter alia*, to minorities, indigenous populations, slavery, and disappearances. It also laid the groundwork for many important normative instruments adopted by the UN, including most recently, the 1992 Declaration of the Rights of Persons Belonging to National or Ethnic, Religious and Linguistic Minorities, adopted by the UN General Assembly on December 18, 1992. *See* Thornberry, "The UN Declaration on the Rights of Persons Belonging to National or Ethnic, Religious and Linguistic Minorities: Background, Analysis and Observations," *in* A. Phillips & A. Rosas (eds.), *The UN Minority Rights Declaration* 11 (1993).

§ 2–21. Commission on the Status of Women

This Commission was established in 1947. It consists of 45 members elected as state representatives along geographic lines similar to those applicable to the Commission on Human Rights. *See generally,* Reanda, "The Commission on the Status of Women," *in* Alston, *supra,* at 265. The Commission's mandate charges it with the preparation of studies, reports and recommendations on human rights and related issues affecting women. It has played an important role in initiating UN programs designed to eradicate *de jure* and *de facto* discrimination against women, including the drafting of the principal contemporary treaties dealing with women's rights. *See* Galey, "Promoting Non–Discrimination Against Women: The UN Commission on the Status of Women," 23 Int'l Studies Q. 273 (1979); Reanda, "Human Rights and Women's Rights: The United Nations Approach," 3 Hum. Rts. Q. 11 (1981). The first few decades of the Commission's existence were devoted to these normative activities. In recent years the Commission has been able to focus more on issues relating to the role and needs of women in contemporary societies and on improving their political, economic, and social status. By serving as the preparatory committee for increasingly more important UN world conferences on the subject, the Commission has gradually gained the political influence it needed but lacked in the past to make a significant impact. On the evolution of the Commission's role, *see* Reanda, "The Commission on the Status of Women," *in* Alston, *supra,* at 265.

Thus far, it has proved much easier for the Commission to engage in promotional activities than to act on specific violations of women's rights. The Commission has had to struggle for a long time to acquire the authority to deal with complaints alleging such violations. In the early 1980's ECOSOC empowered the Commission to undertake a limited review of communications charging specific violations of women's rights. The Commission has used these communications principally as a source of information for its studies rather than as an instrument designed to prod governments to address the specific complaints. Efforts are under way to reform the communications procedures and give the Commission more power to act on complaints. It remains to be seen how successful these efforts will be. *See* Byrnes, "Toward More Effective Enforcement of Women's Human Rights Through the Use of International Human Rights Law and Procedure," *in* R.J. Cook (ed.), *Human Rights of Women: National and International Perspectives* 189, 205–6 (1994). For a telling historical review of the early efforts, see Galey, "International Enforcement of Women's Rights," 6 Hum. Rts. Q. 463 (1984). *See also,* Guggenheim, "The Implementation of Human Rights by the UN Commission on the Status of Women: A Brief Comment," 12 Tex. Int'l L.J. 239 (1977).

§ 2–22. Procedures for Dealing With Gross Violations of Human Rights

The establishment of the UN created great expectations and gave hope to millions of oppressed peoples the world over who believed that the Organization would bring them the freedom and justice for which they had been waiting so long. It is not surprising, therefore, that almost as soon as the UN came into being, it began to receive a large number of petitions from individuals and non-governmental organizations alleging violations of human rights and seeking UN intervention. From 1947 to 1957, for example, some 65,000 such communications were received by the UN. Buergenthal, "The United Nations and the Development of Rules Relating to Human Rights," Proceedings of the Am. Soc. Int'l L. 132, 135 n.7 (1965). These numbers increased even more in later years, at times reaching more than 20,000 communications annually. Tardu, "United Nations Response to Gross Violations of Human Rights: the 1503 Procedure," 20 Santa Clara L. Rev. 559 (1980). But the UN Commission on Human Rights, logically the most appropriate body within the Organization to deal with these petitions, decided in 1947 that it had "no power to take any action in regard to any complaints concerning human rights." L. Sohn & T. Buergenthal, *International Protection of Human Rights* 747 (1973). This decision was confirmed by ECOSOC in Resolution 75(V) of August 5, 1947, which also established a method for classifying the petitions and provided that they be included in a confidential list. Access to that list was so severely restricted that the information contained in it could not even be used by members of the Commission to initiate any action in specific cases. *Id.*, at 748–50.

Between 1947 and 1959, various efforts were made to get ECOSOC to reverse its 1947 decision and empower the Commission to act on communications alleging violations of human rights. Although these efforts were not successful, they led to the adoption of ECOSOC Resolution 728F (XXVIII) of July 30, 1959. It consolidated existing UN procedures for classifying communications while at the same time reaffirming the decision of the Commission that "it has no power to take any action in regard to any complaints concerning human rights." In principle this general rule remains in force to this day, although the exceptions that have been engrafted on it have limited its scope significantly by empowering the Commission to deal with and act on certain very serious types of human rights violations. *See* Sohn, "Human Rights: Their Implementation and Supervision by the United Nations," *in* T. Meron (ed.), *Human Rights in International Law: Legal and Policy Issues* 369, 385 (1984); Rodley, "United Nations Non–Treaty Procedures for Dealing with Human Rights Violations," *in* H. Hannum (ed.), *Guide to International Human Rights Practice* 60 (2d ed. 1992). These changes were ushered in by two ECOSOC resolutions: Resolution 1235 (XLII) of June 6, 1967, and Resolution 1503 (XLVIII) of May 27, 1970. *See generally* Alston, "The Commission on Human

Rights," *in* Alston, *supra*, at 138. Resolution 1235 permits the Commission to examine certain gross violations of human rights that come to its attention, whereas Resolution 1503 establishes a limited petition system for dealing with communications that "reveal a consistent pattern" of such violations. The latter procedure is confidential, the former is not.

ECOSOC Resolution 1235 authorizes the Commission and its Sub–Commission on Prevention of Discrimination and Protection of Minorities

> to examine information relevant to gross violations of human rights and fundamental freedoms, as exemplified by the policy of *apartheid* as practised in the Republic of South Africa ... and to racial discrimination as practised notably in Southern Rhodesia, contained in the communications listed ... pursuant to ... resolution 728F (XXVIII) of 30 July 1959. (Paragraph 2).

When this examination discloses the existence of "situations which reveal a consistent pattern of violations of human rights, as exemplified by the policy of *apartheid* ... and racial discrimination," the Commission is empowered to undertake a "thorough study" and to report its conclusions to the Economic and Social Council. (Paragraph 3).

While some countries sought to limit the application of the 1235 procedure to *apartheid* and related policies, these efforts did not succeed. Today it is no longer disputed that the 1235 procedure applies to any situation involving large-scale violations of human rights, and the Commission has so interpreted it in recent years. The working groups and special rapporteur systems established by the Commission to report on these types of violations, *see* § 2–19, *supra*, and the measures adopted by the Commission to deal with them, derive their legal basis principally from Resolution 1235 and to a lesser extent Resolution 1503. *See, e.g.*, the resolutions adopted by the Commission under agenda item 12 ("Question of the violations of human rights and fundamental freedoms in any part of the world, with particular reference to colonial and other dependent countries and territories)," Commission on Human Rights, Report of the Fiftieth Session, E/1994/24, E/CN.4/1994/132, at 372 (1994). It is also clear today that situations falling within the scope of the 1235 procedure may be placed on the Commission's agenda by its members and that they need not first have to be considered by the Sub–Commission.

Resolution 1503 authorizes the Sub–Commission to establish a small working group to examine the communications received from individuals and other private groups by the UN with a view to identifying those that "appear to reveal a consistent pattern of gross and reliably attested violations of human rights and fundamental freedoms within the terms of reference of the Sub–Commission." For the terms of reference of the Sub–Commission, see § 2–19, *supra*. The resolution also provides that these communications, together with any relevant comments thereon from the governments concerned, should be reviewed by the Sub–Commission "in private meetings ... with a view to determining whether to refer to the Commission on Human Rights particular situations which appear to reveal a consistent pattern of gross and reliably attested violations of human rights requiring consideration by the Commission." Under Resolution 1503 the Commission, when acting on any communication referred to it by the Sub–Commission, is empowered to make a determination whether a) to undertake a "thorough study" thereof in accordance with the provisions of paragraph 3 of Resolution 1235, *supra,* or b) to make it the "subject of an investigation by an *ad hoc* Committee to be appointed by the Commission which shall be undertaken only with the consent of the State concerned...."

On August 13, 1971, the Sub–Commission adopted Resolution 1 (XXIV) establishing specific procedures for the application of ECOSOC Resolution 1503. One noteworthy aspect of this resolution is that it provides, in setting standards and criteria of admissibility, that

communications shall be admissible only if ... there are reasonable grounds to believe that they reveal a consistent pattern of gross and reliably attested violations of human rights and fundamental freedoms, *including* policies of racial discrimination and segregation and of apartheid, *in any country, including* colonial and other dependent countries and peoples. (Emphasis added.)

The words "including" and the phrase "in any country," used in the Sub–Commission's Resolution 1 of 1971, were inserted to make clear that the procedures for dealing with communications are applicable to any gross violations of human rights, whether or not they are related to policies of racial discrimination or *apartheid.* Although some governments sought in the past to limit the application of the 1503 procedures to racial discrimination, they did not prevail. *See* Tardu, *supra,* at 583. Today it is no longer disputed that Resolution 1503 applies to all situations revealing a pattern of gross violations of human rights wherever they might be committed.

Here it should be emphasized that the 1503 procedure does not establish an individual petition system as that concept is usually understood. For a detailed analysis of the 1503 procedure, *see* UN Doc. E/CN.4/1994/42. Although individuals have standing to file petitions, their cause of action is based on a showing of "a consistent pattern of gross and reliably attested violations." The procedure is thus applicable to large-scale or systematic denials of human rights rather than to violations of one individual's rights. Of course, to the extent that one or a series of individual cases are symptomatic of the large-scale violations taking place in a particular country, they state a cause of action under the 1503 procedure.

The petitioner does not have to be the victim of the violation as long as he/she has "direct and reliable knowledge of those violations." Sub–Commission, Res. 1 (XXIV), para. 2(a). Non-governmental organizations may also submit communications. Petitioners must show, however, that domestic remedies have been exhausted "unless it appears that such remedies would be ineffective or unreasonably prolonged." *Id.*, at para. 4(b). Resolution 1503 requires that the proceedings envisaged by it "remain confidential until such time as the Commission may decide to make recommendations to the Economic and Social Council." ECOSOC Res. 1503(8). The confidentiality aspect of the 1503 procedure is its greatest defect. It is carried to such an extreme that the petitioner is not even kept informed of the status of the communication beyond the initial acknowledgement of its receipt, which is not the way any mechanism for the protection of human rights should operate.

A petition received under the 1503 procedure is first examined by a working group of the Sub–Commission. The working group may refer it to the Sub–Commission, which has the power to decide that the petition should be referred to the Commission. The Commission, in turn, has its own working group—the so-called Working Group on Situations—to screen the petitions before they are taken up by it. Although all the proceedings in the Commission relating to a complaint take place in closed sessions, the Commission now identifies the countries whose conduct it found to be governed by the 1503 procedures. Once that finding has been made, the Commission may refer these situations to the Economic and Social Council. ECOSOC as well as

the General Assembly may adopt appropriate resolutions calling on the governments concerned to
remedy the situation and comply with their Charter
obligations not to violate human rights. At this
stage of the proceedings, all debates are public.
Neither ECOSOC nor the General Assembly have
the power to do more than condemn a government's
failure to comply with their resolutions. In extreme cases, the Assembly may recommend that the
Member States impose voluntary sanctions on the
recalcitrant government.

The Commission has now also initiated a practice
that enables it to transform 1503 situations into
1235 cases. *See, e.g.*, its actions on the Sudan and
Zaire, with regard to which the Commission's 1993
annual report notes that the Commission's "Chairman ... announced that the Commission will no
longer examine the human rights situation in the
Sudan and Zaire under the confidential procedure
governed by Council resolution 1503 (XLVIII), in
view of the public procedures concerning both countries established by Commission resolutions 1993/60
and 1993/61, respectively." Commission on Human
Rights Report on the Forty–Ninth Session, UN Doc.
E/1993/23, E/CN.4/1993/122, at 376 (1993). The
two resolutions relating to the Sudan and Zaire are
reproduced in *id.*, at 188 and 190, respectively. As
this example indicates, the Commission can now
"go public" with a particularly serious human
rights situation that it had been considering under
the 1503 procedure by transforming it into a 1235
case. In this fashion the Commission remains

seized of the situation and is free to act on it without being bound by the confidentiality requirement of the 1503 procedure. *See* Bossuyt, "The Development of Special Procedures of the United Nations Commission on Human Rights," 6 Hum. Rts. L.J. 179 (1985). On the interaction between the 1503 and 1235 procedures, see Cook, "International Human Rights Mechanism: The Role of the Special Procedure in the Protection of Human Rights—The Way Forward After Vienna," I.C.J. Rev., No. 50, at 31 (1993).

§ 2–23. High Commissioner for Human Rights

This office was established pursuant to UN General Assembly Resolution 48/141 of January 7, 1994. Earlier efforts to create the position, dating back to the 1950's and 1960's, failed largely for reasons related to the Cold War and superpower opposition. The subject was also considered at the 1993 Vienna World Conference on Human Rights. There a group of Asian countries blocked the adoption of a consensus recommendation calling for the establishment of the office of the UN High Commissioner for Human Rights. The conference did recommend, however, that the subject be considered by the General Assembly "as a matter of priority." UN World Conference on Human Rights, Vienna Declaration and Programme of Action, UN Doc. A/Conf. 157/23, part II, para. 18 (1993). The General Assembly complied and, after weeks of negotiations, adopted the resolution creating the position of High

Commissioner for Human Rights. See G.A. Res. 48/141 (1994). Ecuador's UN representative, José Ayala Lasso, who had chaired these negotiations, was thereafter named to the post by the Secretary–General acting with the approval of the General Assembly.

As stipulated by the General Assembly, the High Commissioner for Human Rights is the "United Nations official with principal responsibility for United Nations human rights activities under the direction and responsibility of the Secretary–General." U.N. G.A. Res. 48/148(4). In discharging his responsibilities, the High Commissioner operates "within the framework of the overall competence, authority and decisions of the General Assembly, the Economic and Social Council and the Commission on Human Rights." *Id.* Among the various functions assigned to the High Commissioner, the most important one is spelled out in paragraph 4(f) of the resolution, which empowers him "to play an active role in removing the current obstacles and in meeting the challenges to the full realization of all human rights and in preventing the continuation of human rights violations throughout the world." *Id.* This language is broad enough to permit him to take on any contemporary human rights problem and to be actively engaged in efforts to prevent human rights violations around the world.

The High Commissioner has the rank of an Under Secretary–General of the United Nations. He is charged with the overall supervision of the Human Rights Centre, which is the human rights secretariat of the UN, as well as with the coordination of the UN's promotional and protection activities. In short, he is the UN's human rights "Czar." How effective he will be depends on many factors, including his diplomatic skill, commitment and creativity, the political will of the Member States of the UN, the resources placed at this disposal and the support he receives from the Secretary–General. While it is too early to say how Mr. Ayala Lasso will perform in his post, it is clear that the creation of the office of High Commissioner of Human Rights marks another important step forward in the struggle to strengthen the ability of the UN to deal with human rights violations.

§ 2–24. Gross Violations of Human Rights and the UN Charter

In establishing "standards and criteria" for the admissibility of human rights complaints, Sub–Commission Resolution 1 (XXIV) of August 13, 1971, *supra* § 2–22, refers to "the relevant principles of the Charter, of the Universal Declaration of Human Rights and of other applicable instruments in the field of human· rights." *Id.,* at para. 1(a). This language has special legal significance given its context: the effort of the UN to establish a UN machinery for dealing with gross violations of human rights. *See* § 2–22, *supra.* Particularly relevant, in this connection, are ECOSOC Resolutions 1235 (XLII) of June 6, 1967, and 1503 (XLVIII) of May 27, 1970, *supra,* as well as UN General Assembly Resolution 2144A (XXI) of October 26, 1966. In the latter resolution, after expressing its conviction "that gross violations of the rights and fundamental freedoms set forth in the Universal Declaration of Human Rights continue to occur in certain countries," the Assembly called on ECOSOC and the Commission on Human Rights "to give urgent consideration to ways and means of improving the capacity of the United Nations to put a stop to violations of human rights wherever they may occur."

These resolutions and the vast human rights practice of UN organs implementing them, and subsequent resolutions, have established an important legal principle applicable to the interpretation of the UN Charter. That principle holds that a state which engages in gross violations of the human rights proclaimed by the Universal Declaration and other relevant human rights instruments, violates the UN Charter obligations spelled out in Articles 55 and 56. It is therefore not illegal for the UN under Article 2(7) of the Charter, which bars intervention in matters essentially within a Member State's domestic jurisdiction, to take appropriate measures designed to compel that state not to engage in gross violations of human rights. The internationalization of human rights and the nature of the obligations the Charter imposes on UN Member States are thus closely linked to the concept of gross violations. That concept is by no means static. Although it is today identified with massive and systematic violations of some of the most fundamental rights proclaimed in the Universal Declaration, see § 2–3, *supra,* many other rights may in time come to be viewed as equally fundamental. Their massive and systematic violation by a government would then also have to be considered a breach of its UN Charter obligations. The required magnitude of the concept of "massive" or "gross" violations may also gradually require a lower threshold of severity as the international community becomes less tolerant of what is lawful behavior under the Charter. Viewed in this light, the human rights provisions of the Charter are "elastic clauses" whose expansion is tied to the evolving standards of international legality and decency.

VI. SPECIALIZED AGENCIES

§ 2–25. Introduction

The Specialized Agencies of the United Nations are functional intergovernmental organizations affiliated with the UN. *See* T. Buergenthal & H. Maier, *Public International Law in a Nutshell* 45–47 (2d ed. 1990). Although they are autonomous entities in the sense that they have their own constitutions and policy-making structure, they have a special institutional relationship with the UN and cooperate with it in areas of mutual concern. This is particularly true as far as the promotion of human rights is concerned. *See* Alston, "The United Nations Specialized Agencies and the Implementation of the International Covenant on Economic, Social and Cultural Rights," 18 Colum. J. Transnat'l L. 79 (1979). The International Labor Organization (ILO) and the United Nations Educational, Scientific and Cultural Organization (UNESCO) are among the specialized agencies that have the most developed human rights systems. The World Health Organization (WHO) and the Food and Agriculture Organization (FAO) also engage in important human rights activities.

§ 2–26. Their Role and Activities: Bibliographic References

Space does not permit us to do more than take note of the human rights work of the specialized agencies. The interaction of these organizations with the UN in the promotion of human rights is described in considerable detail in various parts of UN Centre for Human Rights, *United Nations Action in the Field of Human Rights,* (1994). *See also* Marks, "Human Rights, Activities of Universal Organizations," in *Encyclopedia of Public International Law,* Instalment 8, at 274 (R. Bernhardt, ed. 1985). There is a vast literature on the highly advanced system developed by the ILO for the protection of labor and related human rights. *See, e.g.,* Valticos, "The International Labour Organisation," in K. Vasak & P. Alston (eds.), *The International Dimensions of Human Rights,* vol. 1, at 363 (1982); Landy, "The Implementation Procedures of the International Labor Organization," 20 Santa Clara L. Rev. 633 (1980); Leary, "Lessons from the experience of the International Labour Organization," *in* P. Alston (ed.), *The United Nations and Human Rights: A Critical Appraisal* 580 (1992); Swepston, "Human Rights Complaint Procedures of the International Labour Organization," *in* H. Hannum (ed.), *Guide to International Human Practice* 99 (2d ed. 1992). *See also* V. Leary, *International Labour Conventions and National Law* (1981).

The human rights activities of UNESCO are considered by Saba, "UNESCO and Human Rights," *in* Vasak & Alston, *supra* at 401, who provide a useful overview. In the late 1970's, UNESCO established a special system for dealing with human rights violations falling within its constitutional mandate which covers science, culture, and education. The application of this enforcement mechanism is examined by Alston, "UNESCO Procedure for Dealing with Human Rights Violations," 20 Santa Clara L. Rev. 665 (1980); Marks, "The Complaint Procedure of the United Nations Educational, Scientific and Cultural Organization," *in* Hannum, *supra*, at 86. For an assessment of the effectiveness of these procedures, see Weissbrodt & Farley, "The UNESCO Human Rights Procedures: An Evaluation," 16 Hum. Rts. Q. 391 (1994). The human rights work of the FAO and WHO is described in *United Nations Action in the Field of Human Rights, supra*. The Economic and Social Council of the UN and its various subsidiary organs coordinate the UN human rights effort with that of the specialized agencies. For a thorough study on the interaction of existing measures of implementation, see A.A. Cancado–Trindade, "Co–Existence and Co–Ordination of Mechanisms of International Protection of Human Rights (At Global and Regional Levels)," 202 Recueil des Cours 10 (1987).

CHAPTER 3

THE EUROPEAN SYSTEM FOR THE PROTECTION OF HUMAN RIGHTS

I. INTRODUCTION

The European system for the protection of human rights was established by the Council of Europe, a regional intergovernmental organization created in 1949 by a group of Western European nations committed to the preservation of individual freedom and democracy. Article 3 of its Statute provides that "every Member of the Council of Europe must accept the principles of the rule of law and of the enjoyment by all persons within its jurisdiction of human rights and fundamental freedoms...." The end of the Cold War has enabled an increasing number of Eastern and Central European nations to join the Council of Europe after declaring their acceptance of the principles spelled out in Article 3.

The Council's human rights system has its legal source in two treaties: the European Convention of Human Rights and the European Social Charter. The Convention guarantees basic civil and political rights; the Charter proclaims a catalog of economic and social rights. Each of these treaties establishes its own institutional framework to supervise compliance. The sections that follow will deal with the evolution of these two systems. It will also examine the impact of the European Convention on the human rights practice of the European Union, formally the European Community, and describe the human dimension system of the Organization for Security and Cooperation in Europe.

II. THE EUROPEAN CONVENTION OF HUMAN RIGHTS: AN OVERVIEW

§ 3–1. Introduction

The European Convention of Human Rights was signed on November 4, 1950 and entered into force on September 3, 1953. *See generally* A.H. Robertson & J.G. Merrills, *Human Rights in Europe* (3rd ed. 1993). Although only Member States of the Council of Europe may become parties to the European Convention, *see* Convention, art. 66(1), the Statute of the Council of Europe does not require its members to ratify the Convention. However, since all Council members had ratified the Convention by the time the Cold War was over and some Central and Eastern European nations began to apply for membership, the Council decided to condition all subsequent admissions on the ratification of the Convention. By the end of 1994, the following states had adhered to the Convention: Austria, Belgium, Bulgaria, Cyprus, Czech Republic, Denmark, Finland, France, Germany, Greece, Hungary, Iceland, Ireland, Italy, Liechtenstein, Luxembourg,

Malta, Netherlands, Norway, Poland, Portugal, Romania, San Marino, Slovakia, Slovenia, Spain, Sweden, Switzerland, Turkey, and the United Kingdom. The Convention has been amplified and amended by means of additional Protocols.

§ 3–2. Rights Guaranteed

As originally adopted, the European Convention guaranteed the following rights: right to life; right not to be subjected to torture, inhuman or degrading treatment and punishment; freedom from slavery; right to liberty, security of person, and due process of law; freedom from ex post facto laws and punishment; right to private and family life; freedom of thought, conscience and religion; freedom of expression and of peaceful assembly; and the right to marry and found a family. The Convention also contains a non-discrimination clause, which is applicable only to the "enjoyment of the rights and freedoms" it proclaims (Art. 14), and a provision requiring that an "effective remedy before a national authority" be provided to anyone whose rights have been violated (Art. 13). The beneficiary of the rights and freedoms which the Convention guarantees is "everyone" within the "jurisdiction" of the States Parties to it (Art. 1), that is, it matters not what a person's nationality may be.

The catalog of rights guaranteed by the Convention has been expanded by additional Protocols. The first Protocol added a right to property, the right to education and the undertaking by the States Parties to hold free and secret elections at

reasonable intervals. Protocol No. 4 enlarged the
list further by prohibiting deprivation of liberty for
failure to comply with contractual obligations and
by guaranteeing the right to liberty of movement.
It also bars forced exile of nationals and the collective expulsion of aliens. Protocol No. 6 abolished
the death penalty, and Protocol No. 7 requires
states to accord aliens various due process safeguards before they may be expelled from a country
where they reside. That instrument also provides
for a right of appeal in criminal proceedings, for
compensation in cases of miscarriage of justice, for
the right not to be subjected to double jeopardy, as
well as for equality of rights and responsibility
between spouses. *See generally* P. van Dijk &
G.J.H. van Hoof, *Theory and Practice of the European Convention on Human Rights*, ch. 6 (2d ed.
1990); Robertson & Merrills, *supra*, chapters 1–6.
See also R. Macdonald, F. Matscher & H. Petzold
(eds.), *The European System for the Protection of
Human Rights* (1993), which contains a thorough
analysis of individual rights guaranteed in the Convention in the light of the relevant caselaw. Other
Protocols deal with institutional changes engrafted
on the Convention.

§ 3–3. The Universal Declaration and the Convention

The decision to draft the European Convention
was made after the UN General Assembly adopted
the Universal Declaration of Human Rights and
when it became clear that it would take the UN a

long time to reach agreement on the instruments designed to transform the Declaration into binding treaty obligations. On this subject, *see* § 2–4, *supra*. The historical relationship between the Declaration and the European Convention finds expression in the latter's preamble. There the signatories declare their resolve "as the Governments of European countries which are like-minded and have a common heritage of political traditions, ideals, freedom and the rule of law, to take the first steps for the collective enforcement of certain of the Rights stated in the Universal Declaration." Today the human rights system established by the Convention is not only the oldest but also the most advanced and effective of those currently in existence. On the origins and legislative history of the Convention, *see* Robertson & Merrills, *supra,* at 1.

§ 3–4. Convention Institutions

The Convention established two institutions "to ensure the observance of the engagements undertaken by the High Contracting Parties" (Art. 19): the European Commission of Human Rights and the European Court of Human Rights. The Convention also confers some supervisory functions relating to the enforcement of the rights it guarantees on the Committee of Ministers of the Council of Europe. Convention, arts. 32 and 54. The Committee of Ministers is the governing body of the Council of Europe. Moreover, since the Convention is a treaty adopted within the framework and under the auspices of the Council of Europe, some of its other organs and institutions also play important roles in facilitating the application and implementation of the Convention. *See, e.g.*, Convention, arts. 15(3), 21(1), 39(1), 57. *See generally* Robertson, "Council of Europe," in *Encyclopedia of Public International Law,* vol. 1, at 843 (R. Bernhardt ed., 1992); Ravaud, "The Committee of Ministers," in Macdonald *et al., supra,* at 645.

The European Commission of Human Rights consists "of a number of members equal to that of the High Contracting Parties" to the Convention. Convention, art. 20. They are elected for a six-year period by the Committee of Ministers and serve in their personal capacities. The European Court of Human Rights is composed "of a number of judges equal to that of the Members of the Council of Europe." Convention, art. 38. The judges are elected for nine-year terms by the Parliamentary Assembly of the Council of Europe from a list of three nominees submitted by each Member State of the Council. (The Assembly is composed of national parliamentarians from Member States of the Council of Europe.) The judges serve in their individual capacities and must be persons of "high moral character," who "possess the qualifications required for appointment to high judicial office or be jurisconsults of recognized competence." Convention, art. 38(3). Similar requirements, not previously provided for in the Convention, now also apply to members of the Commission. Protocol No. 8, art. 2 (amending Article 21 of the Convention). The Convention does not require the judges and

Commission members to be nationals of the Member States of the Council of Europe. This explains the presence on the Court of a Canadian national, Professor R. St. J. Macdonald, who was elected on the nomination of Liechtenstein.

The Commission and Court have their seat in Strasbourg, France, which is also the seat of the Council of Europe. Each Convention organ has its own professional staff. The Commission's staff is headed by its Secretary; the Registrar is the chief clerk of the Court.

III. THE ENFORCEMENT MECHANISM OF THE CONVENTION

§ 3–5. Introduction

The rights guaranteed in the European Convention are enforced on the national and international level. In a substantial number of the States Parties, the Convention enjoys the status of domestic law. *See generally* A. Drzemczewski, *European Human Rights Convention in Domestic Law: A Comparative Study* (1983); Polakiewicz & Jacob–Foltzer, "The European Human Rights Convention in Domestic Law: The Impact of the Strasbourg Case–Law Where Direct Effect is Given to the Convention," 12 Hum. Rts. L.J. 65 and 125 (1991); Bernhardt, "The Convention and Domestic Law," *in* Macdonald *et al., supra,* at 25. In these countries the Convention may be invoked as law in the national courts and creates rights directly enforceable by individuals. In States Parties where the Convention as such does not enjoy domestic law status, implementing legislation may be required to enforce the rights it guarantees unless existing national law already ensures the protection of comparable rights. The United Kingdom and some Scandinavian countries, for example, have thus far not accorded the Convention the status of domestic law. *See* J.P. Gardner (ed.), *Aspects of Incorporation of the European Convention of Human Rights into Domestic Law* (1993). But even in these countries the national courts frequently look to the Convention when interpreting and applying domestic law in order to avoid, if at all possible, violating this treaty. *See* Higgins, "The European Convention on Human Rights," in T. Meron (ed.), *Human Rights in International Law: Legal and Policy Issues* 495, 503–05 (1984); Buergenthal, "Self–Executing and Non–Self–Executing Treaties in National and International Law," 235 Recueil des Cours 303, 359 (1992).

Only when domestic law does not provide relief capable of remedying a violation of the Convention may recourse be had to the international institutions described below. This proposition has its basis in the requirement stipulated in all human rights treaties, including the Convention, that before international remedies may be invoked, available domestic remedies must be exhausted. Convention, art. 26. In a broader sense, it can also be said to be derived from the principle of subsidiarity.

See Petzold, "The Convention and the Principle of Subsidiarity," *in* Macdonald *et al.*, *supra*, at 41.

A. THE EUROPEAN COMMISSION OF HUMAN RIGHTS

§ 3–6. Inter–State Complaints

By ratifying the European Convention, a state is deemed to have accepted the jurisdiction of the Commission to receive complaints from other States Parties alleging a violation of the treaty. Convention, art. 24. The Applicant State does not have to demonstrate any special interest in or relationship to the victim of the violation or in its subject matter. Austria v. Italy, Application No. 78/8/60, 4 *Yearbook of the European Convention of Human Rights* [hereinafter cited as Yearbook] 116 (1961). The European Court put the matter as follows: " ... the Convention allows Contracting States to require the observance of these obligations [contained in the Convention] without having to justify an interest deriving, for example, from the fact that a measure they complain of has prejudiced one of their nationals." Ireland v. United Kingdom, Judgment of January 18, 1978, 25 *Publ. Eur. Court H.R.* 1, at 91 (1978).

Inter-state complaints are not subject to the same admissibility requirements prescribed for private petitions other than the obligation to exhaust domestic remedies. Convention, arts. 27 and 26; Denmark *et al.* v. Greece, Applications Nos. 3321–23/67 & 33–44/67, 11 *Y. B.* 690 (1968). Nevertheless, only a small number of inter-state complaints have been lodged with the Commission. With minor exceptions, *see, e.g., Ireland v. United Kingdom, supra,* such applications have been filed against states that had not as yet recognized the right of private petition and thus could only be held internationally accountable for a breach of the Convention by means of an inter-state proceeding. *See Greece v. United Kingdom*, Application No. 17/6/56, 2 *Y. B.* 182 (1958–59); *Greece v. United Kingdom*, Application No. 29/9/57, 2 *Y. B.* 186 (1958–59); *Austria v. Italy, supra; Denmark et al. v. Greece, supra; Denmark et al. v. Greece*, Application No. 44/48/70, 13 *Y. B.* 108 (1970); *Cyprus v. Turkey*, Application Nos. 678/0/74 and 69/50/75, 18 *Y. B.* 82 (1975); *Cyprus v. Turkey*, Application No. 8/007/77, 21 *Y. B.* 100 (1978); *Denmark et al. v. Turkey*, Application No. 99/40/82, 35 Decisions and Reports of the European Commission on Human Rights 143 (1984).

That a number of inter-state complaints were politically motivated cannot be denied. Other such cases have been filed for humanitarian reasons. This was true, for example, of the proceedings which were instituted against Greece and Turkey by various Scandinavian nations. For an overview of these cases, see European Commission of Human Rights, *Stock-Taking on the European Convention on Human Rights: The First Thirty Years: 1954 until 1984,* at 7 (1984) and the periodic *Supplements* thereto. As a general rule, however, states are reluctant to file cases against other states, fearing that this action will be interpreted as an unfriendly act and adversely affect their diplomatic relations. Van Dijk & Van Hoof, *supra*, at 36.

§ 3–7. Private Petitions

The right of an individual to file a complaint with the Commission against a State Party charging it with a violation of the Convention is conditioned on that state's prior recognition of the right of private petition. That recognition is not deemed to be automatic when the state ratifies the Convention; it requires a special declaration. Convention, art. 25(1). An overwhelming majority of the States Parties have to date accepted the Commission's jurisdiction to deal with private petitions.

Private petitions may be filed by "any person, non-governmental organisation or group of individuals claiming to be the victim of a violation ... of the rights set forth in [the] Convention" alleged to have been committed by a State Party which has accepted the jurisdiction of the Commission to receive such petitions. Convention, art. 25(1). The requirement that the petitioner must be "a victim of a violation" has been interpreted by the European Court to mean that "an individual applicant should claim to have been actually affected by the violation he alleges.... Article 25 does not institute for individuals a kind of *actio popularis* for the interpretation of the Convention...." Case of Klass and Others, Judgment of September 6, 1978, 28 *Publ. Eur. Court H.R.* 5, at 17–18 (1979). The right to file private petitions extends to both natural and legal persons whose rights have been violated. *See, e.g.,* The Sunday Times Case, Judgment of April 1979, 30 *Publ. Eur. Court H.R.* 5 (1979); Agrotexim Hellas, S.A. v. Greece, Application No. 14807/89, Eur. Comm. H.R., Decision of Feb. 12, 1992, 13 Hum. Rts. L.J. 318 (1992). *See also* Krüger & Norgaard, "The Right of Application," *in* Macdonald, *supra* at 657, 665–66.

The admissibility of private petitions is governed by the provisions of Article 27 of the Convention, which reads as follows:

(1) The Commission shall not deal with any petition submitted under Article 25 which

(a) is anonymous, or

(b) is substantially the same as a matter which has already been examined by the Commission or has already been submitted to another procedure of international investigation or settlement and if it contains no relevant new information.

(2) The Commission shall consider inadmissible any petition submitted under Article 25 which it considers incompatible with the provisions of the present Convention, manifestly ill-founded, or an abuse of the right of petition.

(3) The Commission shall reject any petition referred to it which it considers inadmissible under Article 26.

The question whether a petition is or is not admissible under Article 27 is determined by the Commission in a preliminary proceeding, which concludes with a ruling on its admissibility. For a thorough analysis of the case law of the Convention relating to admissibility, see Van Dijk & Van Hoof, *supra*, at 61.

As Article 27 indicates, in order for private petitions to be admissible, they must meet all the requirements spelled out in this provision. This is not true of inter-state complaints, which must comply only with Article 27(3). While the meaning of Article 27(1)(a) is obvious, that is not true of subparagraph (b), which declares that the Commission may not deal with a petition that "has already been submitted to another procedure of international investigation or settlement and if it contains no relevant new information." The vagueness of this provision raises questions about its intended meaning. Although by its terms it could be interpreted to bar the admissibility of any case that was previously submitted to another international body, regardless of the action taken by that body, that can hardly have been its intention. It is more reasonable to assume that the provision applies only to cases that have been "adjudicated" on the merits by such a body or deemed by it to have been inadmissible on the same grounds the Commission would apply. It could also mean that the Commission may not deal with a case as long as it is still pending before another international institution. The European Commission has thus far not had an opportunity to interpret this language. It is interesting to note, in this connection, that in ratifying the Optional Protocol to the International Covenant on Civil and Political Rights, some States Parties to the European Convention made reservations to prevent considerations of cases by the UN Human Rights Committee that had already been considered by the European Convention organs. On this subject, see Communication No. 121/1982, UN Human Rights Committee, *Selected Decisions under the Optional Protocol (Second to Sixteenth Sessions)*, at 32 (1985) (holding an application against Denmark inadmissible). The most common grounds for the inadmissibility of individual petitions are those set out in Article 27(2) and (3). *See* §§ 3–8 and 3–9, *infra.*

§ 3–8. Admissibility: Incompatible,   Ill–Founded, or Abuse of the Right of Petition

Under Article 27(2) a petition must be considered inadmissible if it is "incompatible with the provisions of the ... Convention, manifestly ill-founded, or an abuse of the right of petition." The Commission will consider a petition to be "incompatible with the provisions of the ... Convention" when, for example, it is filed against a state that has not recognized the right to private petition or when it involves rights that are not guaranteed by the Convention. *See, e.g.,* X v. Sweden, Application No. 209/5/63, 17 *Collection of Decisions of the European Commission of Human Rights* [hereinafter cited as Collection], 12 (1966). This ground of inadmissibility is jurisdictional in character and relates to the Commission's jurisdiction over the parties or the subject matter of the claim. *Confédération Française Démocratique du Travail v. European Communities,* Application No. 8/030/77, 13 Decisions and Reports 231 (1978).

The requirement that a petition not be "manifestly ill-founded" calls for a determination whether the petition states a *prima facie* case. *Aire Case,* Judgment of October 9, 1979, 32 *Publ. Eur. Court H.R.* 4, 10 (1979); F. Jacobs, *The European Convention on Human Rights* 243–44 (1975); Robertson & Merrills, *supra,* at 272–73. Thus, the Commission often rejects petitions as manifestly ill-founded after concluding that the Application "does not disclose . . . any appearance of a violation" by the Respondent State of the right invoked by the Applicant. *See, e.g., X v. Federal Republic of Germany,* Application No. 27/28/66, 10 *Y. B.* 337 (1967). This conclusion is not always as evident on the face of the petition as the Commission's language suggests; at times it is arrived at after a rather extensive analysis of the merits of the case, which would appear to contradict the meaning of "manifestly." *See Iverson v. Norway,* Application No. 146/8/62, *6 Y. B.* 278 (1963); Jacobs, *supra,* at 245; *W., X., Y. and Z. v. Belgium,* Applications Nos. 6745 and 67/46/74, 18 *Y. B.* 236 (1975). Recent decisions suggest that the Commission is increasingly more likely than in the past to hold these type of cases admissible. Thus, in *Air Canada v. United Kingdom,* Application No. 18465/91, Decision of April 1, 1993, 14 Hum. Rts. L.J. 226 (1993), the Commission held that because the complaint raised "serious questions of fact and law ... which can only be resolved by an examination of the merits," the case "cannot ... be declared manifestly ill-founded within the meaning of Article 27, para. 2 of the Convention." *Id.*, at 228.

"Abuse of the right of petition" is the third ground for holding a petition inadmissible under Article 27(2). It refers to conduct such as, for example, knowingly making false or groundless allegations, repeatedly using abusive and defamatory language about the Respondent Government, or intentionally breaching the rule of confidentiality applicable to the proceedings. *See Rafael v. Austria*, Application No. 24/24/65, 9 *Y. B.* 426 (1966); *X v. Austria & Germany*, Application No. 347/9/69, 28 *Collection* 132 (1969). But the mere fact that a petitioner may have had political motives in filing the case does not constitute an abuse of the right of petition, provided that the complaint otherwise states a valid cause of action. *Lawless v. Ireland*, Application No. 3/32/57, 2 *Y. B.* 308 (1958–59).

§ 3–9. Exhaustion of Domestic Remedies and the Six–Months Rule

Article 27(3) of the Convention provides that "the Commission shall reject any petition referred to it which it considers inadmissible under Article 26." That article reads as follows: "The Commission may only deal with the matter after all domestic remedies have been exhausted, according to the generally recognised rules of international law, and within a period of six months from the date on which the final decision was taken." This language does not distinguish between private and inter-state applications. Hence, to be admissible, both must comply with the requirement for the exhaustion of domestic remedies spelled out in Article 26. *Ireland v. United Kingdom,* Judgment of January 18, 1978, 25 *Publ. Eur. Court H.R.* 5, 64 (1978).

Article 26 establishes two requirements: exhaustion of domestic remedies and the so-called six-months rule. *See generally* Van Dijk & Van Hoof, *supra,* at 81, for a detailed analysis of the relevant caselaw. The European Court has explained the first requirement as follows: "the rule of exhaustion of domestic remedies ... dispenses States from answering before an international body for their acts before they have had an opportunity to put matters right through their own legal system...." *DeWilde, Ooms and Versyp Cases,* Judgment of June 18, 1971, 12 *Publ. Eur. Court H.R.* 12, 29 (1971). In short, you do not make an international case out of a matter that can be resolved on the local level. A case will, therefore, be dismissed for failure to exhaust domestic remedies when it appears that issues relevant to it, raised for the first time before the Convention institutions, were not brought to the attention of the national courts and could there have affected the result. *Cardot v. France,* Judgment of March 19, 1991, 200 Publ. Eur. H.R. 1, 18–19 (1991). For the manner in which this role is applied in practice, see *Castells v. Spain,* Judgment of April 23, 1992, 236 Publ. Eur. Court H.R. 1, 19–20 (1992).

The international law on this subject, and the Commission's and Court's caselaw indicate that remedies, which are not effective or which are unduly prolonged, need not be exhausted. "The only remedies which Article 26 of the Convention requires to be exhausted are those that relate to the breaches alleged and at the same time are available and sufficient...." *Van Oosterwijck Case*, Judgment of November 6, 1980, 40 *Publ. Eur. Court H.R.* 5, at 13 (1981). A remedy is "sufficient" if it is capable of redressing the wrong complained of. *Stögmüller Case*, Judgment of November 10, 1969, 12 *Y. B.* 364 (1969). The failure of a petitioner to resort to a domestic remedy, which has been consistently unsuccessful, will not result in the rejection of the petition. Neither will the failure to file an appeal against a law that prior judgments suggest will be upheld; this is so even in countries where the courts are free to depart from such precedent. *Sigurjonsson v. Ireland,* Application No. 16130/90, Eur. Comm. H.R., Decision of July 10, 1991, 12 Hum. Rts. L.J. 402 (1991). The Court reached the same conclusion in a case where the national courts reversed themselves while the case was being considered by the Commission. *DeWilde, Ooms and Versyp Cases*, Judgment of June 18, 1971, 12 *Publ. Eur. Court H.R.* 12, 34 (1971). However, if the domestic law on the subject is open to conflicting interpretations, a reasonable effort to exhaust potential remedies must be made. *Van Oosterwijck Case*, Judgment of November 6, 1980, 40 *Publ. Eur. Court H.R.* 4, 18–19 (1981).

The domestic remedies requirement may be waived by the Respondent State because it is deemed to be procedural in nature. *Bozano Case*, Judgment of December 18, 1986, 111 *Publ. Eur. Court H.R.* 6, 19–20 (1987). According to the European Court, "there is nothing to prevent States from waiving the benefit of the rule of exhaustion of domestic remedies, the essential aim of which is to protect their national legal order." *DeWilde, Ooms and Versyp Cases*, *supra,* at 31. The waiver may be express, but more often than not it will be inadvertent, for example, when the Respondent State raises the issue for the first time before the European Court without having done so when the case was being considered by the Commission. *Case of De-Jong, Baljet and Van den Brink*, *supra,* at 18–19.

An important issue relating to exhaustion of domestic remedies concerns the burden of proof. The Convention organs have traditionally dealt with this problem in two stages. First, the Commission subjects all petitions it receives to a preliminary *ex officio* examination bearing on its admissibility, which includes a determination whether domestic remedies have been exhausted. This determination is made by reference to the allegations contained in the complaint and the accompanying documents. If it appears at this stage that the petitioner has not exhausted available domestic remedies, the Commission has the power to reject the case summarily. *See* Rules of Procedures of the European Commission of Human Rights [hereinafter cited as Commission Rules], rule 44.

The second stage is reached when the complaint has not been rejected at the preliminary stage and the Respondent State seeks its dismissal by pleading the non-exhaustion of domestic remedies. Here the state has the burden of proof. *DeWeer Case*, Judgment of February 27, 1980, 35 *Publ. Eur. Court H.R.* 4, 15 (1980). The matter has been explained as follows by the European Court:

> The only remedies which Article 26 of the Convention requires to be exhausted are those that relate to the breaches alleged; the existence of such remedies must be sufficiently certain not only in theory but also in practice, failing which they will lack the requisite accessibility and effectiveness; and it falls to the respondent State, if it pleads non-exhaustion, to establish that these various conditions are satisfied....

Case of Johnston and Others, Judgment of December 18, 1986, 112 Publ. Eur. Court H.R. 8, 22 (1987). *See also Case of DeJong, Baljet and Van den Brink*, Judgment of May 22, 1984, 77 *Publ. Eur. Court H.R.* 6, 19 (1984). The six-months rule spelled out in Article 26 requires that the petition be filed with the Commission "within a period of six months from the date on which the final decision was taken." Its purpose is to ensure there be an end to litigation within a reasonable period of time or, to put it another way, "to prevent the past judgments being constantly called into question." *DeBecker v. Belgium*, Application No. 2/14/56, 2 *Y. B.* 214, at 244 (1958–59).

Reading the six-months rule together with the requirement for the exhaustion of domestic remedies helps to clarify what is meant by the "final decision" from which the six-month period is measured. That is, in any given case, the final decision must be determined by reference to the last domestic remedy that must be exhausted pursuant to Article 26. *Nielson v. Denmark*, Application No. 3/43/57, 2 *Y. B.* 412 (1958–59). Thus, for example, if under the applicable domestic law all available domestic remedies are exhausted with an appeal to the superior court of X, then the judgment of that tribunal is the "final decision" for purposes of the six-months rule. But a decision from an appeal to a domestic court, which clearly lacks the power or jurisdiction to grant the relief sought under the Convention, will not be taken into account for purposes of the six-month rule. *Nielson v. Denmark*, *supra*. Hence, if more than six months have passed after the "final decision," but the petitioner thereafter nevertheless appeals to a higher or special court which clearly lacks the power to affect that decision, the petition will be deemed inadmissible barring some very special circumstances. *Id. See also Sibson v. United Kingdom*, Application No. 14327/88, Europ. Comm'n H. R., Decision of April 9, 1991, 12 Hum. Rts. L.J. 351 (1991) (dealing with "special circumstances" applicable to the six-months rule). But the six-month rule is inapplicable when a violation of the Convention is continuous and there exist no domestic remedies to challenge it. *DeBecker v. Belgium*, Application No. 2/14/56, 2 *Y. B.* 214 (1958–59).

§ 3–10. Commission *Modus Operandi*

With the entry into force in 1990 of Protocol No. 8 to the Convention, the manner in which the Commission deals with petitions, both at the admissibility and post-admissibility stage, has undergone significant changes. To take account of the changes, the Commission amended its Rules of Procedure in that same year. *See* Krüger, "Revised Rules of Procedure of the European Commission of Human Rights," 12 Hum. Rts. L.J. 43 (1991). For the text of the revised Rules, *see id.,* at 44.

The examination of private petitions is now handled, at different stages of the proceedings, by individual Rapporteurs, Committees, Chambers, or the plenary Commission. Convention, art. 20 (as amended). (All subsequent cites are to the Convention as amended by Protocol No. 8.). *See also* Commission Rules, rules 47–49. All incoming private petitions are assigned to a Commission member designated as Rapporteur, who prepares a report on its admissibility and decides whether to refer it to a Committee or a Chamber. The Committees have the power, by unanimous vote, to declare a petition inadmissible. The Chambers deal with cases, which "can be dealt with on the basis of established caselaw or which raise no serious question affecting the interpretation or application of the Convention." Convention, art. 20(2). Petitions raising important issues are dealt with by the plenary Commission, which also has the power to assume jurisdiction of cases being considered by a Chamber. Inter-state complaints go directly from a Rapporteur to the plenary Commission, which has exclusive jurisdiction over these cases. Convention, art. 20(5).

Once individual petitions have been declared admissible, they are dealt with by one of the Chambers or the plenary Commission, usually assisted by one or more Rapporteurs. Commission Rules, rules 53–54. On the *modus operandi* of the Commission, see Fribergh & Villiger, "The European Convention of Human Rights," *in* Macdonald *et al., supra,* at 605.

§ 3–11. Post–Admissibility Proceedings

Only a small number of cases—roughly ten to fifteen percent—is ruled admissible and enters the post-admissibility stage of the proceedings before the Commission. In dealing with these cases, the Commission performs a number of different functions. *See generally* Krüger, "The European Commission of Human Rights," 1 Hum. Rts. L.J. 66, 80–84 (1980); Van Dijk & Van Hoof, *supra,* at 107. First, the Commission undertakes an investigation of the facts. Convention, art. 28(1)(a). To that end, it holds hearings, receives written submissions, examines witnesses both at its seat in Strasbourg and, if necessary, by interviewing them in prisons or wherever they may be. *See generally* Frowein, "Fact–Finding by the European Commission of Human Rights," *in* R. Lillich (ed.), *Fact-Finding Before*

International Tribunals 237 (1990). Here it should be noted that at this stage of the proceedings, the Commission has the power, after it has reviewed all the evidence in the case, "to reject the petition if, in the course of its examination, it finds that the existence of one of the grounds for non-acceptance provided for in Article 27 has been established." Convention, art. 29(1). This decision used to require a unanimous vote. Protocol No. 8 amended the provision to require only a two-thirds majority. Article 29(1) is designed for exceptional circumstances where, on closer examination of the petition, it appears that it should not have been admitted in the first place.

Second, while examining the facts, the Commission is also required to "place itself at the disposal of the parties concerned with a view to securing a friendly settlement of the matter on the basis of respect for Human Rights as defined in the Convention." Convention, art. 28(1)(b). Some ten to fifteen percent of cases ruled admissible are disposed of by means of the friendly settlement procedure provided for in Article 28(1)(b). *See generally* Kiss, "Conciliation," *in* Macdonald *et al., supra*, at 703. For a list and summary of these cases, see European Commission of Human Rights, *Stock-Taking on the European Convention on Human Rights: The First Thirty Years 1954–1984*, at 115–44 (1984), and its periodic *Supplements*. For more recent data, see the Commission's *Information Sheets*, published by the Council of Europe. If a friendly settlement has been reached, it usually consists of an agreement whereby the Respondent State undertakes to pay compensation or to make some other amends without, however, admitting responsibility for a violation of the Convention. *See e.g., Amekrane v. United Kingdom*, 16 *Y. B.* 357 (1973); *Nagel v. Federal Republic of Germany*, 21 *Y. B.* 554 (1978); *Hazar v. Turkey,* Report of December 10, 1992, 14 Hum. Rts. L.J. 195 (1993). The friendly settlement is recorded in a report of the Commission, which is published and which contains "a brief statement of the facts and of the solution reached." Convention, art. 28(2).

Cases that have not been settled or discussed move to the third stage of the proceedings. Here the Commission is required to "draw up a Report on the facts and state its opinion as to whether the facts found disclose a breach by the State concerned of its obligations under the Convention." Convention, art. 31(1). This Report, which may contain concurring and dissenting opinions, is drafted in the form of a judicial opinion. *See, e.g., Antonio Diaz Ruano v. Spain*, Report of August 31, 1993, 15 Hum. Rts. L.J. 213 (1994). It is not a judgment, however, because the Commission lacks the power to formally adjudicate the case. That power is reserved to the Committee of Ministers or the Court. Once the Commission's Report has been drawn up, it is transmitted to the Committee of Ministers together with any proposals the Commission wishes to make. Convention, arts. 31(2) and 31(3). At this point, and assuming that the States concerned have accepted the jurisdiction of the

Court, the Commission and the parties have three months within which to refer the case to the Court. If this has not been done, the Committee of Ministers must decide "whether there has been a violation of the Convention." Convention, art. 32. *See* § 3–12, *infra*.

The decision whether or not it should refer a case to the Court is left to the discretion of the Plenary Commission. The Convention does not prescribe any guidelines on that subject. Moreover, until the entry into force in 1994 of Protocol No. 9, individuals could not refer a case to the Court and had no means of compelling the Commission to submit their case to the Court. That situation continues to be a problem for individuals who have filed cases against states that have not as yet ratified Protocol No. 9. The Commission does, however, refer an ever increasing number of cases to the Court. Over the years, it has tended to bring three types of cases with the Court: those where it has found a violation of the Convention, those that raise important legal issues, and those in which there is a significant divergence of views in the Commission regarding their outcome. If one of these considerations is not present, the Commission will as a rule let the Committee of Ministers decide the case. Of course, the Committee must also pass on all cases that cannot be referred to the Court because the state concerned has not accepted its jurisdiction. *See generally* Melander, "Responsibilities for the Organs of the European Convention, including the

Committee of Ministers," Council of Europe Doc. H/Coll(85)4, at 11 (1985).

B. THE COMMITTEE OF MINISTERS

§ 3–12. **Adjudicating Complaints Under Article 32**

When a case is not referred to the Court within three months after the Commission has transmitted its Report to the Committee of Ministers, the latter must decide "whether there has been a violation of the Convention." Convention, art. 32(1). On the role of the Committee of Ministers, *see* Leuprecht, "The Protection of Human Rights by Political Bodies—the Example of the Committee of Ministers of the Council of Europe," *in* M. Nowak *et al, Progress in the Spirit of Human Rights* 95 (Festschrift for Felix Ermacora, 1988); Ravaud, "The Committee of Ministers," in Macdonald *et al., supra*, at 645. This decision requires a two-thirds majority vote in which the states parties to the dispute have a right to participate. *See* Rules Adopted by the Committee of Ministers for the Application of Article 32 of the European Convention on Human Rights [hereinafter cited as Committee of Ministers (Article 32) Rules], rule 10.

The significance of the Committee of Ministers' role under Article 32 must be understood in light of the fact that the Committee is a political body, consisting of the foreign ministers or their deputies of each Member State of the Council of Europe. Its principal function is to serve as the governing board or decision-making body of the Council. The role Article 32 of the Convention assigns to the Committee is secondary to its other functions and was conferred because the Convention does not require the States Parties to accept the jurisdiction of the Court. In the 1950's, when the Convention was being drafted, it was assumed that few states would recognize the Court's jurisdiction and that more states would be willing to ratify the treaty if the final decision on whether the Convention had been violated was left to their political peers.

It is fair to say that, on the whole, the Committee of Ministers has not seriously politicized the application of Article 32. In general, it has tended to rubber stamp findings contained in the Commission's report. *See* Marijnissen Case, Report of the European Commission of Human Rights of March 12, 1984 and Committee of Ministers Resolution DH(85)4 of February 25, 1985, Council of Europe Doc. E89.809, at 1 and 26 (1986). But there are exceptions to this practice. For example, in the *Case of Dores and Silva,* the Commission unanimously determined that Portugal had violated the Convention. The Committee of Ministers failed to adopt this finding because the two-thirds majority vote necessary for the decision could not be obtained. *Case of Dores and Silva*, Rep. Eur. Comm'n Hum. Rts. July 6, 1983; Comm. of Ministers Resolution DH(85)7, April 11, 1985, Council of Europe Doc. E89.808, at 1 and 49 (1986). Here it should be noted that Protocol No. 10 to the European Convention, which was opened for signature in 1992 but is not yet in force, would abolish the two-thirds majority requirement in favor of a simple majority. In some cases, the Committee will accept the Commission's view that the Convention has been violated, and then vote to take no further action. The Committee adopts this approach when, as frequently happens, the Respondent State takes legislative or executive measures designed to ensure that the violation not be repeated or that it be rectified. *See, e.g., Neubede Case*, Rep. Eur. Comm'n Hum. Rts.; December 3, 1983; Committee of Ministers Resolution DH(85)8, April 11, 1985, Council of Europe Doc. E89.807, at 1 and 78 (1986). For a critical view of the Committee's practice, see Tomuschat, "Quo Vadis Argentorum? The Success Story of the European Convention on Human Rights—and a Few Dark Stains," 13 Hum. Rts. L.J. 401 (1992).

The decisions the Committee of Ministers is empowered to adopt pursuant to Article 32 are binding on the States Parties to the Convention. This is true of decisions that a state has violated the Convention and of decisions regarding the measures which the Committee has prescribed as well as the effect to be attributed to these measures. Convention, arts. 32(2) and 32(3). Because of the dilatory tactics of some states in complying with Committee decisions, it has now begun to fix specific time-limits for compliance. *See, e.g., Azzi v. Italy*, Comm. of Ministers Resolution DH (92), February 20, 1992, 13 Hum. Rts. L. J. 181 (1992), and editors' note on the same page. *See generally* Drzemczewski, "Decisions on the Merits: By the Committee of Ministers," *in* Macdonald *et al.*, *supra*, at 733.

§ 3–13. Enforcing Judgments Under Article 54

Article 54 of the Convention empowers the Committee of Ministers to ensure the enforcement of judgments of the European Court of Human Rights. That provision reads as follows: "The judgment of the Court shall be transmitted to the Committee of Ministers which shall supervise its execution." In order to discharge this obligation, the Committee has adopted "Rules Concerning the Application of Article 54 of the European Convention on Human Rights." They provide that as soon as a judgment of the Court has been transmitted, it shall be inscribed on the Committee's agenda (Rule 1). The state concerned must then inform the Committee what steps it has taken to comply with the judgment. If the state has not taken the requisite action, the case is automatically placed on the Committee's agenda for consideration by it within the next six months. (Rule 2).

When the award consists of money damages, it is usually quite easy for the state to pay the injured party and to so inform the Committee. The Committee will then pass a resolution that might, in part, read as follows:

Having satisfied itself that the Government of Belgium has awarded the just satisfaction provided for in the judgment of the Court of 24 October 1983,

Declares, after taking note of the information supplied by the Government of Belgium, that it has exercised its functions under Article 54 of the Convention in this case.

Committee of Ministers, Resolution D.H.(85)14, 28 June 1985, concerning the judgments of the European Court of Human Rights of 10 February 1983 and 24 October 1983 in the Albert and Le Compte Cases, Council of Europe, *Collection of Resolutions Adopted by the Committee of Ministers in Application of Articles 32 and 54 of European Convention on Human Rights 1984–85* [hereinafter cited as *Committee of Ministers Resolutions*], 38–39 (1986).

Sometimes the Court's judgment may declare that certain national laws or practices are in conflict with the Convention and that appropriate legislation needs to be adopted. Compliance with this type of judgment is much harder to police. Often the state will require more time, since the domestic legislative process moves at its own pace. *See, e.g.,* Committee of Ministers, Final Resolution DH (89) 31 (concerning the judgments of the European Court of Human Rights of 21 February 1984 and 23 October 1984 in Öztürk Case, *Committee of Ministers Resolutions*, at 86–87 (Supp. 1988–1989)). It is also not always easy for the Committee, which is not a judicial body, to determine whether the legislative measures do in fact fully comply with the Court's mandate. On this subject, see Robertson & Merrills, *supra,* at 340–41; Committee of Ministers Resolution DH(82)2, 24 June 1982, Concerning the Judgment of the European Court of Human Rights of 24 October 1979 in the Winterwerp Case, *Committee of Ministers Resolutions 1959–1983,* 128–29 (1984). It remains to be decided whether a case can come back to the Court on that issue; such an approach would make a great deal of sense.

C.   THE EUROPEAN COURT OF HUMAN RIGHTS

§ 3–14.   Jurisdiction

Initially, the Convention conferred only contentious jurisdiction on the Court. It now also has limited advisory jurisdiction, which was added by Protocol No. 2. This section considers both types of jurisdiction.

1.   *Contentious Jurisdiction*

The Court's contentious jurisdiction extends to cases that are referred to it by the Commission and the States Parties. With the entry into force in 1994 of Protocol No. 9, individuals also have standing to refer a case to the Court against States that have ratified the Protocol. Convention, art. 44 (as amended). A case is ripe for adjudication by the Court only "after the Commission has acknowledged the failure of efforts for a friendly settlement and within the period of three months provided for in Article 32." Convention, art. 47. A case must consequently have been ruled admissible by the Commission and gone through its post-admissibility proceedings before the Court can be seized of it.

The ratification of the Convention does not automatically subject a State Party to the Court's contentious jurisdiction. A further declaration accepting that jurisdiction is required. Convention, art. 46. An overwhelming majority of the States Parties have now subscribed to the Court's jurisdiction. Most states accept the jurisdiction for a specified period of time, usually three to five years, and renew it regularly.

Article 48(1) of the Convention (as amended) provides that

> the following may bring a case to the Court ...: (a) the Commission; (b) a High Contracting Party whose national is alleged to be a victim; (c) a High Contracting Party which referred the case to the Commission; (d) a High Contracting Party against which the complaint has been lodged; [and] (e) the person, non-governmental organization or group of individuals having lodged the complaint with the Commission.

Article 48(1)(e) is a new provision. Added to the Convention by Protocol No. 9, it is applicable only with regard to states that have ratified the Protocol. Moreover, even with regard to these states, individuals do not have the same rights in filing cases with the Court as do the Commission and the States Parties. That is the consequence of a new paragraph 2 added to Article 48. That provision establishes a panel of three judges which has the task of determining whether the case raises "a serious question affecting the interpretation or application of the Convention" or whether there is any other reason to warrant its consideration. If the panel answers these questions unanimously in the negative, the case cannot be considered by the Court and will have to be decided by the Committee of Ministers. No such conditions limit the rights of states or the Commission to submit cases to the Court.

Although the Convention entered into force in 1953, the Court was not established until 1959. It took that long to obtain the eight acceptances that were required under Article 56 before the election of the judges could take place. The first eight states to subject themselves to the Court's jurisdiction were Belgium, Denmark, Germany (Federal Republic), Ireland, Netherlands, Luxembourg, Austria and Iceland. The first case to reach the Court was the *"Lawless" Case,* Judgment of July 1, 1961 (Merits), 4 *Y. B.* 438 (1961), which was referred to it by the Commission in 1960. That same year the Commission also filed the *"DeBecker" Case,* Judgment of March 27, 1962, 5 *Y. B.* 321 (1962). Five years elapsed before another case reached the Court. *See Case Relating to Certain Aspects of the Laws on the Use of Languages in Education in Belgium*, Judgment of July 23, 1968 (Merits), 11 *Y. B.* 833 (1968). Thereafter the Court's business increased gradually, albeit quite slowly. In the early 1980's, the caseload began to climb significantly. Today the Court decides between 50 to 100 cases annually. On the work of the Court generally, see Walsh, "The European Court of Human Rights," 2 Conn. J. Int'l L. 271 (1987). Bernhardt,

"Commentary: The European System," *id.*, at 299; Callewaert, "The Judgments of the Court: Background and Context," *in* Macdonald *et al., supra*, at 713.

2. *Advisory Jurisdiction*

The Court obtained its advisory jurisdiction in 1970 with the entry into force of Protocol No.2 to the Convention. The Protocol empowers only the Committee of Ministers to request advisory opinions. The power is limited, moreover, to "legal questions concerning the interpretation of the Convention and the Protocols thereto." Protocol No. 2, art. 1(1). In exercising its advisory jurisdiction, the Court may not, however, interpret "the content or scope of the rights or freedoms" that are guaranteed by the Convention and its Protocols. It may not deal with "any other question which the Commission, the Court or the Committee of Ministers might have to consider in consequence of any such proceedings as could be instituted in accordance with the Convention." In short, excluded from the Court's advisory jurisdiction is the interpretation of all questions within the scope of its contentious jurisdiction. Thus, for example, the Court's advisory jurisdiction would extend to the interpretation of Article 35 of the Convention, which provides that "the Commission shall meet as the circumstances require. The meetings shall be convened by the Secretary General of the Council of Europe." This provision does not deal with a right that is guaranteed in the Convention, nor does it concern a subject likely to arise in contentious proceedings. For the legislative history of the Court's advisory power, *see* Council of Europe, *Explanatory Reports on the Second to Fifth Protocols to the European Convention for the Protection of Human Rights and Fundamental Freedoms,* Doc. H (71)11, at 3–18 (1971); Robertson & Merrills, *supra,* at 315.

§ 3–15.   The Individual's Participation in the Proceedings

The Convention, as originally drafted, empowered only states and the Commission, but not individuals, to file cases with the Court. It also made no provisions for the individual's participation in proceedings before the Court. However, in addition to the changes brought about by Protocol 9, *supra* § 3–14, which permits individuals to refer cases to the Court against states that have ratified it, the individual claimant has gradually acquired an ever more important status before the Court. In the very first case to be heard by the Court, the Commission sought permission to present to the Court the individual Applicant's observations. Addressing this motion, the Court acknowledged that "it is in the interest of the proper administration of justice that the Court should have knowledge of and, if need be, take into consideration, the Applicant's points of view. . . ." The Court emphasized, however, that it could obtain this information from the Commission, "which, as the defender of the public interest, is entitled of its own accord . . . to make known the Applicant's views to the Court. . . ."

Moreover, "the Court may also hear the Applicant in accordance with Rule 38 of the Rules of Court...." "Lawless" Case, Judgment of November 14, 1960 (Preliminary Objections and Questions of Procedure), 3 *Yearbook* 492, at 516 (1960). Rule 38 (now Rule 40, as amended) authorized the Court, proprio motu, at the request of a State Party or of the Commission "to hear as a witness or expert or in any other capacity any person whose evidence or statements seem likely to assist it in the carrying out of its task," including, presumably, the Applicant.

In a 1970 ruling, the Court took a further step forward by holding that the Commission was free to include Applicant's counsel on its team of attorneys appearing before the Court in the case and that this practice did not violate Article 44 of the Convention, which gave only states and the Commission the right to file such cases. *DeWilde, Ooms and Versyp Cases*, Judgment of November 18, 1970 (Question of Procedure), 12 *Publ. Eur. Court H.R.* 6 (1971). The Commission used this approach through 1982. Then, in 1983, the Court amended its rules of procedure and authorized individuals to appear in their own right and to be separately represented in proceedings before the Court. Revised Rules of Court, rules 30 and 33. This practice continues to be applicable to individuals who have filed complaints against states that have not as yet ratified Protocol No. 9. Although these individuals lack standing to refer to their case to the Court, they are entitled to be fully represented before it once the case has reached the Court.

§ 3–16. Judgments of the Court

The Convention declares that the judgments of the Court are final and that "the High Contracting Parties undertake to abide by the decisions of the Court in any case to which they are parties." Convention, arts. 52 and 53. The Committee of Ministers supervises the execution of the Court's judgments. Convention, art. 54. On this subject, *see* § 3–13, *supra*. The fact that the judgment of the Court is law only for the party to the case means that the Court's decisions are not formally binding precedent (*stare decisis*) for the States Parties in general. But since the Court traditionally follows its case law, these judgments establish important precedents the States Parties and national courts look to ascertain what the law is. *See generally* Buergenthal, "The Effect of the European Convention on Human Rights on the Internal Law of Member States," in Int'l & Comp. L.Q. Supp. Publ. No. 11, 79, 94 (1965); Sundberg, "The European Experience of Human Rights: The Precedent Value of the European Court's Decisions," 20 Akron L. Rev. 629 (1987); Bernhardt, "The Convention and Domestic Law," in Macdonald et al., supra, at 25, 36–37. On the question whether the Commission and Committee of Ministers are bound by the Court's decisions, *see* A. Drzemczewski, *The European Human Rights Convention in Domestic Law: A Comparative Study* 266 (1983).

Article 50 of the Convention provides that when the Court finds a state responsible for a violation of the Convention, it may "afford just satisfaction to the injured party." The Court lacks the power, however, to reverse domestic judicial decisions or to annul national laws. It also does not have the power to grant any remedies other than "just satisfaction." Despite the fact that the language of Article 50, which conditions this remedy on a breach of the Convention and a finding that the "internal law of the said Party allows only partial reparation" for the breach, might be read to require a prior domestic proceeding on the subject, the Court has rejected this interpretation whenever it has been advanced. *De Wilde, Ooms and Versyp Cases*, Judgment of March 10, 1970 (Question of the Application of Article 50 of the Convention), 14 Publ. Eur. H.R. 1, 8 (1972); *Ringeisen Case*, Judgment of June 22, 1972 (Question of the Application of Article 50 of the Convention), 15 *Publ. Eur. Ct. H.R.* 1, 9 (1972). On Article 50 generally, see M. Enrich Mas, "Right to Compensation," *in* Macdonald *et al., supra*, at 775. Depending upon the procedural posture of the case, the Court either awards "just satisfaction" in its judgment on the merits or in a separate proceeding.

Just satisfaction may consist of monetary damages where no other relief is available. *See, e.g., Bronisch Case*, Judgment of June 2, 1986, 103 Publ. Eur. Court H.R. 1 (1986). In recovering such damages, an injured party is not limited to compensation for specific money damages suffered, but may also receive compensation for non-pecuniary damages. *Case of Colozzo and Rubinat*, Judgment of February 12, 1985, 89 Publ. Eur. Court H.R. 7 (1985). Sometimes the mere finding of a violation of the Convention, together with an award to cover actual costs and expenses, will be deemed to amount to "just satisfaction." *Campbell v. United Kingdom*, Judgment of March 25, 1992, 233 Publ. Eur. Court H.R. 1, at 23 (1992).

§ 3–17. Interpretation of the Rights Guaranteed

The European Court of Human Rights has today for all practical purposes become the constitutional court for civil and political rights of Europe. It has decided more than 400 cases since its establishment and has now had an opportunity to interpret most rights guaranteed by the Convention. For an analysis of these decisions, see Bossuyt & Vanden Bosch, "Judges and Judgements: 25 Years Judicial Activity of the Court of Strasbourg," [1984–85] Rev. Belge de Droit Int'l 695; Frowein, "The European Convention on Human Rights as the Public Order of Europe," 1 *Collected Courses of the Academy of European Law,* (Book 2), at 267 (1992). For the most extensive analysis to date by leading European scholars, see the section on "rights and freedoms," in Macdonald *et al., supra,* at 207–601.

The largest number of cases the Court has had to consider thus far have raised due process issues, that is, they have dealt with the interpretation and application of Article 5 (right to liberty and security of person) and Article 6 (right to a fair hearing). *See, e.g., Stögmüller Case*, Judgment of 10 November 1969, *Publ. Eur. Court H.R.* (Series A: Judgments and Decisions) 4 (1969); Golder Case, Judgment of 21 February 1975, 18 *Publ. Eur. Court H.R.* 5 (1975); *Case of Engel and Others*, Judgment of 8 June 1977, 22 *Publ. Eur. Court H.R.* 4 (1977); *Sramele Case*, Judgment of 22 October 1984, 84 *Publ. Eur. Court H.R.* 6 (1984); *Sanchez-Reisse Case*, Judgment of 21 October 1986, 107 *Publ. Eur. Court H.R.* 1 (1987); *Mats Jacobson Case*, Judgment of June 28, 1990, 180 Publ. Eur. Court H.R. 1 (1990); *Letellier v. France*, Judgment of June 26, 1991, 207 Publ. Eur. Court H.R. 1 (1991); *Kraska Case*, Judgment of April 19, 1993, 254 Publ. Eur. Court H.R. 42 (1993). *See generally* S. Stavros, *The Guarantees for Accused Persons under Article 6 of the European Convention on Human Rights* (1993). The Court has rendered a number of important decisions bearing on questions of freedom of expression, which is guaranteed in Article 10 of the Convention. *See, e.g., The Sunday Times Case*, Judgment of 26 April 1979, 30 *Publ. Eur. Court H.R.* 5 (1979); *Barthold Case*, Judgment of 25 March 1985, 90 *Publ. Eur. Court H.R.* 1 (1985); *Lingens Case*, Judgment of 8 July 1986, 103 *Publ. Eur. Court H.R.* 11 (1986); *Sunday Times v. United Kingdom*, Judgment of November 26, 1991, 217 Publ. Eur. Court H.R. 7 (1992). Freedom of association, proclaimed by Article 11, has been considered by the Court in, *inter alia, Case of Young, James and Webster*, Judgment of 13 August 1981, 44 *Publ. Eur. Court H.R.* 5

(1981); *Case of Le Compte, Van Leuven and De Meyere*, Judgment of 23 June 1981, 43 *Publ. Eur. Court H.R.* 5 (1981); *Ezelin v. France,* Judgment of April 26, 1991, 202 Publ. Eur. Court H.R. 1 (1991). The Court has also addressed difficult issues involving the right to privacy and interference with the right to a family life, protected by Article 8 of the Convention. *See, e.g., Dudgeon Case*, Judgment of 22 October 1981, 45 *Publ. Eur. Court H.R.* 5 (1982); *Malone Case,* Judgment of 2 August 1984, 82 *Publ. Eur. Court H.R.* 7 (1984); *Case of Johnston and Others*, Judgment of 18 December 1986, 112 *Publ. Eur. Court H.R.* 8 (1987); *Niemitz v. Germany*, Judgment of December 16, 1992, 251 Publ. Eur. Court H.R. 25 (1993). For an analysis of the caselaw relating to Articles 8 through 11, see the essays by Cohen–Jonathan, Shaw, Lester, and Tomuschat *in* Macdonald *et al., supra*, at 405 *et seq*.

Article 3 of the Convention provides that "no one shall be subjected to torture or degrading treatment or punishment." The leading case on this subject remains the Court's decision in *Ireland v. United Kingdom*, Judgment of January 18, 1978, 25 Publ. Eur. Court H.R. 1 (1978). For a thorough analysis of the Commission's and Court's caselaw relating to this provision, see Cassese, "Prohibition of Torture and Inhuman or Degrading Treatment of Punishment," *in* Macdonald *et al., supra*, at 225; Van Dijk & Van Hoof, *supra*, at 226. In a very interesting decision involving the application of Article 3, the Court determined that the United Kingdom would violate this provision were it to extradite Mr. Soering to Virginia, where he would be subject to the death penalty. *Soering Case*, Judgment of July 7, 1989, 161 Publ. Eur. Court H.R. 8 (1989). Here the Court did not hold that the death penalty as such violated Article 3, but that the "death row phenomenon" to which Soering would be exposed once capital punishment was imposed, would violate that provision given his youth and mental state. Soering was subsequently extradited to Virginia, but only after an undertaking by the State of Virginia that he would not be charged with a capital crime. Steinhardt, "Recent Developments in the Soering Litigation," 11 Hum. Rts. L.J. 453 (1990). For a critical analysis of the case, see Lillich, "The *Soering* Case," 85 Am. J. Int'l L. 128 (1990). It is interesting to note, in this connection, that Article 2 of the Convention, which deals with the right to life, permits the imposition of the death penalty. Protocol No. 6 subsequently outlawed the death penalty, but the United Kingdom was not a party to the Protocol at the time of the *Soering* litigation. Had it been, the Court could have relied on the Protocol rather than Article 3 of the Convention to bar the extradition. Van den Wyngaert, "Applying the European Convention on Human Rights to Extradition: Opening Pandora's Box?" 39 Int'l & Comp. L.Q. 757, 769 (1990).

Over the years, the Court has had to rule on a number of interesting questions concerning the right to property, which is guaranteed by Article 1 of Protocol No. 1 to the Convention. Thus, for example, in *Case of Lithgow and Others*, Judgment of 8 July 1986, 102 *Publ. Eur. Court H.R.* 9 (1987), the Court dealt with issues arising out of the nationalization of the British shipbuilding industries. In *Case of James and Others*, Judgment of 21 February 1986, 98 *Publ. Eur. Court H.R.* 14 (1986), the Court determined that the British Leasehold Reform Act of 1967, which affected the property interests of the Duke of Westminster, among others, did not violate Article 1 of Protocol No. 1 to the Convention. *See also Pine Valley Development Ltd. v. Ireland*, Judgement of November 29, 1991, 222 Publ. Eur. Court H.R. 1 (1992) (involving a discriminatory taking of property).

In the first case to reach the Court, *Lawless Case* (*Merits*), Judgment of 1 July 1961, *Publ. Eur. Court H.R.* (Series A: Judgments and Decisions 1960–61), at 24 (1961), the Court had to interpret and apply Article 15, which permits the States Parties to derogate, in time of war or other national emergency, from some of their obligations under the Convention. This provision and its implications were the subject of a much more extensive analysis in the *Ireland v. United Kingdom*, Judgment of 18 January 1978, 25 *Publ. Eur. Court H.R.* 5 (1978), which remains the leading case on the subject. Here the Court made clear that, although the States Parties had "a margin of appreciation" in assessing the facts bearing on the existence of a public emergency and the need for suspending certain rights which the Convention guarantees,

the States do not enjoy an unlimited power in this respect. The Court, which, with the Commission, is responsible for ensuring the observance of the States' engagements (Article 19) is empowered to rule on whether the States have gone beyond the 'extent strictly required by the exigencies' of the crisis.... The domestic margin of appreciation is thus accompanied by a European supervision.

Id., at 79. In a 1993 case, the Court reiterated this principle almost *verbatim* while emphasizing that "in exercising its supervision the Court must give appropriate weight to such relevant factors as the nature of the rights affected by the derogation, the circumstances leading to, and the duration of, the emergency situation." *Brannigan and McBride v. United Kingdom*, Judgment of May 26, 1993, 14 Hum. Rts. L.J. 184, 186 (1993). On the application of the margin-of-appreciation concept, see Frowein, "The European Convention on Human Rights as the Public Order of Europe," *in 1 Collected Courses of the Academy of European Law*, (Book 2), 267, 345 (1992).

Although Article 64 of the Convention permits the States Parties to attach reservations when adhering to the Convention, it subjects the right to a number of conditions. Article 64(1) specifies that such reservations may be made only with regard to any provision of the Convention that is incompatible with any laws "then in force" within the reserving state; it also prohibits "reservations of a general character." Article 64(2) requires the reserving state to accompany the reservation with "a brief statement of the law" motivating the reservation.

In *Belilos v. Switzerland*, Judgment of April 29, 1988, 132 Publ. Eur. Court H.R. 1 (1988), the Court was called upon to apply Article 64 to an "interpretative declaration," which the Swiss Government made in adhering to the Convention. The Court concluded that the declaration was in fact a reservation and that, as such, it was invalid because it met neither the requirements of paragraphs 1 nor 2 of Article 64. Addressing the question of the effect of the invalidity of the reservation on Switzerland's continued membership in the Convention, the Court declared that " ... it is beyond doubt that Switzerland is, and regards itself as, bound by the Convention irrespective of the validity of the declaration." *Id.*, at 28. This language leaves open the question whether Switzerland would have been bound by the Convention even if it had considered the validity of the reservation an indispensable condition of its adherence to the treaty. On this subject, see Bourguignon, "The Belilos Case: New Light on Reservations to Multilateral Treaties," 29 Va.J. Int'l L. 347 (1989); Van Dijk & Van Hoof, *supra*, at 606. *See also* Tomuschat, "Turkey's Declaration under Article 25 of the European Convention on Human Rights," *in* Nowak *et al.*, *supra*, at 119.

IV. THE CONVENTION AND THE EUROPEAN UNION

§ 3–18. Incorporation by Absorption

The treaties establishing the European Community (now the European Union), a supranational orga-

nization distinct from the Council of Europe, created various institutions, including its own Court of
Justice. This Court was given the function of ensuring the observance of law in the interpretation
and application of these treaties. The treaties, with
minor exceptions, did not contain any human rights
guarantees. As the role and powers of the European Community expanded, its legislative and administrative activities increasingly affected the rights of
individuals and companies. While the domestic
constitutional law of the Member States of the
Community and the European Convention on Human Rights provided for the protection of these
rights against the acts of states, the treaties creating the European Community did not establish a
parallel protective system against their violation by
Union institutions. Since these institutions were
supranational in character and hence not bound by
the domestic constitutional law of any of its Member States, the risk existed that they might deprive
individuals and companies subject to the jurisdiction of the Community of human rights guaranteed
them under their own domestic law and under the
European Convention without there being a remedy
against such action.

The European Community institutions began to
take this problem seriously when the constitutional
courts of some of the Member States suggested that
the Union's failure to abide by basic human rights
principles might force them to declare Community
acts unconstitutional and hence null and void in
their territories. *See* Stein, "Lawyers, Judges and

the Making of a Transnational Constitution," 75 Am. J. Int'l L. 1, 16 (1981). This threat was gradually averted as the Court of Justice of the European Community declared in a series of decisions that respect for fundamental rights formed an integral part of the general principles of law the Court was required to apply in interpreting the Community treaties and that in ascertaining the nature of these rights it would look to the European Convention of Human Rights. The Court has adhered to this view with increasing frequency and, in doing so, has relied on the caselaw of the European Court of Human Rights. For a discussion of the relevant caselaw, see Weiler, "Protection of Fundamental Human Rights within the Legal Order of the Communities," *in* R. Bernhardt & J.A. Jolowicz (eds.), *International Enforcement of Human Rights* 113 (1987); F.G. Jacobs, "Protection of Human Rights in the Member States of the European Community: Impact of the Case Law of the Court of Justice," *in* J. O'Reilly, *Human Rights and Constitutional Law (Essays in Honor of Brian Walsh)* 243 (1992). This interactive process has been greatly facilitated by the fact that all Member States of the European Union have ratified the European Convention of Human Rights and accepted the jurisdiction of the Human Rights Court. (Note, however, that not all parties to the European Convention are members of the European Union.)

Attempts have been made over the years to work out some form of association agreement between the European Union and the Council of Europe, which would enable the former to join the European Convention of Human Rights. For a discussion of the implications of such an association, see Jacqué, "The Convention and the European Convention," *in* Macdonald *et al., supra,* at 889, 901. Whether this will ever happen, given the complex legal and political issues that would have to be resolved to bring it about, remains to be seen. It is interesting to note, however, that the preamble to the Maastricht Treaty, which transformed the European Community into the European Union, declares that "the Union shall respect fundamental rights, as guaranteed by the European Convention [of] ... Human Rights ... and as they result from the constitutional traditions common to the Member States, as general principles of Community law." Treaty on European Union, Preamble, para. F(2). 36 Int'l Legal Mat. 253, at 256 (1992). This is the very language the Community Court used repeatedly in the past to justify its reliance on the European Convention. Its inclusion in the treaty thus constitutes the express acceptance of the Community Court's approach by the Member States of the Union. *See generally* H. Schermers & D. Waelbroeck, *Judicial Protection in the European Communities* 37 (5th ed. 1992), which examines the practice of the Community Court by reference to specific provisions of the Convention.

V. THE EUROPEAN SOCIAL CHARTER

§ 3–19. Introduction

The European Social Charter, like the European Convention of Human Rights, was drafted under the auspices of the Council of Europe. It complements the Convention, which guarantees only civil and political rights, by establishing a regional European system for the protection of economic and social rights. The Charter was opened for signature on October 18, 1961 and entered into force on February 26, 1965. More than one half of the Member States of the Council of Europe are parties to the Charter. An Additional Protocol to the Charter, expanding its catalog of rights, was concluded on May 5, 1988. Although it entered into force on September 4, 1992, very few states have thus far ratified the Protocol, which required only three ratifications to bring it into effect. On October 21, 1991 the Protocol Amending the European Social Charter was signed. This instrument, which amends the supervisory mechanism of the Charter, is not yet in force. *See generally* D. Harris, *The European Social Charter* (1984); Robertson & Merrills, *supra,* at 349; Fuchs, "The European Social Charter: Its Role in Present–Day Europe and Its Reform," *in* K. Drzewicki, C. Krause & A. Rosas, *Social Rights as Human Rights: A European Challenge* 151 (1994). *See also* R. Goebel, "Employee Rights in the European Community: A Panorama from the 1974 Social Action Program to the Social Charter of 1989," 17 Hastings Int'l & Comp. L.

Rev. 1, 58 (1993); Lundberg, "The Protection of Social Rights in the European Community: Recent Developments," in Drzewicki *et al., supra,* at 169, on the distinction between the European Community's Social Charter and the European Social Charter of the Council of Europe. (Here we examine only the latter instrument.)

§ 3–20. The Catalog of Rights

The Charter proclaims a list of 19 categories of "rights and principles," including the right to work, to just conditions of work, to safe working conditions, to fair remuneration, to organize, and to bargain collectively. It proclaims the right of children, of young people, and of employed women to protection. Also recognized are the right of the family to social, legal and economic protection, the right of mothers and children to social and economic protection, and the right of migrant workers and their families to protection and assistance. Additional rights listed in the Charter are the right to vocational guidance and training, to protection of health, to social security, to social and medical assistance, and the right to benefit from social welfare services. It establishes the right of physically and mentally handicapped persons to training and rehabilitation, and the right to engage in gainful occupations in the territory of other Contracting Parties.

The Additional Protocol supplements this list with four further "rights and principles," including the right of workers to equal treatment and non-discrimination on the grounds of sex; and the right to take part in the determination and improvement of the working conditions and environment in their place of employment. It also provides that "every elderly person has the right to social protection."

These rights are proclaimed in general terms in Part I of the Charter and the Additional Protocol, where the High Contracting Parties declare that they " ... accept as the aim of their policy, to be pursued by appropriate means, both national and international in character, the attainment of conditions in which ... [these] rights and principles may be effectively realised." Hence, despite the fact that the catalog enumerated in Part I of these instruments speaks of "rights and principles," what we have here are policy objectives. The purpose of the Charter is to transform them into enforceable rights.

Part II of the Charter and the Additional Protocol defines and spells out the meaning of the "rights and principles" proclaimed in only general terms in Part I. Thus, the right to safe and healthy working conditions, which is merely identified as such in paragraph 3 of Part I of the Charter, finds expression in the following undertaking contained in Article 3 of Part II:

1.   to issue safety and health regulations;

2.   to provide for the enforcement of such regulations by measures of supervision;

    3. to consult, as appropriate, employers' and
workers' organisations on measures intended to
improve industrial safety and health.

As we shall see in § 3–21, *infra,* this bifurcated
drafting approach, used both in the Charter and in
the Additional Protocol, was devised to establish
various types of obligations and to give states different compliance options.

§ 3–21. Legal Obligations Assumed by the Contracting Parties

    Article 20 (Part III) of the Charter specifies the
obligations the States Parties assume by ratifying
the Charter. The instrument gives the states a set
of options. First, by becoming a party to the Charter, a state undertakes "to consider Part I of this
Charter as a declaration of the aims which it will
pursue by all appropriate means . . . ." Charter, art.
20(1)(a). Second, the state must accept as binding
upon it the undertakings contained in at least five
out of seven articles found in Part II. The seven
provisions are Article 1 (right to work), Article 5
(right to organize), Article 6 (right to bargain collectively), Article 12 (right to social security), Article
13 (right to social and medical assistance), Article
16 (right of the family to social, legal and economic
protection), and Article 19 (right of migrant workers and their families to protection and assistance).
Third, each State Party has a further obligation to
select another specified number of rights or sub-
categories of rights with which it agrees to comply.
See Charter, art. 20(1)(c). The Additional Protocol

adopts the same approach in its Article 5 (Part III), except that it requires states to accept only one or more of the rights set forth in Part II.

This option system encourages states to ratify the Charter without forcing them either to accept all the rights it proclaims or to make complex reservations. It is also drafted so as to ensure that all States Parties will at the very least be bound to guarantee some of the most basic rights. Very few states have accepted all the rights the Charter proclaims.

§ 3–22. International Measures for Enforcement of Charter Rights

The Charter establishes a reporting system, which is also applicable to the Additional Protocol, to monitor the compliance by states with their obligations. It calls for two types of reports. The first is due every two years and must address the domestic implementation of those Part II rights that the particular state has accepted. Charter, art. 21. The second report deals with the status of Part II rights that the particular State Party did not accept. Both of these reports must be provided at specific intervals determined by the Committee of Ministers of the Council of Europe. Charter, art. 22.

The state reports are examined by different Council of Europe bodies. The initial review is by the Committee of Experts, which consists of seven independent experts "of the highest integrity and recognized competence in international social questions," elected by the Committee of Ministers. Charter, art. 25. The Committee of Experts is assisted by a consultant assigned to it by the International Labor Organization. Charter, art. 26. The conclusions of the Committee of Experts, together with the state reports, are referred to the Governmental Committee of the Council of Europe, which presents its findings thereon to the Committee of Ministers. Charter, art. 27. The Parliamentary Assembly of the Council of Europe also receives the conclusions of the Committee of Experts and gives its views thereon to the Committee of Ministers. The latter may, on the basis of the report of the Governmental Committee, and after consultation with the Parliamentary Assembly, make the necessary recommendations to any of the High Contracting Parties. Charter, art. 29.

Over the years, a considerable tug of war has developed between the independent experts, supported by the Parliamentary Assembly, on the one hand, and the Committee of Ministers, on the other, with the former urging the latter to demand more effective compliance by various governments. Rather than pointing out specific instances of noncompliance by individual states, the Committee of Ministers has tended to prefer general recommendations addressed to all states. The Assembly has criticized this practice on various occasions. *See, e.g.,* Parliamentary Assembly, Recommendation 1022 on the "European Social Charter: A Political Appraisal," *in* Council of Europe, *Information Sheet*, No. 19, Doc. H/INF(86)1, at 72–74 (1986).

The Protocol Amending the European Social Charter, which was concluded in 1991 but has not yet entered into force, was designed to address some of these charges by making the supervisory mechanism of the Charter more effective. The most important changes made by the Protocol would give the Committee of Independent Experts the power to render legal opinions determining whether the national laws and practices of the States Parties are in compliance with their obligations under the Charter, and to publish these opinions. Amending Protocol, art. 2. It would also enlarge the Committee to at least nine members elected by the Parliamentary Assembly on the nomination of the States Parties. Amending Protocol, art. 3. Currently, they are elected by the Committee of Ministers. This change would ensure that the membership of the Committee of Independent Experts would not be determined exclusively by governments. The Amending Protocol would also give greater power to the Parliamentary Assembly in reviewing the manner in which the Committee of Ministers discharges its functions under the Charter and, in general, make the entire review process more transparent. Amending Protocol, art. 6. Finally, in addition to requiring the Committee of Ministers to adopt individual recommendations, the Protocol also changes its voting procedure to permit only States Parties to the Charter to vote (by a two-thirds majority) on issues relating to its implementation. Amending Protocol, art. 5. This stipulation would amend the provision of the Charter which permits all Member

States of the Council of Europe, whether or not they have ratified the instrument, to participate in the two-thirds vote in the Committee of Ministers. Some of these changes, among them the voting procedure, have apparently already been implemented by the Committee of Ministers without waiting for the Amending Protocol to enter into force. *See* Fuchs, *in* Drzewicki *et al.*, *supra*, at 164–66.

Despite the criticism levelled against the Charter and its supervisory machinery, it must be emphasized that the States Parties to the Charter have over the years adopted important legislative and other measures with a view to complying with their obligations under that instrument. *See* Strasser, "European Social Charter," *in Encyclopedia of Public International Law,* Instalment No. 8, at 211, 213–14 (R. Bernhardt ed., 1985). Although the Charter has thus contributed to the greater enjoyment of economic and social rights in the territories of the States Parties to it, various proposals have been advanced in the past to give the European Commission and Court of Human Rights jurisdiction to supervise the enforcement of these rights. *See, e.g.,* Berenstein, "Economic and Social Rights: Their Inclusion in the European Convention on Human Rights/Problems of Formulation and Interpretation," 2 Hum. Rts. L.J. 257 (1981). The adoption of the Amending Protocol suggests, moreover, that the Council of Europe has effectively rejected that idea. Instead, it has opted to maintain two quite distinct mechanisms for the implementation of civil and political rights, on the one hand, and economic and social rights, on the other. *See generally* Pellonpää, "Economic, Social and Cultural Rights," *in* Macdonald *et al., supra*, at 855.

VI. ORGANIZATION FOR SECURITY AND COOPERATION IN EUROPE (OSCE)

§ 3–23. Introduction

The Conference on Security and Cooperation in Europe (CSCE), which in 1994 became the Organization for Security and Cooperation in Europe (OSCE), is not strictly an European organization. Although its members now include all European nations, the United States and Canada are also members and were so from its very inception. One could therefore deal with the OSCE in this book either in a separate chapter or include it here. We have chosen the latter approach because the OSCE works closely with the Council of Europe when it comes to the promotion of human rights.

The CSCE was created by the Helsinki Final Act (HFA), which was signed in 1975 by 33 European nations, including the Soviet Union, plus the United States and Canada. At the time only Albania refused to join. With the end of the Cold War, the membership of the OSCE has grown to more than 50 nations, including Albania and the newly independent former Soviet Republics. Conceived as a compromise instrument to bridge the ideological chasm that divided East from West in the 1970's, the HFA ushered in a negotiating process that established a highly imaginative linkage between human rights and security concerns. *See generally* J. Maresca, *To Helsinki: The Conference on Security and Cooperation in Europe*, 1973–1975 (1987); W. Korey, *The Promise to Keep: Human Rights, the Helsinki Process and American Foreign Policy* (1993). This linkage, which gave human rights an important place on the political agenda of East–West relations, has not lost its significance with the end of the Cold War. It has enabled the OSCE to continue to play a major role in today's Europe and to influence the human rights policies of many of its nations.

§ 3–24. The Helsinki Final Act

The OSCE's human rights system as we know it today consists of an ever expanding catalog of human rights and related guarantees and of multifaceted supervisory institutions that have evolved over time from the HFA. This evolution was possible because of the manner in which the HFA was drafted, the follow-up mechanism it established, and its character as a political rather than legally-binding instrument. *See generally* A. Bloed & P. van Dijk (eds.), *Essays on Human Rights in the Helsinki Process* (1985); Buergenthal, "The CSCE Rights System," 25 Geo. Wash. J. Int'l & Econ. L. 333 (1993) [hereinafter cited as Buergenthal, "CSCE Rights System"].

The HFA is a massive document, consisting of four chapters or so-called "baskets." Basket I, entitled "Questions Relating to Security in Europe," consists of two sections ("Principles Guiding Relations Between Participating States," and "Confidence–Building Measures and Certain Aspects of Security and Disarmament"). Basket II deals with "Cooperation in the Field of Economics, of Science and Technology and of the Environment." The subject of Basket III is "Cooperation in Humanitarian and Other Fields." Basket IV, the final chapter of the instrument, spells out the so-called "followup" process. *See* Russell, "The Helsinki Declaration: Brobdingnag or Lilliput," 70 Am. J. Int'l L. 242 (1976).

Human rights issues are addressed primarily in the Guiding Principles proclaimed in Basket I and to some extent also in Basket III, although over time the latter has become less important because the subjects it deals with—human contacts, family reunification, etc.—no longer have the importance they had when the Cold War was in full bloom. Of the ten Guiding Principles set out in the HFA, two deal with human rights. One is Principle VII ("Respect for human rights and fundamental freedoms, including the freedom of thought, conscience, religion or belief") and Principle VIII ("Equal rights and self-determination of peoples"). The remaining principles deal with sovereignty, the use of force, inviolability of frontiers, territorial integrity, peaceful settlement of disputes, non-intervention in internal affairs, cooperation of states, and fulfillment in good faith of international legal obligation.

Principle VII consists of eight unnumbered paragraphs. In the first two the participating States undertake to "respect human rights and fundamental freedoms" and to "promote and encourage the effective exercise of civil, political, economic, social, cultural and other rights and freedoms...." This principle also deals with freedom of religion, rights of individuals belonging to national minorities, and the "right of the individual to know and act upon his rights and duties in this field." The last paragraph of Principle VII reads as follows:

In the field of human rights and fundamental freedoms, the participating States will act in conformity with the purposes and principles of the Charter of the United Nations and with the Universal Declaration of Human Rights. They will also fulfil their obligations as set forth in the international declarations and agreements in this field, including inter alia the International Covenants on Human Rights, by which they may be bound.

The significance of this paragraph, at the time it was adopted, lay in the fact that until then some of the participating States, including the Soviet Union, had never formally acknowledged an obligation to conform their conduct to the Universal Declaration of Human Rights. (The Soviet Union had abstained when the UN General Assembly adopted the Universal Declaration, and Principle VII appears to have been its first unambiguous recognition of the "normative" character of this instrument.)

Principle VIII devotes four paragraphs to the subject of "equal rights and self-determination of peoples." After undertaking to respect the equal rights of peoples and their right to self-determination, the participating States recognize that "all peoples always have the right, in full freedom, to determine, when and as they wish, their internal and external political status, without external interference...." *See generally* H. Hannum, *Autonomy, Sovereignty, and Self–Determination: Accommodation of Conflicting Rights* (1990); C. Tomuschat (ed.), *The Modern Law of Self–Determination* (1993); R. Steinhardt, *International Law and Self–Determination* (The Atlantic Council, 1994).

It took quite a while before the Soviet Union and its allies fully acknowledged that these two Guiding Principles had in fact placed human rights issues on the agenda of the on-going East–West political dialogue. Their efforts to silence that debate by the invocation of the doctrine of non-intervention in internal affairs, enshrined in Principle VI, at times threatened to break up the CSCE. They relented gradually and by the latter part of the 1980's the discussion of specific human rights violations had become routine during CSCE follow-up meetings. Moreover, as we shall see, these meetings also dramatically expanded the human rights catalog of the HFA. *See* § 3–27, *infra*.

§ 3–25. The OSCE Process

The important impact the CSCE has had in the human rights area is partially attributable to the follow-up process provided for by Basket IV of the HFA, which has come to be known as the OSCE process. It consists of the convening by the participating States of periodic intergovernmental conferences for the purpose of achieving "a thorough exchange of views both on the implementation of the provisions of the Final Act ... as well as ... on the deepening of their mutual relations, the improvement of security and the development of cooperation in Europe, and the development of the process of détente in the future." These follow-up conferences have been used for the dual purpose of providing a conference forum to review compliance with human rights commitments and a mechanism for the expansion of the human rights catalog. The existence of this negotiating process has permitted the HFA to be amplified, reinterpreted, and extensively revised at successive conferences. These meetings have of course also been used to focus public attention on the failure of certain states to live up to their human rights commitments. *See* Helgesen, "Between Helsinkis—and Beyond? Human Rights in the CSCE Process," in A. Rosas & J. Helgesen (eds.), *Human Rights in a Changing East/West Perspective* 241 (1987).

The aforementioned normative evolution is accomplished by the so-called "concluding document" which is adopted by consensus at these conferences. *See* Schlager, "The Procedural Framework of the CSCE: From the Helsinki Consultation to the Paris Charter, 1972–1990," 12 Hum. Rts. L.J. 221 (1991). These documents are used to proclaim new OSCE commitments or to expand, modify or interpret the scope and meaning of existing ones. What we have here is a dynamic and creative process that has produced a growing body of OSCE human rights commitments. To understand their nature and evolution, it is necessary to examine the concluding documents of each OSCE follow-up conference at which human rights issues were taken up. Buergenthal, "CSCE Rights System," *supra*, at 344.

§ 3–26. The Non-binding Character of OSCE Commitments

The HFA is not a treaty and it was not intended by the participating States to create binding legal obligations. They conceived it as a non-binding instrument proclaiming political commitments. A state's failure to comply with any of these commitments will therefore have political but not legal consequences. Put another way, non-compliance will not give rise to a cause of action under international law, but it could have very serious political repercussions. Subsequent OSCE concluding documents are also not intended to be legally binding unless the contrary is made express. *See generally* Kiss & Dominick, "The International Significance of the Human Rights Provisions of the Helsinki Final Act," 13 Vand. J. Trans. L. 293 (1980); Van Dijk, "The Implementation of the Helsinki Final Act: The Creation of New Structures or the Involvement of Existing Ones," 10 Mich. J. Int'l 110, 113–15 (1989); Buergenthal, "CSCE Rights System," *supra,* at 375. *See also* Schachter, "The

Twilight Existence of Nonbinding International Agreements," 71 Am. J. Int'l L. 296 (1977).

The history of the HFA and of the instruments it has spawned suggests that their non-binding character has not proved detrimental to the objectives they were designed to achieve. In the past, they frequently proved useful as standards that could be invoked on the international and national plane to prod states to remedy human rights violations. National governments and legislatures, domestic courts and administrative bodies have looked to them in making, interpreting and applying national laws and regulations. They have also proved to be a useful tool for national and international nongovernmental organizations seeking to promote the observance of human rights.

§ 3–27.　The OSCE Catalog of Rights

What distinguishes the rights catalog of the OSCE from that of traditional human rights treaties—the European Convention of Human Rights or the International Covenants, for example—is that in addition to proclaiming basic individual human rights, it also deals with the rights of minorities, rule of law issues, democratic values, elections, etc. In short, when one looks at the entire body of commitments that have found expression over a period of years in the various concluding documents and in the HFA, what emerges is a blueprint for a free and democratic Europe where human rights and the rule of law are observed. This being said, it should nevertheless be obvious that it is one thing to draw up a blueprint and quite another to put it into effect. At the same time, however, it cannot be denied that the OSCE has pioneered this holistic approach to human rights, which proceeds on the assumption that individual rights are best protected in states which adhere to the rule of law and democratic values and are so constituted as to permit these concepts to flourish. With the end of the Cold War, this notion is gaining support elsewhere in the world. *See* Franck, "The Emerging Right to Democratic Governance," 86 Am. J. Int'l L. 46 (1992). *See also* Steiner, "Political Participation as a Human Right," 1 Harv. Hum. Rts. Y.B. 77 (1988).

Although the Madrid (1983) and Vienna (1989) concluding documents expanded the OSCE human rights catalog somewhat, the real breakthrough came with the adoption of Copenhagen Concluding Document (1990). *See generally* Buergenthal, "The Copenhagen CSCE Meeting: A New Public Order for Europe," 11 Hum. Rts. L. J. 217 (1990). In addition to a section on human rights and fundamental freedoms, this instrument contains chapters dealing with the rule of law, free elections and democratic values that added entirely new dimensions to the OSCE human rights catalog. It also enlarged upon prior OSCE commitments on the rights of minorities. Subsequent OSCE documents, from the Charter of Paris for a New Europe (1990), the Moscow Concluding Document (1991), the 1992 Helsinki Document ("Challenges for Change"), through the 1994 Budapest Document ("Towards a Genuine Partnership in a New Era") have refined, reinforced and expanded upon these commitments, which today also include commitments relating to international humanitarian law, and the rights of refugees, migrant workers, and indigenous populations, among others. While it is impossible here to enumerate what has in fact become a vast human rights catalog, its essence is captured in Chapter VIII, para. 2, of the Budapest Document, which reads in part as follows:

> Human rights and fundamental freedoms, the rule of law and democratic institutions are the foundation of peace and security, representing a crucial contribution to conflict prevention. The protection of human rights, including the rights of persons belonging to national minorities, is an essential foundation of democratic civil society.

The OSCE has thus moved from traditional international human rights concerns to the articulation of those basic democratic constitutional principles and legal remedies which seek to ensure that all instrumentalities of the state exercise their powers in conformity with laws adopted by the people through their democratically elected representatives.

§ 3–28. The Human Dimension Mechanism

The Vienna Concluding Document (1989) consolidated the subject of human rights, previously dealt with as a Basket I item, with the human contact and related humanitarian topics set out in Basket III, and it subsumed both topics under the heading of the "Human Dimension of the CSCE." It also established the Human Dimension Mechanism for dealing with the non-observance by states with their human dimension commitments. Subsequent OSCE conferences, among them the Copenhagen (1990), Moscow (1991) and Helsinki (1992) Concluding Documents, have expanded the scope of the Mechanism in order to make it more effective. *See* Buergenthal, "CSCE Rights System", *supra,* at 369.

The Mechanism now consists of a multi-stage process of negotiations, mediation, and fact-finding, involving bilateral and multilateral negotiations, OSCE missions of experts and rapporteurs assisted by the OSCE Office for Democratic Institutions and Human Rights (ODIHR). The process usually begins with claims by one or more states that another state is not living up to its OSCE human dimension commitments. There follows a diplomatic exchange between the states concerned for which specific time-limits are provided. If the matter is not resolved between them, the states may bring it to the attention of all OSCE states and place the matter on the agenda of OSCE follow-up or human dimension conferences. If this process does not produce results, OSCE expert missions or rapporteur missions may be appointed to investigate the charges. These perform the role of third-party fact-finders and mediators. As a rule, the missions are established by mutual consent of the states concerned, although such consent is not necessary in serious situations. In such cases a mission may be convoked whenever a group of states or the OSCE Senior Council considers it necessary. *See* Bloed, "The Between Conflict Prevention and Implementation Review," 4 Helsinki Monitor, No. 4, at 36 (1993).

§ 3–29. The High Commissioner on National Minorities

Although the HFA makes a passing reference to the rights of individuals belonging to national minorities, it was the Copenhagen Concluding Document which in 1990 proclaimed a series of important OSCE commitments on this subject. These commitments were expanded upon in the Report of the Geneva Meeting of Experts on National Minorities (1991). That report, in turn, was incorporated by reference into the Moscow Concluding Document (1991). Having thus laid the normative foundation for a system to protect national minorities, the OSCE in 1992 established the office of the High Commissioner on National Minorities (HCNM). *See CSCE Helsinki Document: The Challenges of Change,* ch. II, at 7 (1992) (spelling out the mandate of the HCNM). *See also* Bloed, "The CSCE and the Protection of Minorities," *in* A. Phillips & A. Rosas (eds.), *The UN Minority Rights Declaration* 95 (1993).

With the end of the Cold War, potential conflicts posed by minority issues began to threaten the peaceful transition to democracy in Eastern and Central Europe and in the former Soviet Republics. *See* Roth, "The CSCE and the New Increase of National, Ethnic and Racial Tensions," 4 Helsinki Monitor, No. 4, at 5 (1993). *See also* L. Sohn (ed.), *The CSCE and the Turbulent New Europe* (GWU–

IRLI, 1993). Concern with these problems is reflected in the mandate of the HCNM, which reads in part as follows:

The High Commissioner will provide "early warning" and, as appropriate, "early action" at the earliest possible stage in regard to tensions involving national minority issues which have not yet developed beyond an early warning stage, but, in the judgement of the High Commissioner, have the potential to develop into a conflict within the CSCE area, affecting peace, stability or relations between participating States, requiring the attention of and action by the Council [of Ministers of Foreign Affairs] or the CSE [Committee of Senior Officials].

As this language indicates, the principal function of the HCNM is to address minority problems before they degenerate into serious conflicts. In discharging this mandate, the High Commissioner is to be guided by "CSCE principles and commitments." He/she is to "work in confidence and ... act independently of all parties involved in the tensions." In 1993, Mr. Max van der Stoel, a former Dutch foreign minister, was appointed High Commissioner for a three-year term. Because of his stature and diplomatic skills, Mr. Van der Stoel has been able to render extremely useful mediating and advisory services to governments and national minorities in a number of countries, resolving potentially explosive conflicts or, at the very least, getting different groups together in the hope of finding solutions. In the process he has transformed and adjusted his mandate to the unexpected demands on his services, and developed a *modus operandi* that has gained him a great deal of respect within the OSCE area. Chigas, "Bridging the Gap Between Theory and Practice: The CSCE High Commissioner on National Minorities," 5 Helsinki Monitor, No 3, at 26 (1994). *See also* Huber, "Preventing Ethnic Conflict in the New Europe: The CSCE High Commissioner on National Minorities," 1 CSCE Bulletin, No. 3, at 17 (ODIHR, 1993).

By formulating a catalog of basic OSCE commitments relating to the rights of national minorities, the Copenhagen CSCE Conference (1990) picked up on a subject which had attracted only sporadic interest on the part of the international community after the demise of the League of Nations minorities system. *See* § 1–5, *supra*. Copenhagen and some of the tragic events in the former Yugoslavia and elsewhere in the world no doubt account for a renewed interest in international norms and institutions for the protection of minorities. As a result, in 1992, the United Nations adopted the "Declaration on the Rights of Persons Belonging to National or Ethnic, Religious and Linguistic Minorities," (UN General Assembly Res. 47/135 of December 18, 1992). *See generally* Thornberry, "The UN Declaration: Background, Analysis and Observations," *in* A. Phillips & A. Rosas (eds.), *The UN Minority Rights Declaration* 11 (1993). In 1994, the Council of Europe adopted and opened for signature the "Framework Convention for the Protection of National Minorities." Council of Europe, Doc. H (94)

10. In the explanatory report to this convention, we find the following paragraph:

The framework Convention is the first legally binding multilateral instrument devoted to the protection of national minorities in general. Its aim is to specify the legal principles which States undertake to respect in order to ensure the protection of national minorities. The Council of Europe has thereby given effect to the ... call [by the Vienna Declaration of the Heads of State and Governments of the Member States of the Council of Europe] ... for the political commitments adopted by the Conference on Security and Cooperation in Europe (CSCE) to be transformed, to the greatest possible extent, into legal obligations.

Explanatory Report, para. 10, *id.*, at 13. These new United Nations and Council of Europe instruments strengthen the normative framework within which the High Commissioner on National Minorities discharges his mandate. Here we also have a fascinating example of the manner in which regional and international institutions interact and complement each other in confronting human rights problems. *See generally* Buergenthal, "International and Regional Human Rights Law and Institutions: Some Examples of Their Interaction," 12 Texas Int'l L.J. 321 (1977); Cancado–Trindade, "Co–Existence and Co–Ordination of Mechanisms of International Protection of Human Rights (At Global and Regional Levels)," 202 Recueil des Cours 9 (1987).

CHAPTER 4

THE INTER–AMERICAN HUMAN RIGHTS SYSTEM

I. INTRODUCTION

This chapter deals with the law and institutions that have been developed by the Organization of American States to promote and protect human rights. The OAS is a regional inter-governmental organization which includes among its 35 members all sovereign states of the Americas. These states are: Antigua and Barbuda, Argentina, The Bahamas, Barbados, Belize, Bolivia, Brazil, Canada, Chile, Colombia, Costa Rica, Cuba, Dominica, Dominican Republic, Ecuador, El Salvador, Grenada, Guatemala, Guyana, Haiti, Honduras, Jamaica, Mexico, Nicaragua, Panama, Paraguay, Peru, St. Kitts and Nevis, St. Lucia, St. Vincent and the Grenadines, Suriname, Trinidad and Tobago, United States, Uruguay, and Venezuela. Although the Castro government was expelled from the Organization in 1962, Cuba remains at least in theory a Member State.

The OAS discharges its functions through various organs, including the General Assembly and Permanent Council. The General Assembly which meets once a year in regular session and in as many special ones as necessary. It is the supreme policy-setting organ of the Organization. Each Member State has one vote in the Assembly. The Permanent Council is composed of the permanent representatives of each Member State to the OAS. The Council serves as the Organization's decision-making organ between Assembly sessions and performs various other functions bearing on the resolution of disputes and peacekeeping. Both organs have jurisdiction to deal with human rights matters. On the OAS in general, see OAS Secretariat, *The Inter–American System*, 2 vols. (F.V. Garcia–Amador, ed., 1982). *See also* V.P. Vaky & H. Muñoz, *The Future of the Organization of American States* (1993).

The inter-American human rights systems has two distinct legal sources: one has evolved from the Charter of the OAS, the other is based on the American Convention on Human Rights. The Charter-based system applies to all 35 Member States of the OAS. The Convention system is legally binding only on the States Parties to it. The two systems overlap and interact in a variety of ways. This makes it difficult at times to determine where one ends and the other begins. In some cases, the legal mechanisms or norms of both systems apply to different aspects of one and the same human rights situation. *See, e.g.*, Advisory Opinion OC–10/89, I.–A. Court H.R., Series A: Judgments and Opinions, No. 10 (1990) (interpreting the normative effect of the American Declaration of the Rights and Duties of Man). Hence, although we shall examine these two systems separately in this chapter because it is conceptually easier to do so, the reader should keep in mind that as a practical matter, the two systems often function as one.

For a complete collection of relevant treaties and related texts, reports, judicial opinions and historical documents bearing on the OAS system, see T. Buergenthal & R. Norris, *Human Rights: The Inter–American System* (5 Looseleaf volumes 1982–1994). Two joint publications of the Inter–American Commission and Court of Human Rights, one entitled *Basic Documents Pertaining to Human Rights in the Inter–American System* [hereinafter cited as *Basic Documents*], OEA/Ser.L/V/II.82, doc. 6, rev. 1 (1992), and the other, *Inter–American Yearbook on Human Rights,* are indispensable research tools on the inter–American system. *See also* T. Buergenthal & D. Shelton, *Protecting Human Rights in the Americas: Selected Problems* (4th ed. 1995) [hereinafter cited as *Protecting Human Rights.*]

II. THE OAS CHARTER–BASED SYSTEM

§ 4–1. Introduction

The Charter-based human rights norms and institutions of the inter-American system have evolved over a 50–year period. Various legal and political considerations contributed to its evolution. The major legal developments include the promulgation of the American Declaration of the Rights and Duties of Man, the establishment of the Inter–

American Commission on Human Rights, the 1970 amendment of the OAS Charter, and the entry into force of the American Convention on Human Rights. *See* A. Schreiber, *The Inter–American Commission on Human Rights* (1970); Cancado Trindade, "The Evolution of the OAS System of Human Rights Protection: An Appraisal," 25 Germ. Y.B. Int'l L. 498 (1982); Medina–Quiroga, "The Inter–American Commission on Human Rights and the Inter–American Court of Human Rights," 12 Human Rts. Q. 439 (1990). The political factors that have played an especially important role include the emergence of the Castro regime and the hemispheric reaction to it. Equally important has been the attitude of the U.S. Government, which initially showed little interest in, if not outright hostility to, the development of an inter-American human rights system, and then championed it at different times and for different reasons. The fall of all but one of the Latin American dictatorships—a relatively recent phenomenon—has also had a significant political impact. See Buergenthal, "Human Rights in the Americas: View from the Inter–American Court," 2 Conn. J. Int'l L. 303 (1987); Vaky & Muñoz, *supra*, at 71.

§ 4–2. The OAS Charter

The Charter, a multilateral treaty which is the constitution of the OAS, was opened for signature in Bogota, Colombia, in 1948 and entered into force in 1951. It was amended by the Protocol of Buenos Aires, which was concluded in 1967 and came into effect in 1970, and by the Protocol of Cartagena de Indias, Colombia. The latter instrument was opened for signature in 1985 and entered into force in 1988. Two later amendments to the Charter, the Protocols of Washington and Managua, have not as yet entered into force.

The 1948 Charter made very few references to human rights. One provision of importance was Article 3(j), now Article 3(k), wherein "the American States proclaim the fundamental rights of the individual without distinction as to race, nationality, creed, or sex" among the principles to which they are committed. Another important reference to human rights appears in Article 13, now Article 16. After declaring that "each State has the right to develop its cultural, political and economic life freely and naturally," this provision prescribes that "in this free development, the State shall respect the rights of the individual and the principles of universal morality." The 1948 Charter did not define "the fundamental rights of the individual" to which Article 3 referred, nor did it create any institution to promote their observance. However, the same diplomatic conference which adopted the 1948 Charter also proclaimed the American Declaration of the Rights and Duties of Man. Promulgated in the form of a simple conference resolution, this instrument proclaims an extensive catalog of human rights. *See* § 4–3, *infra.*

In amending the OAS Charter, the Protocol of Buenos Aires introduced some important changes bearing on human rights: it established the Inter–

American Commission on Human Rights as an OAS Charter organ and prescribed that the Commission's principal function should be "to promote the observance and protection of human rights...." OAS Charter, as amended, arts. 51(e) and 112, now arts. 52(e) and 111. With these amendments, the Commission acquired the constitutional legitimacy it had heretofore lacked. *See* § 4–4, *infra.* These changes also significantly strengthened the normative character of the American Declaration. *See* § 4–3, *infra.*

§ 4–3. The American Declaration of the Rights and Duties of Man

The Declaration was proclaimed on May 2, 1948 by the Ninth International Conference of American States, antedating by a few months the Universal Declaration with which it has much in common. The preamble of the American Declaration emphasizes that "the international protection of the rights of man should be the principal guide of an evolving American law."

The American Declaration proclaims a list of some 27 human rights and ten duties. The catalog of rights embraces civil and political as well as economic, social and cultural rights. These include the right to life, liberty and security of person, to equality before the law, to residence and movement, to a fair trial, to protection from arbitrary arrest, to due process of law, to nationality and asylum. Freedom of religion, expression, assembly and association are proclaimed. Protected, too, is the right to privacy, to property, to health, to education, to the benefits of culture, to work, to leisure time, and to social security. The list of duties includes a duty to society, toward children and parents, to receive instruction, to vote, to obey the law, to serve the community and the nation, to pay taxes, and to work. Also proclaimed are duties with respect to social security and welfare, as well as the duty to refrain from political activities in a foreign country.

The Declaration was adopted as a non-binding conference resolution that was deemed by those who drafted it to have no legal effect. *See* Buergenthal, "The Revised OAS Charter and the Protection of Human Rights," 69 Am. J. Int'l L. 828, at 829 (1975). Very gradually, however, the legal status of the American Declaration began to change. Today it is deemed to be the normative instrument that embodies the authoritative interpretation of "the fundamental rights of the individual," which Article 3(k) of the OAS Charter proclaims. On this subject, the inter-American Court of Human Rights has found that "for the member states of the Organization, the Declaration is the text that defines the human rights referred to in the Charter.... [T]he Declaration is for these States a source of international obligations related to the Charter of the Organization." Advisory Opinion OC–10/89, I–A. Court H.R., Series A: Judgments and Opinions, No. 10, para. 45 (1989). This conclusion finds strong support in the human rights practice of the OAS and of its Member States, which the Court reviewed in considerable detail in that advisory opinion. *Id.*, at par. 43. *See also* Buergenthal, "The Inter–American System for the Protection of Human Rights," *in* T. Meron (ed.), *Human Rights in International Law: Legal and Policy Issues* 438, 470–79 (1984); Shelton, "Abortion and the Right to Life in the Inter–American System: the Case of 'Baby Boy'," 2 Hum. Rts. L.J. 309, 312–13 (1981). For a discussion of the implications of the normative character of the Declaration, see Buergenthal, "The American Human Rights Declaration: Random Reflections," *in* K. Hailbronner, G. Ress & T. Stein (eds.), *Staat und Völkerrechtsordnung* (*Festschrift für Karl Doehring*) 133 (1989).

§ 4–4. Commission as Charter Organ: Its Institutional Evolution

The establishment of the Inter–American Commission on Human Rights was mandated in 1959 by the Fifth Meeting of Consultation of Ministers of Foreign Affairs. The OAS Council complied with that mandate in 1960 by adopting the Statute of the Commission and electing the first seven Commission members. Since the 1948 OAS Charter did not provide for the establishment of the Commission, the Council designated it as an "autonomous entity" of the OAS, "the function of which it is to promote respect for human rights." 1960 Commission Statute, art. 1. These rights were defined as follows in Article 2 of the Statute: "for the purpose of this Statute, human rights are understood to be those set forth in the American Declaration of the Rights and Duties of Man." The adoption of the

Statute of the Commission and the language it employed set in motion the long process that transformed the Declaration into the important normative instrument it has become.

Article 9 of the 1960 Statute gave the Commission various powers to promote human rights, including the power to prepare studies and reports and "to make recommendations to the governments of the member states in general ... for the adoption of progressive measures in favor of human rights within the framework of their domestic legislation...." The Commission, in its first session, interpreted this language to authorize it to address general recommendations to individual states. In reliance on this interpretation and on its power to prepare studies, the Commission ushered in the practice of undertaking so-called country studies, a practice it follows to this day. *See, e.g., Annual Report of the Inter–American Commission on Human Rights 1993*, at 399 (1994).

The Second Special Inter–American Conference authorized the Commission in 1965 to receive and act on individual petitions charging OAS Member States with violations of some, but not all, rights proclaimed in the American Declaration. The new powers, which the Commission incorporated into its Statute in 1966 as Article 9(*bis*), applied to the following "preferred" rights: the right to life, liberty and security of person (Article I), equality before the law (Article II), freedom of religion (Article III), freedom of expression (Article IV), freedom from arbitrary arrest (Article XXV), and the right to due process of law (Article XXVI). In this fashion, Article 9(*bis*) authorized the Commission to establish a limited individual petition system. That system had its legal source in powers implied in the OAS Charter, rather than in any specific human rights treaty.

The status of the Commission changed in 1970 with the entry into force of the Protocol of Buenos Aires. It amended the 1948 OAS Charter and transformed the Inter–American Commission on Human Rights into a formal organ of the OAS, whose "principal function shall be to promote the observance and protection of human rights and to serve as a consultative organ of the Organization in these matters." OAS Charter, as amended, arts. 51 and 112(1), now arts. 52 and 111(1). The Protocol added two other provisions applicable to the new Charter organ it created. The first was Article 112(2), now 111(2), which provides that "an inter-American convention on human rights shall determine the structure, competence and procedures of this Commission. . . ." The other was Article 150, which remains in force and reads as follows: "Until the inter-American convention on human rights, referred to in . . . [Article 111], enters into force, the present Inter–American Commission on Human Rights shall keep vigilance over the observance of human rights." By becoming an OAS Charter organ, the Commission acquired an institutional and constitutional legitimacy it had not previously enjoyed. The reference in Article 150 to "the present" Commission, read in conjunction with Article

112, now Article 111, can also be deemed to have legitimated the practices and procedures the Commission developed under Articles 9 and 9(*bis*) of its Statute. *See generally,* Buergenthal "The Revised OAS Charter and the Protection of Human Rights," 69 Am. J. Int'l L. 828 (1975); Cancado Trindade, "Co–Existence and Co–Ordination of Mechanisms of International Protection of Human Rights (At Global and Regional Levels)," 202 Recueil des Cours 10, at 190 (1987); C. Medina–Quiroga, *The Battle of Human Rights: Gross, Systematic Violations and the Inter–American System* 85 (1988).

The "inter-American convention" to which the amended OAS Charter referred was adopted in 1969 and entered into force in 1978, whereas the amendments to the OAS Charter were drafted in 1967. That is why those who drafted the Convention, being aware of the references which the amended OAS Charter made to the Convention, assigned two distinct functions to the Inter–American Commission on Human Rights. There are first the functions the Commission performs in relation to all Member States of the OAS, spelled out in Article 41(a)–(e) and (g) of the Convention, and, second, the functions applicable only to States Parties to the Convention. Convention, arts. 41(f), 44–51. The former functions for all practical purposes track the Commission's preexisting powers as OAS Charter organ. *See* Advisory Opinion OC–13, I.–A. Court H.R., Series A: Judgments and Opinions, No. 13 (1993) (interpreting Articles 41–42, 46–47, and 50–51 of the Convention).

The entry into force of the Convention required the OAS General Assembly to adopt a new Statute for the reconstituted Commission. Convention, art. 39. This it did in 1979. *See* Norris, "The New Statute of the Inter–American Commission on Human Rights," 1 Hum. Rts. L.J. 379 (1980). That Statute remains in force today. It takes account of the different functions the Commission performs as an OAS Charter organ and as a Convention organ. To this end, it spells out the Commission's powers as they apply (a) to all OAS Member States (Article 18); (b) to the States Parties to the Convention (Article 19); and (c) to OAS Member States that are not parties to the Convention (Article 20). Articles 18 and 20 of the Statute thus preserve for the Commission the powers it had under Articles 9 and 9(*bis*) of its old Statute. *See generally*, Shelton, "The Inter–American System for the Protection of Human Rights: Emergent Law," *in* I. Cotler & F.P. Eliades (eds.), *International Human Rights Law: Theory and Practice* 369, 370 (1992). Moreover, in defining "human rights," Article 1(2) of the new Statute provides as follows:

For the purposes of the present Statute, human rights are understood to be:

(a) The rights set forth in the American Convention on Human Rights, in relation to the States Parties thereto;

(b) The rights set forth in the American Declaration of the Rights and Duties of Man, in relation to the other Member States.

This reference to the Declaration reinforces its normative character and legitimates the authority of the Commission in relation to states that are not parties to the Convention. For these states, the OAS Charter and the Declaration impose human rights obligations which the Commission has the authority to enforce under its Statute. Inter–American Commission on Human Rights [hereinafter I.–A. Comm. H.R.], Rep. No. 31/93 (Case No. 10.573/United States), Decision of October 14, 1993, I–ACHR, *Annual Report 1993*, OEA/Ser.L/V/II.85, Doc. 9 rev., at 312 (1993).

§ 4–5. The Commission as Charter Organ: Its Practice

As a Charter organ, the Commission performs a variety of functions, including promotional and consultative activities. The Commission has helped draft OAS human rights instruments, including the American Convention on Human Rights, and it is regularly consulted by the OAS Permanent Council and the General Assembly on human rights issues. The Commission also sponsors conferences and publishes human rights documents and pamphlets. *See, e.g.,* I–ACHR, *Ten Years of Activities 1971–1981* (1982); I–ACHR, *25 Years of Struggle for Human Rights in the Americas 1959–1984* (1984). On different occasions during its existence, the Commission has played an important role in mediating and protecting human rights in civil war situations, in international armed conflicts, and hostage seizures. *See* I–ACHR, "Reports of the Activities of the Inter–

American Commission on Human Rights in the Dominican Republic (June 1 to August 31, 1965 and September 1, 1965 to July 6, 1966)," in *The Organization of American States and Human Rights 1960– 1967* at 359 and 439 (1972) (civil war); I–ACHR, "Report of the Inter–American Commission on Human Rights on the Situation regarding Human Rights in El Salvador and Honduras," *in The Organization of American States and Human Rights 1969–1970,* at 291 (1976) (international armed conflict); I–ACHR, Report on the Situation of Human Rights in the Republic of Colombia, OEA/Ser.L/V/ II.53, doc.22, at 22 (1981) (hostage seizure). Country studies and the examination of individual petitions have, however, occupied most of its time. *See, e.g.,* [1985] *Inter-American Yearbook of Human Rights* 263 (1987); [1989] *id.,* at 52 (1993). *See also* Padilla, "The Inter–American Commission on Human Rights of the Organization of American States: A Case Study," 9 Am. U.J. Int'l L. & Pol'y 95, 104 (1993) (reporting that "the Commission has conducted more than fifty on-site visits to sixteen member states").

1. *Country Studies and On–Site Investigations*

A country study is an investigation of the human rights conditions of a state. The Commission usually initiates such a study when it receives individual communications or other credible evidence, often from non-governmental human rights organizations, suggesting that a government is engaging in large-scale violations of human rights. The first country reports were prepared in the early 1960's and dealt with Cuba, Haiti and the Dominican Republic. Cuba and Haiti refused to allow the Commission to visit their countries; the Dominican Republic gave permission to enter and became the first country to be the subject of an on-site investigation. The reports relating to these countries are reproduced in *The Organization of American States and Human Rights 1960–67,* Part III (1972). In its initial country study concerning Cuba, the Commission established the precedent of hearing witnesses and receiving evidence. In that case, it held hearings in Miami and interviewed many refugees. During its visits to the Dominican Republic, the Commission criss-crossed the country, held hearings, met with government and opposition leaders, and interviewed representatives of various church, business and union groups as well as private individuals; it also set up offices in the country for the receipt of written and oral complaints. The *modus operandi* adopted by the Commission during its visits to the Dominican Republic in the 1960's became a model which it has followed with minor variations to this day in its on-site investigations. *See, e.g.,* I–ACHR, *Report on the Situation of Human Rights in Argentina,* OEA/Ser.L/V/II.49, doc. 19, corr. 1 (1980); I–ACHR, *Report on the Situation of Human Rights in the Republic of Nicaragua,* OEA/Ser.L./V/II.53, doc.25 (1981); I–ACHR, *Fourth Report on the Situation of Human Rights in Guatemala*, OEA/Ser.L/V/II. 83, Doc. 16 rev. (1993); I–ACHR, *Second Report on the Situation of Human*

Rights in Colombia, OEA/Ser.L/V/II.84, Doc. 39 rev. (1993); I–ACHR, *Report on the Situation of Human Rights in El Salvador*, OEA/Ser.L/V/II.85, Doc. 28 rev. (1994); I–ACHR, *Report on the Situation of Human Rights in Haiti*, OEA/Ser.L/V/II.85, Doc. 9 rev. (1994). *See also* I–ACHR, *Annual Report 1992–1993*, OEA/Ser.L/V/II.83, Doc. 14, at 16 (1993); I–ACHR, *Annual Report 1993*, OEA/Ser.L./V/II.85, Doc. 9 rev., at 17 (1994).

On-site investigations are usually arranged by an exchange of letters and cables between the chairman of the Commission and the government concerned. As a rule, the Commission requests permission to visit a particular country, but some governments have extended invitations for such visits on their own initiative. *See, e.g.,* I–ACHR, *Report on the Situation of Human Rights in Panama,* OEA/Ser.L/V/II.44, doc. 38 rev.1, at 1–3 (1978). *See generally* Norris, "Observations *In Loco:* Practice and Procedure of the Inter–American Commission on Human Rights, 1979–1983," 19 Tex. Int'l L.J. 285 (1984); Padilla, *supra*, at 103. Prior to 1977, the rules governing on-site visits were negotiated on an *ad hoc* basis. Thereafter the Commission adopted a set of rules on the subject. These are now codified in Articles 55 through 59 of the Commission's Regulations. Article 58 of the Regulations requires the host government to put at the disposal of the Commission all facilities necessary for the accomplishment of its mission and to pledge that it will impose no punitive measures against individuals who cooperate with or supply information to the Commission. The right of members of the Commission and its staff to travel freely in the host country, to meet with any individuals whatsoever, and to visit prisons is provided for in Article 59 of the Rules. This provision also establishes the government's obligation to ensure the safety of the Commission and its staff, and to provide the Commission with whatever documents or other information it may request. On-site investigations are now generally undertaken by a so-called "Special Commission" of the Commission. To avoid conflict of interest problems, Article 56 of the Regulations provides that members of the Commission, who are nationals of or reside in a country in which the investigation is to be carried out, shall be ineligible to serve on the "Special Commission."

In preparing its country studies, whether or not on-site investigations are involved, the Commission proceeds in stages. Initially, after the relevant information has been gathered, the Commission prepares a draft report. That document examines the conditions in the country by reference to the human rights standards set out in the American Declaration of the Rights and Duties of Man or of the American Convention on Human Rights, depending upon whether or not the state is a party to the Convention. The draft report is then submitted to that country's government for its comments. The government's response is analyzed by the Commission to determine whether the report should be amended in light of the information brought to its attention by the government. After reassessing its findings, the Commission decides whether to publish the report. The Regulations of the Commission require the publication of the report if the government does not respond to the request for observations (Art. 62). The Commission does not have to publish the report, however, if the government either agrees to comply with the recommendations or demonstrates that it is not committing any violations. The reports published by the Commission in the past few years usually have reproduced in full the government's observations.

In addition to publishing the report, the Commission may also transmit it to the OAS General Assembly. Because debates in the Assembly attract considerable public attention, reference to and discussion by the Assembly of a country report, followed by an appropriate resolution, can have a significant impact on the behavior of a government that has been charged by the Commission with human rights violations. Although OAS General Assembly resolutions are not legally binding, they are acts emanating from the highest political organ of the Organization and, consequently carry considerable moral and political weight. Governments tend to take these considerations into account before they decide how to react to recommendations made by the Commission in its country studies. Ultimately, as in all efforts to enforce internationally guaranteed human rights, the effectiveness of the Commission's country-study practice depends on the Commission's prestige and credibility, on the public opinion pressure its recommendations are likely to generate, and on the resolutions that the OAS General Assembly is willing to adopt to back the Commission. In the past, the attitude of the Assembly has varied, depending upon whether a substantial number of the governments represented in it were military dictatorships or democracies. *See generally* Farer & Rowles, "The Inter–American Commission on Human Rights," *in* J. Tuttle (ed.), *International Human Rights Law and Practice* 47 (1978). But now that most members are represented by freely elected governments, one might have assumed that the Assembly would strongly support the Commission. That has unfortunately not been the case. Instead, the General Assembly has increasingly adopted "boiler plate" resolutions that fail to fully address the recommendations of the Commission based on its country reports. These resolutions are moreover often drafted in such a way as to either disguise the names of the countries that were the subjects of these reports or to name them without taking note of the charges against them. *See, e.g.*, AG/Res. 1269(XXIV–O/94), OAS Gen. Ass. Doc. OEA/Ser.P./XX.O.2, vol. 1, at 75 (1994); AG/Res. 1213 (XXIII–O/93), OAS Gen. Ass. Doc. OEA/Ser.P/XXIII.O.2, vol. 1, at 31 (1993). This regrettable practice is quite obviously designed to protect governments against adverse publicity.

2. *Individual Petitions*

Prior to the entry into force of the American Convention, the Commission examined and acted formally on only those private communications that alleged a violation of one of the "preferred" freedoms enumerated in Article 9(*bis*) of its old Statute. *See* § 4–4, *supra*. This practice changed with the promulgation of its current Statute. The Commission's Regulations now no longer distinguish between the "preferred freedoms" and other rights proclaimed in the American Declaration. Instead they establish a procedure, based on Article 20 of the Statute, that allows the Commission to receive and act on individual petitions charging a violation of any of the rights enumerated in the Declaration. *See* Commission Regulations, arts. 51–54.

The Commission processes these petitions in much the same way as the private communications it receives under the Convention. *See* § 4–9, *infra*. The two types of petitions are treated differently only at the final stages of the proceedings. That is, the petition process applicable to states not parties to the Convention concludes with a report, denominated a "final decision." Commission Regulations, art. 53. This decision usually contains a finding of facts and the Commission's conclusions and recommendations. If a state does not comply with the recommendation, the Commission may publish the decision. The Commission's annual report to the OAS General Assembly usually contains a chapter in which some of its decisions are reproduced. *See, e.g., I–ACHR, Annual Report 1993,* OEA/Ser.L/V/II.85, doc. 9 rev. 1, Chapter III (1994) (containing 23 decisions involving States Parties to the Convention and states, such as the United States and Canada, which are not parties).

This Charter-based individual petition system is plagued by two serious weaknesses. The first has to do with the fact that, since the petitions are directed against states which are not parties to the Convention, the Court has no contentious jurisdiction to deal with them. Second, although the Commission transmits its decisions in these cases to the General Assembly, this body has shown little interest in dealing with individual petitions. Non-compliance by states with the decisions of the Commission in these cases consequently attracts little notice, which deprives the system of its effectiveness.

III. THE CONVENTION–BASED SYSTEM

§ 4–6. Introduction

The American Convention on Human Rights was opened for signature on November 20, 1969 at an inter-American diplomatic conference held in San Jose, Costa Rica. It entered into force on July 18, 1978 and has to date been ratified by 25 OAS Member States. The following states are parties to the Convention: Argentina, Barbados, Bolivia, Brazil, Chile, Colombia, Costa Rica, Dominica, Dominican Republic, Ecuador, El Salvador, Grenada, Guatemala, Haiti, Honduras, Jamaica, Mexico, Nicaragua, Panama, Paraguay, Peru, Suriname, Trinidad and Tobago, Uruguay and Venezuela. Missing from the list are Canada, the United States, and some of the smaller English-speaking Caribbean nations. The United States signed the Convention and President Jimmy Carter referred it to the Senate for its advice and consent to ratification. *See* § 7–3, *infra*. The Senate did not act on the request, which has not been renewed by subsequent administrations. Two Additional Protocols, one dealing with Economic, Social, and Cultural Rights (1988) and the other with the Abolition of the Death Penalty (1990), have not as yet entered into force. *See generally* Shelton, "The Inter–American System," in H. Hannum (ed.), *Guide to International Human Rights Practice* 119, 120 (2d ed. 1992).

§ 4–7. The Convention and its Guarantees

The Convention guarantees some two dozen broad categories of civil and political rights. These include the following: the right to juridical personality, right to life, right to humane treatment, freedom from slavery, right to personal liberty, right to a fair trial, freedom from ex post facto laws, right to compensation for miscarriage of justice, right to privacy, freedom of conscience and religion, freedom of thought and expression, right of reply, right of assembly, freedom of association, rights of the family, right to a name, rights of the child, right to nationality, right to property, freedom of movement and residence, right to participate in government, right to equal protection of the law, and right to judicial protection. These guarantees are supplemented by a broad non-discrimination clause and an undertaking by the States Parties to take progressive measures for "the full realization of the rights implicit in the economic, social, educational, scientific, and cultural standards set forth in the Charter of the Organization of American States as amended by the Protocol of Buenos Aires." (Art. 26.)

Article 1(2) declares that the term "person" as used in the Convention means "human being." Corporations and other juridical persons are thus not the intended beneficiaries of the rights the Convention guarantees. The States Parties to the Convention have an obligation not only "to respect" the rights guaranteed in the Convention, but also "to ensure" their free and full exercise. (Art.1(1).) They consequently have both positive and negative duties, that is, they have the obligation not to violate the rights which the Convention guarantees and are required to adopt whatever measures may be necessary and reasonable under the circumstances "to ensure" their full enjoyment. For an extensive interpretation of the obligations states have under Article 1 of the Convention, see Velasquez Rodriguez Case, I.–A. Court H.R., Judgment of July 29, 1988, Series C: Decisions and Judgments, No. 4, paras. 159 *et seq.* (1988).

Article 27 of the Convention allows the States Parties to derogate from their obligations "in time of war, public danger, or other emergency that threatens [their] independence or security". *See* Grossman, "A Framework for the Examination of States of Emergency Under the American Convention on Human Rights," 1 Am. U. J. Int'l L. & Pol. 35 (1986). Derogation is not permitted, however, from the application of the more basic human rights which the Convention guarantees. The catalog of non-derogable rights is longer than that of the European Convention of Human Rights and the International Covenant on Civil and Political Rights. Unlike these treaties the American Convention also declares that "the judicial remedies essential for the protection" of the non-derogable rights may not be suspended. On this subject, *see* Advisory Opinion OC–8/87, I.–A. Court H.R., *Series A: Judgments and Opinions,* No. 8 (1987); Advisory Opinion, OC–1987, I.–A. Court H.R., Series A: Judgments and Decisions, No. 9 (1987). *See generally* Hartman, "Derogation from Human Rights Treaties in Public Emergencies," 22 Harv. Int'l L.J. 1 (1981); T. Meron, *Human Rights Law–Making in the United Nations* 86 (1986); J. Fitzpatrick, *The International System for Protecting Rights During States of Emergency* (1994).

The Convention also contains a so-called "federal clause," which enables a federal state to assume more limited obligations by binding itself only in relation to matters over which it "exercises legislative and judicial jurisdiction." (Art.28.) This provision was included in the Convention at the urging of the U.S. delegation to the San Jose Conference, which argued that the clause was needed to enable the U.S. to become a party to the Convention. *See* Buergenthal, "The Inter–American System for the Protection of Human Rights," *in* T. Meron (ed.), *Human Rights in International Law: Legal and Policy Issues* 438, 445 (1994).

§ 4–8. The Convention Organs

The Convention provides for the establishment of the Inter–American Commission on Human Rights and the Inter–American Court of Human Rights, and confers on them "competence with respect to matters relating to the fulfillment of the commitments made by the States Parties" thereto. (Art.33.) *See generally* Shelton, "Implementation Procedures of the American Convention on Human Rights," 26 Germ. Y.B. Int'l L. 238 (1983); Buergenthal, "Implementation in the Inter–American Human Rights System," *in* R. Bernhardt & J.A. Jolowicz (eds.), *International Enforcement of Human Rights* 57, 61 (1987). Both institutions consist of seven members each, elected in their personal capacities. The members of the Commission are elected by all OAS Member States, but only the States Parties to the Convention have the right to nominate and vote in the election of the judges of the Court. Since the Commission is both a Convention and an OAS Charter organ, *see* § 4–4, *supra,* it is logical to give all OAS Member States, whether or not they have ratified the Convention, a vote in the selection of the Commissioners.

The Commission has its seat at the headquarters of the OAS in Washington, D.C.; the Court sits in San Jose, Costa Rica. The Court and the Commission hold at least two regular sessions annually, and may meet in special sessions as often as necessary. Membership on the Court and Commission is not a full-time position, but both institutions have a small permanent professional staff.

A. THE INTER–AMERICAN COMMISSION ON HUMAN RIGHTS

§ 4–9. The Commission as Convention Organ

The functions of the Commission are spelled out in Article 41 of the Convention. It codifies the Commission's preexisting functions as an OAS organ, *see* § 4–4, *supra,* and mandates it "to take action on petitions and other communications pursuant to its authority under the provisions of Articles 44 through 51 of this Convention." (Article 41(f).) These provisions apply only to the States Parties to the Convention and deal with the petition system it establishes. It should not be confused with the petition system the Commission administers as an OAS Charter organ. *See* § 4–5, *supra.*

1. *Examination of Petitions*

The Convention empowers the Commission to deal with individual petitions and inter-state communications. (Arts. 44 and 45.) By becoming a party to the Convention, a State is deemed to have accepted the jurisdiction of the Commission to examine private complaints lodged against that state. (Art. 44.) The Commission may deal with inter-state complaints—complaints filed by one State Party against another—only if both states, in addition to ratifying the Convention, have also recognized the inter-state jurisdiction of the Commission. (Art. 45.) In adopting this approach, the American Convention departs from the more traditional scheme utilized by the European Convention, for example, which establishes an optional individual petition system and a mandatory inter-state complaint procedure. *See* Frowein, "The European and American Conventions on Human Rights: A Comparison," 1 Hum. Rts. L.J. 44 (1980); Buergenthal, "The American and European Conventions on Human Rights: Similarities and Differences," 30 Am. U. L. Rev. 155 (1980). Moreover, unlike some other human rights treaties, the American Convention does not give only victims of violations the right to file private petitions. Any person or group of persons and nongovernmental organizations may do so also. (Art. 44.)

The admissibility of a petition is conditioned, *inter alia,* on (1) the exhaustion of domestic remedies "in accordance with the generally recognized principles of international law;" and (2) the requirement that the petition be submitted to the Commission within a period of six months from the date on which the victim of the alleged violation was notified of the final domestic judgment in his case. (Art. 46(1).) These requirements do not prevent the admissibility of a petition, however, if it can be shown that (1) there exist no domestic remedies to protect against the violation of the rights at issue; (2) there has been a denial of access to or interference with respect to the applicable domestic remedies; or (3) the domestic remedies have been subjected to unwarranted delay. (Art. 46(2).) The Inter-American Court of Human Rights has interpreted the requirement for the exhaustion of domestic remedies in a number of cases and advisory opinions, including *inter alia, Godinez*

Cruz Case *(Preliminary Exceptions), I–A. Court H.R., Series C: Judgments and Decisions, No. 3, paras. 81* et seq. *(1987); Advisory Opinion OC– 11/90,* id., *Series A: Judgments and Opinions (1992);* Caballero Delgado v. Colombia *(Preliminary Objection),* id., *Series C: Judgments and Decisions, No. 17, paras. 56* et seq. *(1994).* See also Velasquez Rodriguez *(Merits), I.–A. Court H.R., Series C: Judgments and Decisions, No. 4, paras. 56* et seq. *(1988). The Commission's rules of procedure provide, moreover, that the respondent government has the burden of demonstrating the non-exhaustion of domestic remedies if it invokes that objection and the complaint alleges that compliance with that requirement was impossible. Commission Regulations, art. 37(3). This proposition is consistent with the Court's caselaw on the subject.* See, e.g., Fairen Garbi Case *(Preliminary Objections), I.–A. Court H.R., Series C: Decisions and Judgments, No. 2, para. 87 (1987).*

A complaint will also be held to be inadmissible if it does not state a *prima facie* case under the Convention or if it is otherwise "manifestly groundless or obviously out of order."   (Art. 47(b) and (c).) Article 47(d) requires the Commission to reject a petition that "is substantially the same as one previously studied by the Commission or by another international organization."   This provision complements Article 46(c), which conditions admissibility on the requirement "that the subject of the petition or communication is not pending in another international proceeding of settlement."   The

Commission interprets these last two requirements in a manner designed to ensure that a complaint will not be rejected when any other international organization, although seized of the matter in general, is or was in no position to grant the petitioner the specific relief he/she seeks from the Commission. Commission Regulations, art. 39(2). On the manner in which the Court has resolved various admissibility issues, *see Velasquez Rodriguez Case* (Preliminary Objections), I.–A. Court H. R., Series C: Decisions and Judgments, No. 1 (1987); *Neira Alegria Case* (Preliminary Objections), I.–A. Court H.R., Series C: Decisions and Judgments, No. 13 (1991); *Cayara Case* (Preliminary Objections), I.–A. Court H.R., Series C: Decisions and Judgments, No. 14 (1993); *Caballero Delgado Case* (Preliminary Objections), I.–A. Court H.R., Series C: Decisions and Judgments, No. 17 (1994).

In dealing with complaints that are not rejected as inadmissible, the Commission examines the allegations, seeks information from the government concerned, and investigates the facts. As part of this process, the Commission may hold hearings in which the government and the petitioners participate. The Commission must also "place itself at the disposal of the parties concerned with a view to reaching a friendly settlement of the matter on the basis of respect for the human rights recognized" in the Convention. (Art. 48(b).) If a friendly settlement is obtained, the Commission prepares a report that describes the facts of the case and the settlement. (Art. 49.) For a precedent-setting friendly settlement that the Commission negotiated with the Government of Argentina, see Report No. 1/93, I–ACHR, *Annual Report 1992–93*, OAS/Ser.L.V./II.83, Doc. 14, at 35 (1993).

If the parties are unable to reach a friendly settlement, the Commission draws up a report, setting out the facts and the conclusions it has reached about the case. (Art. 50.) For a finding that no violation of the Convention was committed, see Report No. 2/92 (Case 10.289/Costa Rica), I–ACHR, *Annual Report 1991*, OEA/Ser.L/V/II.8 Doc. 6 rev. 1, at 73 (1992). The report, containing a finding that a violations has been committed, which may also include whatever recommendations the Commission wishes to make, is transmitted to the states concerned. They have three months within which to comply with or react to the recommendations of the Commission. During that period, the case may also be referred to the Inter–American Court of Human Rights by the Commission or the interested states. For a Commission decision referring a case to the Court, see Case No. 7920 (Honduras), Resolution No. 22/86 of April 18, 1986, I–ACHR, *Annual Report 1985–86*, OEA/Ser.L/V/II.68, Doc. 8 rev. 1, 40. Individuals do not have standing to refer a case to the Court. *See* § 4–11, *infra*.

In dealing with a case that has not been taken to the Court or settled by the parties, "the Commission may, by the vote of an absolute majority of its members, set forth its opinion and conclusions concerning the question submitted for its consideration." (Art. 51(1).) If it has concluded that the

Convention was violated, the Commission must set out its "recommendations," if any, and "prescribe a period within which the state is to take the measures that are incumbent upon it to remedy the situation examined." (Art. 51(2).) Once this period has expired it "shall decide by a vote of an absolute majority of its members whether the state has taken adequate measures and whether to publish its report." (Art. 51(3).) *See, e.g.*, Report No. 32/92 (Case 10.454/Colombia), I–ACHR, *Annual Report 1992–93*, OEA/Ser.L/V/II.83/Doc. 14, at 52 (1993). For a discussion of the relationship between Articles 50 and 51, see Advisory Opinion OC–13, I.–A. Court H.R., Series A: Judgments and Opinions, No. 13 (1993); *Caballero Delgado Case* (Preliminary Objections), I.–A. Court H.R., Series C: Decisions and Judgments, No. 17 (1994).

The Commission's rules of procedure permit it to include in its annual report to the OAS General Assembly the final report on a specific case. This rule, which does not prevent the publication of the case report as a separate document as well, gets the matter on the agenda of the General Assembly, where the state's failure to comply with the Commission's recommendations may be discussed and acted upon. It should be noted, however, that individual cases have thus far not led to any OAS General Assembly action.

The Commission may deal with inter-state communications only if the applicant and respondent states have recognized its jurisdiction to receive such complaints. (Art. 45.) Jurisdiction may be accepted on an *ad hoc* basis for a specific case or in general. About one half of the States Parties to the Convention have made the requisite general declaration, but to date no such inter-state proceeding has been instituted. The admissibility requirements and procedures for dealing with inter-state applications are in all respects the same as those that are prescribed for individual petitions.

A ruling by the Commission that a petition is inadmissible is a quasi-judicial decision, which is final and not subject to appeal. The Convention is silent on the legal effect of an opinion of the Commission, rendered pursuant to Article 51, holding that a state has violated the Convention. Although this decision is not formally binding as is a judgment of the Court, it is an authoritative legal determination by a body to which the Convention assigns "competence ... relating to the fulfillment" of the obligations assumed by the States Parties. These states and the OAS are, consequently, entitled to treat the Commission's findings under Article 51 as an authoritative ruling that a State Party has violated its treaty obligation and to act accordingly.

2. *Role Before the Court*

The Convention gives the Commission standing to refer cases to the Court and provides, in addition, that "the Commission shall appear in all cases before the Court." (Arts. 61 and 57.) The quoted language mandates the participation of the Commission in all contentious proceedings before the Court, whether or not they originated as private petitions or as actions by one state against another. The Commission is thus more than a mere party in proceedings before the Court. Even when the Commission refers a case to the Court, it is deemed to do so not on its behalf, but on behalf of an individual or a state. The Commission need not, moreover, adopt as its own the contentions of the victim or state whose case it has referred to the Court. When the Commission appears before the Court, it does so not as "party", but as "the 'Ministerio Publico' of the inter-American system." *In the Matter of Viviana Gallardo*, Case No. G 101/81, Decision of Nov. 13, 1981, I.–A. Court H.R., *Series A: Judgments and Opinions* 77, at para. 22 (1984). The Court's reference to the Latin American legal institution known as "ministerio publico" was designed to make clear that the Commission appears before the Court as protector of the legal order established by the Convention. Its function before the Court, in short, is to promote the legal and institutional integrity of the Convention system.

The Commission has standing also to request advisory opinions from the Court. *See* § 4–14, *infra*. Moreover, the temporary restraining orders, which the Court has power to enter, § 4–13, *infra,* may in certain circumstances be granted only "at the request of the Commission." (Art. 63(2).) Thus, in addition to the multitude of functions the Commission performs in dealing with petitions, it also plays an important role in assisting the Court in discharging its judicial responsibilities. The Commission's Annual Reports as a rule contain a chapter or subchapter entitled "Activities of the I–ACHR in connection with the Inter–American Court of Human Rights," which reports on pending cases, requests for provisional measures, advisory opinion requests, and the Commission's role relating thereto.   *See, e.g.*, I–ACHR, *Annual Report 1993*, OEA/Ser.L/V/II.85, Doc. 9, rev. at 21 (1994).

B.   THE INTER–AMERICAN COURT OF HUMAN RIGHTS

§ 4–10.   Jurisdictions of the Court

The Court has contentious jurisdiction, which is jurisdiction to adjudicate cases involving charges that a State Party has violated the Convention.   It also has jurisdiction to render advisory opinions interpreting the Convention and certain other human rights treaties.   *See* Buergenthal, "The Inter–American Court of Human Rights," 76 Am. J. Int'l L. 231 (1982); Cerna, "The Inter–American Court of Human Rights," *in* M. Janis (ed.), *International Courts for the Twenty–First Century* 117 (1992); S. Davidson, *The Inter–American Court of Human Rights* (1992).   *See also* Frost, "The Evolution of the Inter–American Court of Human Rights: Reflections of Present and Former Judges," 14 Hum. Rts. Q. 171 (1992).

§ 4–11.   Contentious Jurisdiction

Article 62 of the Convention delimits the Court's contentious jurisdiction as follows:

1. A State Party may, upon depositing its instruments of ratification or adherence to this Convention, or at any subsequent time, declare that it recognizes as binding, *ipso facto,* and not requiring special agreement, the jurisdiction of the Court on all matters relating to the interpretation or application of this Convention.

2. Such declaration may be made unconditionally, on the condition of reciprocity, for a specified period, or for specific cases. It shall be presented to the Secretary General of the Organization, who shall transmit copies thereof to the other member states of the Organization and to the Secretary of the Court.

3. The jurisdiction of the Court shall comprise all cases concerning the interpretation and application of the provisions of this Convention that are submitted to it, provided that the States Parties to the case recognize or have recognized such jurisdiction, whether by special declaration pursuant to the preceding paragraphs, or by a special agreement.

This provision indicates that a State Party does not accept the contentious jurisdiction of the Court merely by ratifying the Convention. To do so, it must either have filed the declarations referred to in paragraphs 1 and 2 of Article 62 or have concluded the special agreement mentioned in paragraph 3. The general declarations accepting the Court's jurisdiction have to date been made by Argentina, Bolivia, Colombia, Chile, Costa Rica, Ecuador, El

Salvador, Guatemala, Honduras, Nicaragua, Peru, Panama, Paraguay, Suriname, Trinidad and Tobago, Uruguay, and Venezuela.

The Convention specifies in Article 61(1) that "only the States Parties and the Commission shall have the right to submit a case to the Court." Individuals who have filed a complaint with the Commission cannot consequently bring the case to the Court and depend on the Commission or a state to do it for them. Moreover, before the case may be filed with the Court, the relevant Commission proceedings applicable to it must be "completed" (Article 61(2).) In the *Gallardo* case, the first contentious case to come before the Court, the government of Costa Rica sought to waive the proceedings before the Commission and take the matter directly to the tribunal. The Court held that it lacked jurisdiction to entertain the case until the Commission had dealt with it, emphasizing that the proceedings before the Commission "have not been created for the sole benefit of the States, but also in order to allow for the exercise of important individual rights, especially those of the victims." *In the Matter of Viviana Gallerdo*, Case No. Gl/01/81, Decision of Nov. 13, 1981, I.–A. Court H.R., *Series A: Judgments and Opinions,* at para. 25 (1984). The Court's concern here was that individuals, unlike a State Party, have no formal standing in the Court, whereas they do in proceedings before the Commission. This consideration would give the state a significant advantage if it were to be permitted to bypass the Commission. Still unresolved is the question whether the States Parties to an inter-state dispute may waive the Commission proceedings. Here no such inequality would exist.

The rule set forth in Article 61(1) that "only the States Parties and the Commission shall have the right to submit a case to the Court," needs further explanation. First, Article 62(3) indicates that a case may only be taken to the Court by one state against another state if both have accepted the Court's jurisdiction. Second, Article 62(2) permits the States Parties to accept that jurisdiction "on the condition of reciprocity," and a number of states have done so. A state which has made such a declaration cannot be taken to the Court by a State Party which has not accepted the tribunal's jurisdiction. However, even if a state has accepted the Court's jurisdiction subject to reciprocity, it can be supposed that this reservation would not deprive the Commission of the right to take the matter to the Court if the case grew out of an individual petition rather than an inter-state complaint. This conclusion finds support in the Court's holding regarding the limited applicability of the principle of reciprocity to human rights treaties. Advisory Opinion OC–2, I.–A. Court H.R., *Series A: Judgments and Opinions,* No. 2 (1982). For an analysis of some of these jurisdictional issues, see Buergenthal, "Interim Measures in the Inter–American Court of Human Rights," *in* R. Bernhardt (ed.), *Interim Measures Indicated by International Courts* 69, 72 (1994). Finally, Article 61(1) leaves open the question whether it permits all States Parties to refer any case to the Court or only the cases in which the Applicant States were parties in the proceedings before the Commission. This issue remains to be resolved by the Court.

§ 4–12. The Court's Powers in Contentious Cases

Once a case has been referred to the Court, it has the power to fully review the Commission's findings of fact and law. *See generally* Gros–Espiell, "Contentious Proceedings Before the Inter–American Court of Human Rights," 1 Emory J. Int'l Disp. Res. 175 (1987); Buergenthal, "Judicial Fact–Finding: The Inter–American Human Rights Court," *in* R. Lillich (ed.), *Fact-Finding before International Tribunals* 261, 263–64 (1992). The Court has the power also to hear any challenges to its jurisdiction based on non-compliance by the Commission with the procedures set out in Articles 48 to 50 of the Convention and any other relevant provisions thereof. *See, e.g., Godinez Cruz Case* (Preliminary Objections), I.–A. Court H.R., Series C: Decisions and Judgments, No. 3 (1987). This means, for example, that the Commission's finding that the petitioner has exhausted all available domestic remedies, as required by Article 46 of the Convention, may also be reviewed. *Fairen Garbi Case* (Preliminary Objections), I.–A. Court H.R., Series C: Decisions and Judgments, No. 2, (1987); *Neira Alegria Case* (Preliminary Objections), I.–A. Court H.R., Series C: Decisions and Judgments, No. 13 (1991).

Article 67 of the Convention provides that the judgment rendered by the Court is "final and not subject to appeal." The same provision also authorizes the Court to interpret its judgments if there is a disagreement as to its "meaning or scope." *See Neira Alegria Case* (Requests for Revision and Interpretation of the Judgment of December 11, 1991 on the Preliminary Objections), I.–A. Court H.R., Series C: Decisions and Judgments, No. 14 (1992); *Velasquez Rodriguez Case* (Interpretation of the Compensatory Damages Judgment), I.–A. Court H.R., Series C: Decisions and Judgments, No. 9 (1990). Moreover, the "States Parties to the Convention undertake to comply with the judgment of the Court in any case to which they are parties." (Art. 68(1).) The types of judgments that the Court may render and the manner in which they are to be enforced are spelled out in two provisions of the Convention. The first is Article 63(1), which reads as follows:

If the Court finds that there has been a violation of a right or freedom protected by this Convention, the Court shall rule that the injured party be ensured the enjoyment of his right or freedom that was violated. It shall also rule, if appropriate, that the consequences of the measure or situation that constituted the breach of such right or freedom be remedied and that fair compensation be paid to the injured party.

The Court is, consequently, empowered to award money damages and render declaratory judgments. The latter may specify not only what rights have been violated, but also how the state should remedy the violation. *See, e.g.*, *Aloeboetoe Case* (Reparations), I.–A. Court H.R., Series C: Decisions and Judgments, No. 15 (1993); *Godinez Cruz Case* (Compensatory Damages), I.–A. Court H.R., Series C: Decisions and Judgments, No. 8 (1989); *Velasquez Rodriguez Case* (Compensatory Damages), I.–A. Court H.R., Series C: Decisions and Judgments, No. 7 (1988).

The second provision is Article 68(2), which deals with money damages. It provides that the "part of a judgment that stipulates compensatory damages may be executed in the country concerned in accordance with domestic procedures governing the execution of judgments against the state." The language of Article 68(2) suggests that the States Parties are not required to establish a mechanism for the domestic execution of the Court's money judgments; it merely permits them to do so. By contrast, Article 27 of the headquarters agreement between the Court and the Government of Costa Rica provides that the Court's judgments shall be enforced in Costa Rica as if they were domestic judgments. For the text, see I.–A. Court H.R., *Annual Report 1981*, OEA/Ser.L/III.5, Doc. 13, at 16 (1981). There has been no occasion to date to apply this provision. A Peruvian law (Law No. 23385 establishing the Peruvian Court of Constitutional Guarantees) provides that judgments of international institutions whose jurisdiction Peru has accepted shall be enforced by the Supreme Court of Peru in accordance with the procedures governing domestic judgments. Although Peru has accepted the Court's jurisdiction, it is unclear whether this provision is being applied.

The Convention does not establish any specific mechanism to supervise the enforcement of the Court's judgments. Article 65 of the Convention does, however, bear on the subject. It reads as follows:

> To each regular session of the General Assembly of the Organization of American States the Court shall submit, for the Assembly's consideration, a report on its work during the previous year. It shall specify, in particular, the cases in which a state has not complied with its judgments, making any pertinent recommendations.

This provision requires the Court to inform the OAS General Assembly of situations involving non-compliance with its decisions, thus permitting the Assembly to discuss the matter and to take whatever political measures it deems appropriate. Although the Assembly lacks the power to adopt resolutions that are legally binding on the Member States, condemnatory OAS resolutions do carry considerable political weight, which can translate into public opinion pressure. Here it should be noted, however, that the Government of Honduras had failed for a number of years to pay the full amount of compensation specified by the Court in its judgments in the *Velasquez Rodriguez* and *Godinez Cruz* cases, the so-called *Honduran Disappearance Cases*. That is, it paid only a part of the sums due to the next of kin of the victims. A review of the Court's annual reports to the OAS General Assembly for the years during which Honduras remained in default indicates that the Court did not bring the noncompliance formally to the Assembly's attention, which, as a consequence, did not adopt a resolution on the subject. The matter was finally resolved in February 1995 when the Honduran Government, headed by a former President of the Court, agreed to pay the amounts due in an official ceremony held at the seat of the OAS in Washington.

§ 4–13. Provisional Measures

The American Convention is the only major human rights treaty that expressly authorizes the issuance of temporary restraining orders. Article 63(2) of the Convention deals with these so-called provisional measures. It provides that:

> In case of extreme gravity and urgency, and when necessary to avoid irreparable damage to persons, the Court shall adopt such provisional measures as it deems pertinent in matters it has under consideration. With respect to a case not yet submitted to the Court, it may act at the request of the Commission.

This provision permits the Court to grant temporary restraining orders in cases pending before it and in cases that have been lodged with the Commission but not yet referred to the Court. For an analysis of the manner in which the Court has applied Article 63(2), see Pasqualucci, "Provisional Measures in the Inter–American Human Rights

System: An Innovative Development in International Law," 26 Vand. J. Transnat'l L. 803 (1993); Buergenthal, "Interim Measures in the Inter–American Court of Human Rights," *in* R. Bernhardt (ed.), *Interim Measures Indicated by International Courts* 69 (1994). In both types of cases brought to it under Article 63(2), the Court will have to determine, if only in a preliminary manner, whether it has jurisdiction over the parties. In cases that are already pending before it, this issue will as a practical matter arise only when the request for the order is made before the question of the Court's jurisdiction to hear the case has been settled. But the jurisdictional issue will always have to be examined in those cases that are still being considered by the Commission. *See* Buergenthal, *supra*, at 71.

In the first category of cases, the Court may act on its own motion or at the request of one of the parties. *See* the Court's Rules of Procedure, art. 24(1). The Court has already granted some requests for provisional measures in these types of cases. *See, e.g.,* Decisions of January 15 and January 19, 1988 in the *Honduran Disappearance Cases*, I.–A. Court H.R., *Annual Report 1988*, OEA/Ser.L/V/III.19, Doc. 13, at 25 and 27 (1988). Provisional measures may be granted in the second category of cases only at the request of the Commission. In the past, the Commission has on a number of occasions requested such orders, but the Court has not always entered them. For example, the Commission was successful, *inter alia*, in the *Bustios-Rojas Case (Peru)*, Decision of August 8, 1990, I.–A. Court H.R.,

Annual Report 1990, OEA/Ser.L/V/III.23, Doc. 12, at 31 (1991); Decision of January 17, 1991, I.–A. Court H.R., *Annual Report 1991*, OEA/Ser.L/V/III.25, Doc. 7, at 15 (1992). But the Court failed to grant the Commission's request in a number of other cases. *See, e.g., Peruvian Prisons Case*, Decision of January 27, 1993, I.–A. Court H.R., *Annual Report 1993*, OEA/Ser.L/V/III.29, Doc. 4, at 21 (1994).

§ 4–14. Advisory Jurisdiction

The scope of the Court's advisory jurisdiction is very broad. *See generally* Buergenthal, "The Advisory Practice of the Inter–American Human Rights Court," 79 Am. J. Int'l L. 1 (1985). This power is spelled out in Article 64 of the Convention, which provides:

1. The member states of the Organization may consult the Court regarding the interpretation of this Convention or of other treaties concerning the protection of human rights in the American states. Within their spheres of competence, the organs listed in Chapter X [now Chapter VIII] of the Charter of the Organization of American States, as amended by the Protocol of Buenos Aires, may in like manner consult the Court.

2. The Court, at the request of a member state of the Organization, may provide that state with opinions regarding the compatibility of any of its domestic laws with the aforesaid international instruments.

Thus, any OAS Member State, and not only the States Parties to the Convention, have standing to request an advisory opinion. The Court's advisory jurisdiction is not limited, moreover, to interpretations of the Convention; it extends to any other treaty "concerning the protection of human rights in the American states." All OAS organs, the General Assembly, the Permanent Council, etc., including the Inter–American Commission on Human Rights, have standing to request advisory opinions. Under Article 64(2) the Court is also empowered, at the request of any Member States of the OAS, to render advisory opinions determining whether the state's domestic laws are compatible with the Convention or the aforementioned human rights treaties. On the relationship between Articles 64(1) and 64(2), see Advisory Opinion OC–14/94, I.–A. Court H.R., Series A: Judgments and Opinions, No. 14 (1995).

Since its establishment in 1979, the Court has rendered a substantial number of advisory opinions. Article 64 has therefore been extensively interpreted. For example, the Court has held that to satisfy the requirement that an advisory opinion request fall "within their spheres of competence," OAS organs must demonstrate a "legitimate institutional interest" in the subject matter of the request. Advisory Opinion OC–2/82 of Sept. 24, 1982, I.–A. Court H.R., *Series A: Judgments and Opinions,* No. 2 (1982). The Court has also ruled that the phrase "other treaties concerning the protection of human rights in the American states" to which Article 64 refers, applies not only to OAS or inter-American treaties, but to any treaty bearing on the enjoyment or enforcement of human rights in a state belonging to the inter-American system. Advisory Opinion OC–1/82, I.–A. Court H.R., *Series A: Judgments and Opinions,* No. 1 (1982).

In interpreting Article 64(2), the Court has held that the reference to "domestic laws" may in certain circumstances be deemed to apply also to proposed or pending legislation and not only to laws already in force. Advisory Opinion OC–4/84, I.–A. Court H.R., *Series A: Judgments and Opinions,* No. 4 (1984). The mere fact that a request for an advisory opinion concerns a matter that is or once was the subject of a contentious proceeding before the Commission will not necessarily result in its rejection by the Court. *See* Advisory Opinion OC–3/83, I.–A. Court H.R., *Series A: Judgments and Opinions,* No. 3 (1983); Advisory Opinion OC–5/85, I.–A. Court H.R., *Series A: Judgments and Opinions,* No. 5 (1985); Advisory Opinion OC–14/94, I.–A. Court H.R., Series A: Judgments and Opinions, No. 14 (1995). But where it appears that a state may have asked for an advisory opinion in order to delay pending contentious proceedings before the Commission or otherwise to gain an unfair advantage over the private parties in such proceedings, the Court will decline to render the requested advisory opinion. Advisory Opinion OC–12/91, I.–A. Court H.R., Series A: Judgments and Opinions, No. 12 (1992). *See* Buergenthal, "The Advisory Practice of the Inter–American Court," *supra,* at 9–12.

§ 4–15. Legal Effect of Advisory Opinions

Advisory opinions are not, as such, legally binding. That conclusion is inherent in the concept of advisory opinions. They are after all, advisory in character. *See* Advisory Opinion OC–3/83, I.–A. Court H.R., Series A: Judgments and Opinions, No. 3 (1983). Moreover, the Convention nowhere states that these opinions are binding. Nevertheless, the Court is a "judicial institution whose purpose is the application and interpretation of the American Convention on Human Rights," Statute of the Court, art. 1, and it is an organ having "competence with respect to matters relating to the fulfillment of the commitments by the States Parties to this Convention." Convention, art. 33. The Court's pronouncements, whether made in a contentious case or advisory opinion, derive their value as legal authority from its character as a judicial institution empowered to interpret and apply that instrument. In short, advisory opinions are not academic exercises; they are judicial pronouncements. The mere fact therefore that the Court has made a pronouncement in an advisory opinion rather than in a contentious case does not diminish the legitimacy or authoritative character of the legal principle enunciated by it.

What then is the difference between an advisory opinion and a judgment in a contentious case? Since a judgment is binding on the parties to the dispute, Convention, art. 68, a state which does not comply with it in a case to which it was a party violates the specific obligation set out in Article 68.

It is also in breach of whatever other provisions of the Convention the Court determined to have been violated by the state. An advisory opinion, on the other hand, is not binding. Consequently, the mere failure of a state to comply with the opinion does not constitute a breach of the Convention. But if a state engages in activities determined by the Court in an advisory opinion to be incompatible with the Convention, the state is on notice that its conduct violates its treaty obligations. This fact will seriously undermine the legitimacy of any legal arguments in conflict with those pronounced in the Court's advisory opinion that the states might assert to justify its position. For the telling consequences of an advisory opinion, see Moyer & Padilla, "Executions in Guatemala as Decreed by the Courts of Special Jurisdiction in 1982–1983," *in* I.–A.C.H.R., *Human Rights in the Americas* 280. *See also* Buergenthal, "Self–Executing and Non–Self Executing Treaties in National and International Law," 235 Recueil des Cours 303, 390–91 (1992) (discussing a decision of the Argentine Supreme Court giving effect to an advisory opinion of the Inter–American Court of Human Rights).

§ 4–16. Emerging Caselaw

Although the Court has to date not rendered a very large number of judgments and opinions, they have already made important contributions to the evolution of the law of the Convention and to international human rights law in general. In one of its first opinions, for example, the Court declared that "modern human rights treaties, in general, and the American Conventions in particular, are not multilateral treaties of the traditional type concluded to accomplish the reciprocal exchange of rights for the mutual benefit of the contracting States." Advisory Opinion, OC–2/82, I.–A. Court H.R., Series A: Judgments and Opinions, No. 2, para. 29 (1982). Since the object and purpose of these treaties "is the protection of the basic rights of individual human beings, irrespective of their nationality, both against the State of their nationality and all other contracting States," *id.*, the concept of reciprocity, which plays an important role in the application of traditional treaties, loses much of its relevance in the application of human rights treaties. The Court consequently determined that a state which had ratified the Convention with a reservation did not have to wait upon the acceptance of the reservation by other contracting parties before it could be considered to be a party to the Convention. *Id.,* at para. 40.

Article 27 of the Convention permits the States Parties, "in time of war, public danger, or other emergency that threatens the independence or security of a State Party," to derogate from some of their treaty obligations. The second paragraph of Article 27 lists the rights which may not be suspended even during such emergencies. The European Convention on Human Rights and the Civil and Political Covenant have comparable derogation clauses. In its Advisory Opinion OC–3/83, I.–A. Court H.R., Series A; Judgments and Opinions, No.

3 (1983), the Court had to interpret the scope of a reservation to Article 4 of the Convention, which deals with the right to life and is one of the non-derogable rights listed in Article 27(2). Although it eventually found that the reservation did not authorize the measures the reserving state had taken, the Court took the position that its inquiry had to start with the question whether the reservation was compatible with the object and purpose of the treaty, which is the test applicable under Vienna Convention on the Law of Treaties. (Art. 19(c).)

Article 27 of the Convention allows the States Parties to suspend, in time of war, public danger, or other emergency that threatens their independence or security, the obligations they assumed by ratifying the Convention, provided that in doing so they do not suspend or derogate from certain basic or essential rights, among them the right to life guaranteed by Article 4. It would follow therefrom that a reservation which was designed to enable a State to suspend any of the non-derogable fundamental rights must be deemed to be incompatible with the object and purpose of the Convention and, consequently, not permitted by it. The situation would be different if the reservation sought merely to restrict certain aspects of a non-derogable right without depriving the right as a whole of its basic purpose. Since the reservation referred to by the Commission in its submission does not appear to be of a type that is designed to deny the right to life as such, the Court concludes that to that extent it can be considered, in principle, as not being incompatible with the object and purpose of the Convention. *Id.,* at para. 61.

Apart from its specific holding, the real importance of this opinion derives from the fact that it is the first unambiguous international judicial articulation of the principle that incompatibility and non-derogability are conceptually interrelated.

In another opinion, the Court was asked to interpret the scope of the last phrase of Article 27(2), which prohibits the suspension "of the judicial guarantees essential for the protection" of the rights that are non-derogable. Here the Court ruled that the writ of habeas corpus and related remedies may not be suspended in emergency situations, even though they are guaranteed in other provisions of the Convention which are not defined as non-derogable rights under Article 27(2). Advisory Opinion OC–8/87, I.–A. Court H.R., *Series A: Judgments and Opinions,* No. 8 (1987).

The Court has also rendered two important opinions dealing with the right to freedom of expression. In the first, it ruled that a Costa Rican law, which required journalists to belong to a professional association in order to be licensed to practice their profession, violated the right to freedom of expression guaranteed in Article 13 of the Convention. Advisory Opinion OC–5/85 I.–A. Court H.R., *Series A: Judgments and Opinions,* No. 5 (1985). The other advisory opinion dealt with the scope and nature of the right of reply, which is guaranteed in

Article 14 of the Convention. Here the Court explored the delicate balance between the right of reply and freedom of expression. Advisory Opinion OC–7/86, I.–A. Court H.R., *Series A: Judgments and Opinions,* No.7, at paras. 24–25 (1986). In these two opinions as well as in Advisory Opinion OC–6/86, I.–A. Court H.R., *Series A: Judgments and Opinions,* No. 6 (1986), the Court analyzed the interrelationship between representative democracy, the protection of human rights, and the inter-American system.

Of the contentious cases decided thus far, the most important ones no doubt are the so-called *Honduran Disappearance Cases,* which constitute the first ever international adjudication of charges implicating a state in a policy of forced disappearances. In the first two of these cases, the Court held Honduras responsible for the disappearances of two Honduran nationals after finding that in the early 1980's there existed in that country a policy of forced disappearances that was tolerated by and imputable to its Government. *Velasquez Rodriguez Cases* (Merits), I.–A. Court H.R., Series C: Decisions and Judgments, No. 4 (1988); *Godinez-Cruz Case* (Merits), I.–A. Court H.R., Series C: Judgments C: Decisions and Judgments, No. 5 (1989). In the third case, *Fairen Garbi and Solis Corrales Case* (Merits), I.–A. Court H.R., Series C: Decisions and Judgments, No. 6 (1989), the Court found that Honduras' responsibility for the disappearance of two Costa Rican national had not been proved. These cases explore the obligations assumed by the States Parties under Article 1(1) of the Convention as well as the difficult evidentiary issues that arise in disappearance cases. *See generally* Shelton, "Judicial Review of State Action by International Courts," 12 Fordham Int'l L.J. 361 (1989); Shelton, "Private Violence, Public Wrongs, and the Responsibility of States," 13 *id.* 1 (1989–90); Buergenthal, "Judicial Fact–Finding: Inter–American Court of Human Rights," *in* R. Lillich (ed.), *Fact-Finding Before International Tribunals* 361, 267 (1990); Grossman, "Disappearances in Honduras: The Need for Direct Victim Representation in Human Rights Litigation," 15 Hastings Int'l & Comp. L. Rev. 363 (1992); Kokott, "No Impunity for Human Rights Violations in the Americas," 14 Hum. Rts. L.J. 153 (1993).

With the increase in the number of contentious cases reaching it, the Court has had to struggle with issues relating to the measure of damages to which victims of human rights violations are entitled and the institutional arrangements that must be made to ensure that they receive the awards to which they are entitled. *See, e.g.*, *Velasquez Rodriguez Case* (Compensatory Damages), I.–A. Court H.R., Series C: Decisions and Judgments, No. 7 (1990); Aloeboetoe Case (Reparations), I.–A. Court H.R., Series C: Decisions and Judgments, No. 15 (1995).

In an advisory opinion rendered in December 1994, the Court ruled that government officials who enforce national laws that violate the Convention will themselves incur international responsibility if the execution of these laws also constitutes an international crime. Advisory Opinion OC–14, I.–A.

Court H.R., Series A; Judgments and Opinions, No. 14 (1995). Since the Court has neither international criminal jurisdiction nor jurisdiction to receive cases charging individuals or other non-state actors with violations of the Convention, it remains to be seen what significance the aforementioned advisory opinion will have. Of course, there is nothing in international law as such that would prevent the State Parties to the Convention from conferring such jurisdiction on the Court by appropriate protocols to that instrument.

CHAPTER 5

THE AFRICAN SYSTEM OF HUMAN AND PEOPLES' RIGHTS

I. INTRODUCTION

The African Charter on Human and Peoples' Rights entered into force on October 21, 1986. Nowak, "The African Charter of Human and Peoples' Rights," 7 Hum. Rts. L.J. 399 (1986). The Charter was adopted by the Organization of African Unity in 1981 and has to date been ratified by 49 states. For the drafting history of the Charter, see Mbaye, "Introduction to the African Charter on Human and Peoples' Rights," *in* International Commission of Jurists, *Human and Peoples' Rights in Africa and the African Charter* 19 (1985); Gittleman, "The African Charter on Human and Peoples' Rights: A Legal Analysis," 22 Va. J. Int'l L. 667 (1982); Ramcharan, "The Travaux Préparatoires of the African Commission on Human and Peoples' Rights," 13 Hum. Rts. L.J. 307 (1992).

The African Charter establishes a system for the protection and promotion of human rights that is designed to function within the institutional framework of the OAU. The OAU is a regional intergovernmental organization which came into being in

1963 and has a membership of 53 states. It operates through a permanent Secretariat, various Ministerial Conferences, a Council of Ministers and the Assembly of Heads of State and Government. The Assembly meets once a year and is the highest policy-making body of the OAU. *See generally* Bello, "Organization of African Unity," *in Encyclopedia of Public International Law, Instalment* 6, at 270 (R. Bernhardt, ed. 1983).

II. THE RIGHTS AND DUTIES

§ 5–1. Introduction

The African Charter differs from the European and American Conventions on Human Rights in a number of respects. *See generally* Okere, "The Protection of Human Rights in Africa and the African Charter on Human and Peoples' Rights: Comparative Analysis with the European and American Systems," 6 Hum. Rts. Q. 141 (1984). First, the African Charter proclaims not only rights but also duties. Second, it codifies individual as well as peoples' rights. Third, in addition to guaranteeing civil and political rights, it protects economic, social and cultural rights. Fourth, the treaty is drafted in a form that permits the States Parties to impose very extensive restrictions and limitations on the exercise of the rights it proclaims. *See* Weston, Lukes & Hnatt, "Regional Human Rights Regimes: A Comparison and Appraisal," 20 Vand. J. Transnat'l L. 585, 608–14 (1987); Flinterman & Ankumah, "The African Charter on Human and Peoples'

Rights," in H. Hannum (ed.), *Guide to International Human Rights Practice* 159 (2d ed. 1992).

The provisions of the Charter reflect the influence of UN human rights instruments and African traditions. Thus, it bears a stronger resemblance to the International Covenants of Human Rights than to the two other regional human rights treaties. *See* van Boven, "The Relations between Peoples' Rights and Human Rights in the African Charter," 7 Hum. Rts. L.J. 183, 186–90 (1986). The emphasis the Charter places on African tradition finds expression in its preamble as well as in the form in which many of its rights and duties are articulated. Mbaye, *supra,* at 26. The preamble speaks of "the virtues of [African] historical tradition and the values of African civilization which should inspire and characterize their reflection on the concept of human and peoples' rights." Other principles that inform of the African Charter are referred to in the following provision of the preamble:

Convinced that it is henceforth essential to pay particular attention to the right to development and that civil and political rights cannot be dissociated from economic, social and cultural rights in their conception as well as universality and that the satisfaction of economic, social and cultural rights is a guarantee for the enjoyment of civil and political rights.

The emphasis on the right to development, which is a peoples' right, and the linking together of different categories of individual rights has its conceptual source in the standard-setting practice of the UN.

§ 5–2. Individual Rights

The Charter contains a broad non-discrimination clause and an equal-protection clause. It guarantees the right to life and it prohibits slavery as well as torture, cruel, inhuman or degrading treatment and punishment. It bars arbitrary arrest and detention as well as *ex post facto* criminal legislation and punishment. The Charter contains provisions designed to ensure due process of law and fair hearings. It guarantees freedom of religion, the right to receive information, to express one's opinions, freedom of association and assembly. In addition to recognizing the right to freedom of movement, the Charter prohibits mass expulsions of non-nationals "aimed at national, racial, ethnic or religious groups." (Art. 12.)

The Charter guarantees the right to property, to work, to equal remuneration for equal work, to the enjoyment of "the best attainable state of physical and mental health" (Art. 16(1)), and the right to education. The provision, which proclaims the right to education and the right to take part in the cultural life of one's community, also declares that "the promotion and protection of morals and traditional values recognized by the community shall be the duty of the State." (Art. 17(3).) A similar concept finds expression in Article 18, which characterizes the family as "the natural unit and basis of society" and declares, *inter alia,* that "the State shall have the duty to assist the family which is the custodian of morals and traditional values recognized by the community." Besides providing that "the aged and the disabled shall ... have the right to special measures of protection in keeping with their physical and moral needs," Article 18 also contains the following provisions:

The State shall ensure the elimination of every discrimination against women and also ensure the protection of the rights of the woman and the child as stipulated in international declarations and conventions.

(Art. 18(3).) Very few, if any, human rights treaties resort to this extremely liberal form of incorporation by reference of other international instruments. On the utility of this approach as far as the rights of women are concerned, see Welch, "Human Rights and African Women: A Comparison of Protection Under Two Major Treaties," 15 Hum. Rts. Q. 548 (1993); Butegwa, "Using the African Charter on Human and Peoples' Rights to Secure Women's Access to Land in Africa," *in* R. Cook (ed.), *Human Rights of Women: National and International Perspectives* 495 (1994). *See also* Beyani, "Toward a More Effective Guarantee of Women's Rights in the African Human Rights System," *in* Cook, *supra*, at 285.

Although the aforementioned catalog of individual rights is very extensive, some of the rights are phrased in language that seems designed to deprive the guarantee of much meaning. *See* Flinterman &

Ankumah, *supra*, at 165–66. Article 8, for example,
which proclaims "freedom of conscience, the profession and free practice of religion," declares that "no
one may, *subject to law and order,* be submitted to
measures restricting the exercise of these freedoms." (Emphasis added.) And Article 10(1) provides that "every individual shall have the right to
free association *provided that he abides by the law.*"
(Emphasis added.) Similarly, Article 9(2) articu-
lates the right to freedom of expression by declaring
that "every individual shall have the right to express and disseminate his opinions *within the law.*"
(Emphasis added.) It should be noted, however,
that other rights, particularly those which concern
the physical integrity of the individual and due
process, do not authorize the restrictions that are
permitted with regard to the rights applicable to the
exercise of political freedoms. Noteworthy, too, is
the fact that the African Charter does not contain a
general derogation clause permitting the States
Parties to suspend the enjoyment of certain rights
during national emergencies. Whether the existence of this power may be implied or whether it is
incorporated by reference through the language of
Article 60 of the Charter, which refers to other
human rights instruments, remains to be seen. On
this subject, see Gittleman, *supra,* at 704. For an
analysis of Article 60, see § 5–7, *infra.* Some commentators suggest that the many "clawback" clauses found in the African Charter make a general
derogation clause unnecessary for states wishing to

impose restrictions during national emergencies. Flinterman & Ankumah, *supra*, at 166.

§ 5–3. Peoples' Rights

It has become fashionable in the human rights field to speak of "generations" of rights. Civil and political rights are characterized as "first generation" rights, whereas economic, social and cultural rights are classified as "second generation" rights. Most of the freedoms which the African Charter denominates as peoples' rights are sometimes described as "third generation" rights. *See generally* Marie, "Relations between Peoples' Rights and Human Rights: Semantic and Methodological Distinctions," 7 Hum. Rts. L.J. 195 (1986); Kiwanuka, "The Meaning of 'People' in the African Charter on Human and Peoples' Rights," 82 Am. J. Int'l L. 80 (1988); Swanson, "The Emergence of New Rights in the African Charter," 12 N.Y. L. Sch. J. Int'l & Comp. L. 307 (1991). Among these are the right of peoples to self-determination and to full sovereignty over their natural resources. Also on the list are the right to development, the right to peace, and "the right to a general satisfactory environment favourable to their development." (Art. 24.) The right to development, which has already been mentioned, is formulated as follows: "All peoples shall have the right to their economic, social and cultural development with due regard to their freedom and identity and in the equal enjoyment of the common heritage of mankind." (Art. 22(1).) This and similar language found in the African Charter reinforces the OAU's political agenda in the UN by giving it treaty status. A few of these rights do, of course, already enjoy that status. *See, e.g.,* Common Article 1 of the International Covenants on Human Rights. *See generally* van Boven, *supra,* at 189–90; Kiss, "The Peoples' Right to Self–Determination," 7 Hum. Rts. L.J. 165 (1986). On the right to development in the Charter, *see* Bello, "Article 22 of the African Charter on Human and People's Rights," *in* E. Bello & B. Ajibola (eds.), *Essays in Honor of Judge Taslim Olawale Elias,* vol. I, at 447 (1991).

§ 5–4. Duties

A distinguished African jurist and former vice president of the International Court of Justice, who played an important role in drafting the African Charter, points out that "in Africa, laws and duties are regarded as being two facets of the same reality: two inseparable realities." Mbaye, *supra,* at 27. *See also* Umozurike, "Autochthony in the African Charter on Human and People's Rights," *in* E. Bello & B. Ajibola (eds.), *Essays in Honour of Judge Taslim Olawale Elias,* vol. I, at 475 (1992). Mbaye suggests that it should therefore come as no surprise to anyone that the African Charter proclaims duties as well as rights. Here it is worth recalling that the American Declaration on the Rights and Duties of Man adopted the same approach, but that the drafters of the American Convention did not follow the same course.

The duties that the African Charter proclaims fall into two broad categories. In the first group are duties which can be characterized as correlatives of rights. The other category might be described as restrictions on the enjoyment of rights disguised as duties. Article 27(2), for example, which declares that "the rights and freedoms of each individual shall be exercised with due regard to the rights of others, collective security, morality and common interest," appears to codify both categories of duties. Here it is evident that the scope of these duties or their impact on the rights guaranteed in the Charter would differ significantly depending upon whether an individual's rights were to be limited by the rights of others or by considerations of collective security; the latter type of duties appear to be dangerously vague. The contrast between these different types of duties is even more striking in Article 29, which imposes on the individual the duty "to respect his parents at all times, to maintain them in case of need" and "to preserve and strengthen social and national solidarity, particularly when the latter is threatened." (Arts. 29(1) and 29(4).) The first two duties differ very considerably from the third, which is an invitation to the imposition of unlimited restrictions on the enjoyment of rights.

Other types of duties reflect the African values which the Charter seeks to advance. Article 29(7) imposes the duty "to preserve and strengthen positive African cultural values in relation with other members of the society, in the spirit of tolerance, dialogue and consultation and, in general, to contribute to the promotion of the moral well-being of society." Whether the inclusion of these duties and those set out in chapter II of the Charter will adversely affect the enjoyment of the rights the treaty guarantees remains to be seen. It cannot be doubted, however, that the catalog of duties which the Charter proclaims carries with it a serious risk of governmental abuse. Umozurike, "The African Charter on Human and Peoples' Rights," 77 Am. J. Int'l L. 902, 911 (1983). The seriousness of this risk will depend, in part at least, on the pace and success of the process of democratization in Africa. On this subject, see Aidoo, "Africa: Democracy Without Human Rights? " 15 Hum. Rts. Q. 703 (1993); Mutua, "Human Rights and Politics in Africa," 1 E. Afr. J. Peace & Hum. Rts. 250 (1993).

III. STATE OBLIGATIONS AND MEASURES OF IMPLEMENTATION

§ 5–5. Introduction

The obligations assumed by the States Parties to the Charter and the measures of implementation or international supervision it establishes are modelled more on the International Covenants on Human Rights than on the American or European Convention. *See generally* Umozurike, "The African Charter ..." *supra*, at 909. Among the striking differences between the African Charter and the other regional systems is the absence of a court and the greater emphasis the African system places on negotiation and conciliation.

According to African conception of the law, disputes are not settled by contentious procedures, but through reconciliation. Reconciliation generally takes place through discussions which end in a consensus leaving neither winners nor losers. Trials are always carefully avoided. They create animosity. People go to court to dispute rather than to resolve a legal difficulty.

Mbaye, *supra,* at 27. Moreover, as we shall see in § 5–8 and § 5–9, *infra,* unlike the international mechanisms of protection of the two other regional systems, the African system is designed to deal with massive denials of human rights and not with individual violations.

§ 5–6. State Obligations

The basic obligation of the States Parties to the African Charter is spelled out in Article 1. It provides that they "shall recognize the rights, duties and freedoms enshrined in this Charter and shall undertake to adopt legislative or other measures to give effect to them." This obligation is complemented by Article 62, which requires the States Parties to report biennially "on the legislative or other measures" they have adopted to give effect to the rights the Charter guarantees. Although the African Commission on Human and Peoples' Rights, *see* § 5–7, *infra,* has begun to review these reports, the process is apparently not as yet working very well. *See* "African Commission on Human and People's Rights," 47 I.C.J. Rev. 51, 53 (1991).

The Charter establishes two other important obligations. One is contained in Article 25, which imposes a "duty" on the States Parties "to promote and ensure through teaching, education and publication, the respect of the rights" the Charter guarantees and "to see to it that these ... rights as well as corresponding obligations and duties are understood." This provision, if acted upon with imagination by the Commission and by non-governmental human rights organizations, could prove helpful in developing a useful program of human rights education in Africa. The other obligation is spelled out in Article 26. In addition to declaring that the States Parties have a duty "to guarantee the independence of courts," it provides that they "shall allow the establishment and improvement of appropriate national institutions entrusted with the promotion and protection" of the rights set forth in the Charter. Although it is not clear whether the phrase "national institutions" refers to governmental as well as non-governmental institutions, both types of bodies could play an important promotional role in legitimating the human rights debate in individual African countries.

§ 5–7. The African Commission on Human and Peoples' Rights

The Charter provides for a Commission, established within the institutional framework of the OAU, "to promote human and peoples' rights and ensure their protection in Africa." (Art. 30.) *See generally* Flinterman & Ankumah, *supra,* at 160.

See also Amoah, "The African Charter on Human and Peoples' Rights—An Effective Weapon for Human Rights?" 4 Afr. J. Int'l & Comp. L. 226 (1992). The Commission is composed of 11 members, elected by the OAU's Assembly of Heads of States and Governments from a list of names presented by the States Parties. Since all OAU Member States are represented in the Assembly, states not parties to the Charter also have a vote in selecting the Commission, although only States Parties may nominate the candidates. The members of the Commission are elected to six-year terms and serve in their individual capacities rather than as government representatives.

The Commission has promotional and quasi-judicial functions. Its promotional mandate is very broad and includes the power to undertake studies, convene conferences, initiate publication programs, disseminate information and collaborate with national and local institutions concerned with human and peoples' rights. As part of this promotional effort, the Commission may "give its views or make recommendation to governments." (Art. 45(1)(a).) This power should enable the Commission to bring to the attention of individual governments "problem areas" revealed by its studies. Here it should be recalled that the system of "country studies" utilized by the Inter–American Commission on Human Rights evolved out of a grant of promotional powers that was weaker than that conferred by the African Charter. *See* Buergenthal, "The Inter–American System for the Protection of Human

Rights," *in* T. Meron (ed.), *Human Rights in International Law: Legal and Policy Issues* 439, 472–73 (1984).

The quasi-judicial powers of the African Commission may be divided into two parts: so-called interpretative powers and powers applicable to the resolution of disputes involving allegations of human rights violations. The Commission's interpretative powers are quite extensive and resemble the advisory jurisdiction of some international courts. The Commission has jurisdiction to "interpret all the provisions of the present Charter at the request of a State Party, an institution of the OAU or an African Organization recognized by the OAU." (Art. 45(3).) The Commission is also empowered, in the context of its promotional activities, "to formulate and lay down, principles and rules aimed at solving legal problems relating to human and peoples' rights and fundamental freedoms upon which African Governments may base their legislations." (Art. 45(1)(b).) This grant of power combines quasi-legislative and quasi-judicial aspects, for it seems to permit the Commission to prepare draft legislation, to propose legal solutions to disputes and to articulate, by means of codification and interpretation, human rights standards. The Commission's other quasi-judicial powers—those dealing with complaints charging violations of human rights—will be discussed in § 5–8, *infra*.

The powers that Article 45 confers on the Commission gain special importance because of the unusual lawmaking mandate embodied in Articles 60 and 61 of the Charter. Article 60 declares that "the Commission shall draw inspiration from international law on human and peoples' rights...." It then lists, by way of illustration, the normative sources of that law, making specific mention of the UN and OAU Charters, the Universal Declaration of Human Rights, African instruments on human and peoples' rights and "other instruments adopted by the United Nations and by African countries in the field of human and peoples' rights as well as from the provisions of various instruments adopted within the Specialized Agencies of the United Nations of which the parties to the present Charter are members." This provision is amplified by Article 61, which permits the Commission "to take into consideration, as subsidiary measures to determine the principles of law," various other human rights agreements to which the Member States of the OAU are parties, together with "African practices consistent with international norms on human and peoples' rights, customs generally accepted as law, general principles of law recognized by African States as well as legal precedents and doctrine." Consequently, in interpreting and applying the African Charter, the Commission has a broad mandate to draw on a vast body of law which Articles 60 and 61 incorporate by reference into the African Charter. These provisions grant the Commission an invaluable tool capable of ensuring that the interpretation of the Charter will keep up with the growth of general international law of human and peoples' rights.

§ 5–8. Interstate Complaints

The African Charter establishes an inter-state complaint mechanism that provides for two distinct methods of dispute resolution. The first permits a State Party, which believes that another state has violated the Charter, to bring the matter to that state's attention in a formal communication which is copied to the Commission. The respondent state has three months within which to present its reply. Either state may submit the matter to the Commission within three months from the date on which the original communication is received by the respondent state, provided that "the issue is not settled to the satisfaction of the two States involved through bilateral negotiations or by any other peaceful procedure." (Art. 48.) The Commission plays no active role in these proceedings and, if the states decide not to take their dispute to it, the negotiations could go on for years without producing any solution. The other option open to a state is set out in Article 47 of the Charter. It permits a State Party to file an interstate complaint directly with the Commission without going through the procedure outlined above.

Once an interstate complaint has been formally referred to the Commission, either under Article 47 or 48, it is treated in an identical fashion and the procedures applicable to it are the same. Here the complaint is subject to the requirement that "all local remedies, if they exist, have been exhausted, unless it is obvious to the Commission that the procedure of achieving these remedies would be unduly prolonged." (Art. 50.) Once the admissibility requirement has been met, the Commission embarks on a fact-finding process, designed to obtain all relevant information bearing on the case. The Commission is not limited to the information provided by the parties and is free to draw on "other sources." (Art. 52.) It may also hold hearings at which the states concerned have the right to present written and oral submissions. If an amicable solution "based on the respect of human and peoples' rights" has not been reached, the Commission must prepare a report, "stating the facts and its findings." (Art. 52.) This report is transmitted to the states concerned and the OAU's Assembly of Heads of State and Government. In it the Commission may also address to the Assembly whatever recommendations it "deems useful." (Art. 53.) The Charter contains no provisions requiring any further action by the Assembly on the Commission's report, although presumably any state represented in the Assembly is free to raise the matter at its annual meetings. It remains to be seen how effective this procedure will be; although for the time being there is little basis for optimism. *See* "Submission of the 4th Activities Report of the African Commission on Human and People's Rights," 12 Hum. Rts. L.J. 277 (1991).

§ 5–9. Individual Complaints

The individual complaint mechanism of the Charter bears a striking resemblance to the procedure established by the UN under ECOSOC Resolution

1503. *See* § 2–22, *supra*. It differs very significantly from the individual petition system of the European and American Conventions.

Article 55 of the African Charter requires the Secretariat of the Commission to compile "a list of communications other than those of [from] States parties to the present Charter and transmit them to the members of the Commission." The language of Article 55 suggests that the communications may originate with private individuals, non-governmental organizations, and various other entities. Although the text is sufficiently general to admit the possibility that it applies also to communications from OAU Member States not parties to the Convention, it is doubtful that this was the intention. *See* Rule 114 of the Rules of Procedure of the African Commission on Human and Peoples Rights, adopted February 13, 1988 (which does not provide for such communications). A simple majority of the Commission's membership is sufficient to take up a communication appearing on the Secretariat list. The communication is, however, subject to various admissibility requirements spelled out in Article 56 of the Charter. Included among them is the obligation to exhaust domestic remedies and the requirement that the claim must not be "based exclusively on news disseminated through the mass media." (Art. 56(4).)

It is important to recognize that the individual petition system of the African Charter is not designed to deal with individual cases of violations of human or peoples' rights. It permits the Commission to act only in relation to "special cases which reveal the existence of a series of serious or massive violations of human and peoples' rights." (Art. 58(1).) In short, if a private communication does not reveal either a series of serious violations or massive violations, it does not state a cause of action under the Charter. Massive violations presumably are those that are large-scale in nature. The concept of a series of serious violations was probably introduced to ensure that the Commission does not deal with isolated violations of the Charter. Conversely, even if a State Party is not engaging in massive violations of human or peoples' rights, a showing that it regularly commits or tolerates serious individual violations, whether related or not, should bring the matter within the jurisdiction of the Commission.

Once the Commission has determined that a complaint is admissible and that it meets the requirements established in Article 58(1), it must be referred by the Commission to the Assembly of Heads of State and Government. Thereafter, it is for the Assembly to decide whether to "request the Commission to undertake an in-depth study ... and make a factual report, accompanied by its findings and recommendations." (Art. 58(2).) Thus even if a complaint reveals, in the opinion of the Commission, "the existence of a series of serious or massive violations," the Commission will be able to investigate the matter only if the Assembly makes the request provided for in Article 58(2). A special exception applies to emergency situations. Here the Charter provides that "a case of emergency duly noticed by the Commission shall be submitted by the latter to the Chairman of the Assembly of Heads of State and Government who may request an in-depth study." (Art. 58(3).) Thus far the Commission apparently has not received the requisite authorization under Article 58(2).

The in-depth study and report that the Commission prepares when authorized to do so by the Assembly remains confidential until such time as the latter decides that it shall be published. Moreover, even the general or annual report of the Commission on its overall activities may only be published "after it has been considered by the Assembly of Heads of State and Government." (Art. 59(3).) This language leaves open the question whether or not the Assembly may prevent the publication of the annual report altogether or merely order changes to be made before publication. It is quite obvious, however, that the Commission's only real sanction—publicity—is severely limited by the powers the African Charter vests in the Assembly, which is a political body that is not likely to be an enthusiastic guardian of human rights as currently constituted.

CHAPTER 6

HUMANITARIAN LAW

I. INTRODUCTION

Although scholars disagree about whether humanitarian law is a distinct branch of international law or an integral part of the international law of human rights, an overview of the latter subject would today be incomplete if it failed to deal with humanitarian law. *See generally* T. Meron, *Human Rights and Humanitarian Norms as Customary Law* (1989); Hampson, "Human Rights Law and International Humanitarian Law: Two Coins or Two Sides of the same Coin? " *Bull. Hum. Rts.* 9½, at 46 (U.N. 1992). This chapter therefore describes the principal elements of modern humanitarian law, focusing on the protection of the individual. On the subject generally, *see* F. Kalshoven, *Constraints on the Waging of War* (1987); Dinstein, "International Humanitarian Law," *in* I. Cotler & F.P. Eliadis (eds.), *International Human Rights Law: Theory and Practice* 203 (1992). For a brief historical introduction, *see* § 1–7, *supra*. *See also*, Boisson de Chazournes, "The Collective Responsibility of States to Ensure Respect for Humanitarian Principles," *in* A. Bloed *et al.* (eds.), *Monitoring Human Rights in Europe* 247 (1993).

Humanitarian law can be defined as "the human rights component of the law of war." *See* § 1–7, *supra*. Thus perceived, it is that branch of human rights law which applies in international armed conflicts and, in certain limited circumstances, in internal armed conflicts. *See* A. H. Robertson & J.G. Merrills, *Human Rights in the World* 277 (3rd ed. 1989). The principal sources of that law, although by no means the only ones, are the four Geneva Conventions of 1949 and the two 1977 Protocols Additional to these treaties. Humanitarian law also consists of some earlier instruments on the subject as well as various rules of customary international law. *See* Dinstein, "Human Rights in Armed Conflict: International Humanitarian Law," *in* T. Meron (ed.), *Human Rights in International Law: Legal and Policy Issues 345* (1984); T. Meron, *Human Rights in Internal Strife: Their International Protection* (1987); L.C. Green, *The Contemporary Law of Armed Conflict* (1993).

II. THE GENEVA CONVENTIONS AND PROTOCOLS

§ 6–1. Introduction

The four Geneva Conventions were concluded in 1949 and entered into force in 1950. They consist of the Geneva Convention for the Amelioration of the Condition of the Wounded and Sick Members of Armed Forces in the Field; the Geneva Convention for the Amelioration of the Condition of Wounded, Sick and Shipwrecked Members of Armed Forces at

Sea; the Geneva Convention relative to the Treatment of Prisoners of War; and the Geneva Convention relative to the Protection of Civilian Persons in Time of War. Most Member States of the United Nations, including the United States, adhere to these treaties. No international human rights instrument has as many States Parties as the Geneva Conventions. Today important parts of the Geneva Conventions are considered to have acquired the status of customary international laws, thus making them obligatory also for states that are not parties to these instruments. Meron, "The Geneva Conventions as Customary Law," 81 Am. J. Int'l L. 348 (1987).

The two Protocols Additional to the Geneva Conventions were opened for signature in 1977. Protocol I deals with the protection of victims of international armed conflicts; Protocol II applies to non-international armed conflicts. To date, the vast majority of the States Parties to the Conventions has ratified both Protocols. The U.S. has not yet ratified either Protocol. In 1987, President Reagan asked the Senate for its consent to the ratification of Protocol II and indicated that the U.S. would not ratify Protocol I. *See* Gasser, "An Appeal for Ratification by the U.S.," 81 Am. J. Int'l L. 912 (1987). At present, the U.S. Government is reexamining its position with regard to Protocol I. Meron, "The Time Has Come for the United States to Ratify Geneva Protocol I," 88 Am. J. Int'l L. 678 (1994). *See also* Aldrich, "Prospects for United States Ratification of Additional Protocol I to the 1949 Geneva Conventions," 85 Am. J. Int'l L. 1 (1991).

For the texts of the Geneva Conventions and the Protocols thereto as well as other relevant information, see International Committee of the Red Cross & League of Red Cross Societies, *International Red Cross Handbook,* which is periodically updated. *See also* A. Roberts & R. Guelff (eds.), *Documents on the Law of War* (2d. ed. 1989). Relevant provisions of the Geneva Conventions are often included either verbatim or incorporated by reference in the military manuals or instructions issued to the armed forces of the States Parties. *See, e.g.*, Department of the Army, *Field Manual FM27–10: The Law of Land Warfare* (1956).

§ 6–2. The Geneva Conventions and International Armed Conflicts

The principal purpose of the 1949 Geneva Conventions was to establish humanitarian rules applicable to international armed conflicts. Thus, common Article 2 of these treaties declares that "the present Convention shall apply to all cases of declared war or any other armed conflict which may arise between two or more of the High Contracting Parties, even if the state of war is not recognized by one of them." For an analysis of the articles that are common to all four Geneva Conventions, *see* H. Coursier, *Course of Five Lessons on the Geneva Conventions* 24–37 (1963).

The individuals who are protected by the Geneva Conventions can be identified, in general terms, by reference to the subjects of the treaties: sick and wounded members of the armed forces, prisoners of war, and civilian populations. In each of the treaties, the States Parties assume a large number of obligations for the benefit of the "protected persons." Thus, the Geneva Convention on Prisoners of War requires, for example, that prisoners of war be treated "humanely" (Art. 13) and that they not be subjected "to physical or mental torture to secure from them information of any kind." (Art. 17.) It prohibits "measures of reprisal against prisoners of war" (Art. 13) and provides that "all prisoners of war be treated alike by the Detaining Power, without any adverse distinction based on race, nationality, religious belief or political opinions, or any other distinction founded on similar criteria." (Art. 16.)

The Fourth Geneva Convention, which seeks to protect civilian populations, establishes a massive code of conduct for the Occupying Power. It prohibits "not only murder, torture, corporal punishment, mutilation ... of a protected person, but also ... any other measures of brutality whether applied by civilian or military agents." (Art 32.) It outlaws the taking of hostages (Art. 34), collective punishment and reprisals (Art. 33) as well as "individual or mass forcible transfers" of protected persons or their deportations to the territory of the Occupying Power. (Art. 49.) This Convention also establishes due process requirements applicable to criminal trials and sentencing of protected persons. (Arts. 66–75.) *See generally* J. Pictet, *Humanitari-*

an Law and the Protection of War Victims 122 (1975).

To ensure that the States Parties comply with their obligations, the Geneva Conventions provide for a system of supervision that is administered by so-called Protecting Powers. *See* L.C. Green, *The Contemporary Law of Armed Conflict* 234 (1993). Each State Party to the Convention has the right to designate a neutral country to serve as its Protecting Power. The functions of the Protecting Powers are "to safeguard the interests of the Parties to the conflict." (Art. 8 of Geneva Convention I, II and III, and Art. 9 of Geneva Convention IV.) The role of the Protecting Power may also be performed by the International Committee of the Red Cross or another comparable and impartial humanitarian organization. (Art. 10 Geneva Conventions I, II and III and Art. 11 of Geneva Convention IV.) The ICRC, which plays a very important role in the development and enforcement of humanitarian law, is described in § 6–7, *infra*.

The Protecting Powers are empowered to perform a variety of functions under each of the four Conventions. For example, under the Geneva Convention on Prisoners of War, the Protecting Powers are entitled to visit all prisoner of war camps and to interview the prisoners. "Visits may not be prohibited except for reasons of imperative military necessity, and then only as an exceptional and temporary measure." (Art. 126.) Similar provisions are found in the Geneva Convention on the Protection of Civilian Populations, which empowers representatives of the Protecting Powers "to go to all places where protected persons are, particularly to places of internment, detention and work." (Art. 143.)

The Conventions also provide for a conciliation procedure designed to deal with conflicts between the States Parties regarding the interpretation or application of any provisions thereof. The conciliation process may be initiated by the Protecting Powers or by one of the parties to the conflict. Here the role of the Protecting Powers is to act as intermediaries and to "lend their good offices with a view to settling the disagreement." (Geneva Conventions I, II and III, Art. 11; Geneva Convention IV, Art. 12.) The Conventions do not, however, establish a mandatory system for the arbitration or adjudication of disputes.

Experience indicates that it is by no means easy to get the parties to an international armed conflict to agree on the designation of Protecting Powers. This has prompted states to resort to the ICRC to perform most of the functions that the Geneva Conventions assign to Protecting Powers. Under certain circumstances, moreover, the designation of the ICRC or a comparable organization is required by the Conventions (Geneva Convention I, Art. 10(3).) Another major obstacle to the implementation of the Geneva Conventions has been the frequent refusal by one or more States Parties to an armed conflict to recognize the international character of the hostilities. By adopting this position, a state can for all practical purposes totally frustrate the application of the protective system the Conventions establish for international armed conflicts. *See generally* Kalshoven, *supra,* at 61–70; Dinstein, "Human Rights in Armed Conflict," *supra,* at 356.

§ 6–3. The Geneva Conventions and Internal Armed Conflicts: Common Article 3

The post-World War II era is replete with examples of internal armed insurgencies. Some reached massive proportions and involved organized military units and large numbers of combatants on all sides. Whenever such conflicts are not "international" in character, the protective system of the Geneva Conventions, described in § 6–2, *supra,* is inapplicable and only common Article 3 of the Conventions may be relevant. *See Case Concerning Military and Paramilitary Activities in and against Nicaragua (Nicaragua v. United States),* Merits, [1986] I.C.J. Rep. 14, at 114–15. Common Article 3 applies "in the case of armed conflicts not of an international character." *See* Pictet, *supra,* at 53; Goldman, "International Humanitarian Law: Americas Watch's Experience in Monitoring Armed Conflicts," 9 Am. U. J. Int'l L. & Pol'y 49, at 56–62 (1993). This provision requires the parties to the conflict—the government and the insurgents—to treat "humanely" all "persons taking no active part in the hostilities, including members of armed forces who have laid down their arms and those placed *hors de combat* by sickness, wounds, detention, or any other cause...." Adverse distinctions in treatment based "on race, colour, religion or faith, sex, birth or wealth, or any other similar criteria" are prohibited. Article 3 also prohibits the following acts:

(a) violence to life and person, in particular murder of all kinds, mutilation, cruel treatment and torture;

(b) taking of hostages;

(c) outrages upon personal dignity, in particular, humiliating and degrading treatment;

(d) the passing of sentences and the carrying out of executions without previous judgment pronounced by a regularly constituted court, affording all judicial guarantees which are recognized as indispensable by civilized peoples.

Article 3 permits the International Committee of the Red Cross to offer its humanitarian services to the parties to the conflict. The ICRC has used this innocuous stipulation with great imagination to provide extensive humanitarian assistance to victims of civil wars and similar hostilities. This work is described in the Annual Reports of the ICRC. *See, e.g.*, ICRC, 1992 *Annual Report* 121–22 (1993), concerning the role of the ICRC in El Salvador.

Although the guarantees spelled out in Article 3 are not very extensive, they do offer some protection in circumstances where any humane treatment, however elementary, is invaluable. Unfortunately, it has not always proved easy to get the governments involved in an internal armed conflict to agree that the provisions of Article 3 are applicable to it. *See* Veuthey, "Implementation and Enforcement of Humanitarian Law and Human Rights

Law in Non–International Armed Conflicts: The Role of the International Committee of the Red Cross," 33 Am. U. L. Rev. 83 (1983). The problem here is both legal and political. There is general agreement that an "armed conflict not of an international character" within the meaning of Article 3 must consist of more than merely a few riots, disturbances or minor armed clashes. On the other hand, a full blown civil war is clearly covered by Article 3. It is more difficult to say at what point a civil disturbance reaches the intensity that is required to transform it into an Article 3 conflict. Moreover, most governments faced with serious internal armed disturbances are reluctant to characterize them as Article 3 conflicts lest they thereby enhance the military, political or legal status of the insurgents whom they would prefer to describe as mere outlaws or bandits. Even though Article 3 provides that its "application ... shall not affect the legal status of the Parties to the conflict," this fact has not significantly increased the willingness of governments to recognize the application of the provision. *See generally* Meron, *Human Rights in Internal Strife, supra,* at 71; Kooijmans, "In the Shadowland Between Civil War and Civil Strife: Some Reflections on the Standard–Setting Process," *in* A.J.M. Delissen & G.J. Tanja (eds.), *Humanitarian Law of Armed Conflict: Challenges Ahead* 225, 227–29 (1991).

§ 6–4. Protocol I

The title of this instrument is "Protocol Additional to the Geneva Conventions of 12 August 1949,

relating to the Protection of Victims of International-
al Armed Conflicts (Protocol I)." The name is
somewhat misleading for the Protocol does not apply only to the international armed conflicts covered
by common Article 2 of the Geneva Conventions,
which are defined as conflicts between two or more
States Parties to the treaty. Instead, Article 1(4) of
the Protocol makes that instrument applicable also
to

> armed conflicts in which peoples are fighting
> against colonial domination and alien occupation
> and against racist regimes in the exercise of their
> right of self-determination, as enshrined in the
> Charter of the United Nations and the Declara-
> tion on Principles of International Law concern-
> ing Friendly Relations and Co-operation among
> States in accordance with the Charter of the
> United Nations.

Moreover, Article 3(a) of the Protocol extends the
coverage of the four Geneva Conventions to the
armed conflicts to which Protocol I applies. For a
State Party to the Conventions which ratifies Protocol I, the meaning of an international armed conflict as defined in the Conventions has thus been
expanded to embrace the wars of national liberation
described in Article 1(4). This broadening of the
scope of the concept of an international armed
conflict has led some countries, notably the U.S., to
oppose the treaty. *See* Agora, "The U.S. Decision
not to Ratify Protocol I to the Geneva Conventions
on the Protection of War Victims," 81 Am. J. Int'l
L. 910 (1987). At the same time, however, the U.S.

considers many of the principles enunciated in Protocol I to be part of customary international law and as such binding on it. *See* Matheson, "The United States Position on the Relation of Customary International Law to the 1977 Protocols Additional to the 1949 Geneva Conventions," 2 Am. U. J. Int'l & Pol'y 419 (1987). With the end of the Cold War and the changed international situation, many of the objections to Protocol I have lost their validity. *See* Aldrich, "Prospects for United States Ratification of Additional Protocol I to the 1949 Geneva Conventions," 85 Am. J. Int'l L. 1 (1991); Meron, "The Time has Come for the United States to Ratify Geneva Protocol I," 88 Am. J. Int'l L. 678 (1994).

The Protocol covers a wide range of subjects. *See generally* M. Bothe, K. Partsch & W. Solf, *New Rules for Victims of Armed Conflicts: Commentary on the Two 1977 Protocols Additional to the Geneva Conventions of 1949* (1982); Y. Sandoz, C. Swinarski & B. Zimmermann (eds.), *Commentary on the Additional Protocols of 8 June 1977 to the Geneva Conventions of 12 August 1949* (ICRC, 1987). It amplifies and expands the obligations established in the four Geneva Conventions and related humanitarian law instruments and, in general, seeks to make warfare less brutal and inhuman. In dealing with methods and means of warfare, for example, Article 35 declares that "the right of the Parties to the conflict to choose methods or means of warfare is not unlimited." It prohibits methods of warfare that "cause superfluous injury or unnecessary suffering" as well as "widespread, long-term and severe damage to the environment." Article 54 of the Protocol outlaws "starvation of civilians as a method of warfare" and bars military attacks on or destruction of "objects indispensable to the survival of the civilian population."

Of special interest to any study of the manner in which international human rights law evolves is Section III, Part IV of the Protocol. Entitled "Treatment of Person in the Power of a Party to the Conflict," Section III declares that the obligations it establishes to be "additional to the rules concerning humanitarian protection of civilians ... contained in the Fourth Convention ... as well as to other applicable rules of international law relating to the protection of fundamental human rights during international armed conflict." (Art. 72.) This provision applies, *inter alia,* to captured guerilla fighters and mercenaries, who do not benefit from more favorable treatment under other provisions of the Geneva Conventions or Protocols. *See generally* Bothe, Partsch & Solf, *supra*, at 440 (1982). The express acknowledgement of the interrelationship between human rights norms and humanitarian law demonstrates the ever greater confluence of these once distinct areas of the law. *See* § 6–6 *infra*. *See also* Sepulveda, "Interrelationship in the Implementation and Enforcement of International Humanitarian Law and Human Rights Law," 33 Am. U. L. Rev. 117 (1983); Symposium on "Human Rights and Humanitarian Law," *in Bull. Hum. Rts.*, 91/1 (U.N. 1992) (containing short essays by a number of experts on this subject).

Article 75 contains the most noteworthy innovations made in Section III of the Protocol. It spells out the fundamental rights to which "persons in the power of a Party to the conflict" are entitled, reaffirming and amplifying the guarantees contained in common Article 3 of the Geneva Conventions. Article 75 provides for humane treatment and contains a pervasive non-discrimination clause. In addition to outlawing "at any time and in any place whatsoever, whether committed by civilian or by military agents," all forms of violence directed against the life or physical or mental well-being of persons, including murder, torture, and corporal punishment, Article 75 establishes extensive due process guarantees for the benefit of persons "arrested, detained or interned for actions related to the armed conflict." These guarantees are very similar in scope and wording to those set forth in major human rights conventions. Section III also contains special guarantees for refugees and stateless persons as well as for women, children and journalists.

Protocol I contemplates the establishment of a 15–member International Fact–Finding Commission. (Art. 90.) The Commission's functions are to investigate "grave breaches" of the Conventions and the Protocol and to "facilitate, through its good offices, the restoration of an attitude of respect for the Conventions and this Protocol." (Art. 90(2)(c).) The Commission's power to undertake these investigations is conditioned on the recognition of its jurisdiction by the respective parties to conflict (Art. 90(2)(a).) The first elections of the members of the Commission were held in 1991 shortly after the requisite twenty States Parties to the Protocol had accepted its jurisdiction. The Commission held its first meeting in 1992, but has to date not been called upon to undertake any investigations. The members of the Commission are elected to five-year terms and serve in their personal capacities.

§ 6–5. Protocol II

This instrument is much shorter than Protocol I and is entitled "Protocol Additional to the Geneva Conventions of 12 August 1949, and relating to the Protection of Victims of Non–International Armed Conflicts (Protocol II)." *See generally* Kalshoven, *supra,* at 137; Bothe, Partsch & Solf, *supra,* at 604; Symposium on "International Humanitarian and Human Rights Law in Non–International Armed Conflicts," 33 Am. U. L. Rev. 9–161 (1983); Green, *supra,* at 306. Since the definition of international armed conflicts adopted by Protocol I includes certain types of wars of national liberation which the Geneva Conventions treated as non-international in character, these internal armed conflicts are not covered by Protocol II. Article 1 of Protocol II limits its scope of application even further. Although it declares that this instrument "develops and supplements" common Article 3 of the Geneva Conventions "without modifying its existing conditions of application," it provides that Protocol II applies to all such armed conflicts which are not covered by Article 1 of Protocol I and "which take place in the territory of a High Contracting Party between its armed forces and dissident armed forces or other organized armed forces." Moreover, Protocol II applies to these conflicts only if the dissident forces are "under responsible command" and "exercise such control over a part of [the High Contracting Party's] territory as to enable them to carry out sustained and concerted military operations and to implement this Protocol." (Art. 1(1).) Article 1(2) narrows the scope of Protocol II even further by declaring that it "shall not apply to situations of internal disturbances and tensions, such as riots, isolated and sporadic acts of violence and other acts of a similar nature, as not being armed conflicts." *See generally* Meron, *Human Rights in Internal Strife, supra,* at 75; Junod, "Additional Protocol II: History and Scope," 33 Am. U. L. Rev. 29 (1983).

Here it should be noted that the language of common Article 3, see § 6–3, *supra,* is less restrictive than Article 1 of Protocol II. That provision expressly declares, however, that it does not change the scope of applicability of common Article 3, which can consequently still be applied to certain internal armed conflicts that do not meet the stricter test of Article 1 of Protocol II. J. Pictet, *Development and Principles of International Humanitarian Law* 48–49 (1985). Common Article 3, however, contains fewer guarantees than does Protocol II. Hence, when internal armed confrontations qualify as Protocol II conflicts, the affected individuals are entitled to greater protection or more rights than they would enjoy under common Article 3. *See* Goldman, "International Humanitarian Law and the Armed Conflicts in El Salvador and Nicaragua," 2 Am. U. J. Int'l L. & Pol'y 539, 543–49 (1987).

Protocol II amplifies the guarantees set out in common Article 3 and contains specific provisions designed to ensure humane treatment of individuals being detained "for reasons related to the armed conflict." (Art. 5.) It proclaims a catalog of due process provisions and other guarantees that are applicable "to the prosecution and punishment of criminal offenses related to the armed conflict." (Art. 6.) The Protocol contains a special section on the protection of civilian populations, which declares, *inter alia,* that "the civilian population as such, as well as individual civilians, shall not be the object of attack." (Art. 13(2).) It also prohibits "acts or threats of violence the primary purpose of which is to spread terror among the civilian population." (*Id.*)

Unlike its companion instrument, Protocol II makes no provision for Protecting Powers, nor does it assign specific functions to the International Committee of the Red Cross. It does provide, however, that "relief societies located in the territory of the High Contracting Party, such as Red Cross ... organizations, may offer their services for the performance of their traditional functions in relation to the victims of the armed conflict." (Art. 18(1).) Protocol II also does not establish any measures of implementation or supervision to ensure compliance with its provisions.   For possible alternative methods of protection, see Ramcharan, "The Role of International Bodies in the Implementation and Enforcement of Humanitarian Law and Human Rights Law in Non–International Armed Conflicts," 33 Am. U. L. Rev. 99 (1983).

§ 6–6.   Humanitarian Law and Human Rights Treaties: Their Interaction

The International Covenant on Civil and Political Rights, the European Convention of Human Rights and the American Convention on Human Rights contain so-called derogation clauses.   Covenant, art. 4, European Convention, art. 15; American Convention, art. 27.   These provisions permit the High Contracting Parties, in time of war or other serious national emergencies, to suspend many of the rights these instruments protect.   Various safeguards limit the exercise of the right of derogation.   Two of these are relevant to the subject here under discussion.

First, all derogation clauses list certain specific fundamental rights which may not be suspended even in time of war or other emergency.   Although the three human rights treaties mentioned above do not establish an identical catalog of non-derogable rights, each prohibits the suspension of the same core group of basic rights.   Among these are the right to life, the right not to be tortured or to be held in slavery, and the right not to be subjected to *ex post facto* laws or punishment.   Second, the derogation clauses also limit the manner in which states may exercise their power to suspend the rights that are derogable. They all provide, *inter alia,* that the derogating states may not adopt measures which are "inconsistent with their other obligations under international law." *See, e.g.,* Covenant, art. 4(1). This stipulation has a special significance for states which have ratified humanitarian law treaties and one or more of the principal human rights instruments. For these states, the humanitarian law treaties form an integral part of the derogation clause of the particular human rights treaty, barring the suspension during armed hostilities of rights whose enjoyment is guaranteed by the Geneva Conventions, for example, or one of the two Protocols. The reverse may also be true. For example, a government may be free under the humanitarian law treaties to adopt a given measure in time of war. If that measure were to adversely affect the enjoyment of a non-derogable right guaranteed in a human rights convention which the state in question has ratified, its government would be barred from taking that action even in time of war even though it was not prohibited by the Geneva Conventions or one of its Protocols. For an analysis of derogation clauses and some of their consequences, *see* Buergenthal, "To Respect and to Ensure: State Obligations and Permissible Derogations," *in* L. Henkin (ed.), *The International Bill of Rights: The Covenant on Civil and Political Rights* 72, at 78 (1981); J. Fitzpatrick, *Human Rights in*

Crisis: The International System for Protecting Rights During States of Emergency (1994).

As has been noted in § 6–4 and § 6–5, *supra,* Protocols I and II expand the guarantees applicable to certain types of internal conflicts beyond those that are provided for under common Article 3 of the Geneva Conventions. A significant number of internal conflicts are, however, excluded from the scope of application of the Protocols because they either do not qualify as so-called wars of national liberation (Protocol I) or because they do not meet the stringent threshold requirements of Protocol II. Individuals involved in internal hostilities which are not covered by the Protocols or common Article 3 can, consequently, look for protection only to international human rights laws. *See* Buergenthal, "The United Nations Truth Commission for El Salvador," 27 Vand. J. Transnat'l L. 497, 526–27 (1994), for an example of how this principle has also been applied to insurgents. On the resulting gaps in the protection of individuals who can benefit neither from humanitarian law nor human rights law, see Meron, *Human Rights in Internal Strife, supra,* at 58–59.

§ 6–7. The International Committee of the Red Cross

This body, which dates back to the 1860's, was established by Henri Dunant, a Swiss businessman and one of the most influential early advocates of international humanitarian law and of its codification. The ICRC is a private humanitarian institution incorporated under the laws of Switzerland. Since the ICRC exercises functions conferred on it by the Geneva Conventions and their Protocols and since these treaties recognize its special status, various commentators contend that the ICRC, although non-governmental in character, is a subject of international law. *See, e.g.,* R. Siegrist, *The Protection of Political Detainees: The International Committee of the Red Cross in Greece 1967–1971,* at 26 (1985) and the authorities cited therein. Whether or not that characterization is sound, it is clear that the ICRC has a *sui generis* international status that distinguishes it from other non-governmental human rights organizations. That status derives from the powers the humanitarian treaties confer on it and from the confidence governments have in its political neutrality and impartiality. Although erroneous, there is a widely held perception that the ICRC is an entity of the Swiss Government, which it is not. The ICRC does, however, have close relations with the Swiss Government, which bolsters its credibility as a neutral body.

Article 4 of the Statutes of the ICRC includes among its functions the performance of the tasks that the Geneva Conventions and their Protocols confer on that organization. For the text of the Statutes of the ICRC, see *International Red Cross Handbook*, which is periodically updated. The Statutes mandate the ICRC to act as a neutral institution in situations of war, civil war or internal strife, and "to endeavour to ensure at all times that the military and civilian victims of such conflicts and of their direct results receive protection and assistance, and to serve, in humanitarian matters, as an intermediary between the parties." (Art. 4(1)(d).) In addition, the ICRC also plays a major role in promoting the development, dissemination and teaching of international humanitarian law. *See generally* Surbeck, "Dissemination of International Humanitarian Law," 33 Am. U. L. Rev. 125 (1983). The ICRC has also come to play an increasingly more important role in rendering humanitarian assistance to political detainees in countries torn by internal civil strife. These activities span the globe.

Unlike the traditional non-governmental human rights organizations, the ICRC does not resort to publicity as a technique to obtain humanitarian treatment for prisoners of war, civilian populations or political detainees. Its *modus operandi* consists of very discreet interventions and negotiations with the responsible authorities and officials. As a rule, the ICRC does not publish its findings on specific violations or abuses; it provides its reports only to the authorities concerned. But if the latter publish distorted or partial versions of ICRC findings, it will release its report to the public. On the effectiveness of this approach as it applies to political detainees, see D. Forsythe, *Present Role of the Red Cross in Protection* 31 (1975). *See also* Veuthey, "Implementation and Enforcement of Humanitarian Law and Human Rights Law in Non–International Armed Conflict: The Role of the International Committee of the Red Cross," 33 Am. U. L. Rev. 83 (1983); Meron, "Internal Strife: Applicable

Norms and a Proposed Instrument," *in* A.J.M. Delissen & G.J. Tanja (eds.), *Humanitarian Law of Armed Conflict: Challenges Ahead* 249, 252 (1991).

§ 6–8. The International Criminal Tribunal for the Former Yugoslavia and Rwanda

By Resolution 827 of May 25, 1993, the Security Council of the United Nations established the "International Tribunal for the Prosecution of Persons Responsible for Serious Violations of International Humanitarian Law Committed in the Territory of the Former Yugoslavia Since 1991." A year later the Security Council expanded the Tribunal's jurisdiction to embrace the Rwandan genocide. *See generally* O'Brian, "The International Tribunal for the Former Yugoslavia," 87 Am. J. Int'l L. 639 (1993). *See also* "Report of the Secretary–General Pursuant to Paragraph 2 of Security Council Resolution 808," Doc. S/2504 of May 3, 1993 (containing an annotated text of the draft Statute of the Tribunal; the draft Statute was adopted by the Security Council without any changes). The Tribunal is the first such international judicial body to be created since the establishment of the Nürnberg and Tokyo war crimes tribunals after World War II. The United Nations is currently also considering proposals for the establishment of a permanent international criminal court. *See* Doc. A/C.N.4/L.491 (1994).

The Statute of the Yugoslav Tribunal confers jurisdiction on it "to prosecute persons responsible for serious violations of international humanitarian law committed in the territory of the former Yugoslavia since 1991 . . . . " (Art. 1) The meaning of the phrase "serious violations of humanitarian law" is spelled out in subsequent provisions of the Statute, which identify the following crimes: grave breaches of the Geneva Conventions of 1949 (Art. 2); violations of the laws and customs of war (Art. 3); genocide (Art. 4); and crimes against humanity (Art. 5). The individual elements comprising these crimes are enumerated in the Statute. Thus, for example, the following acts are defined as crimes against humanity "when committed in armed conflict, whether international or internal in character, and directed against any civilian population:" murder, extermination, enslavement, deportation, imprisonment, torture, rape, persecutions on political, racial and religious grounds, and other inhuman acts. On crimes against humanity in general, see C. Bassiouni, *Crimes Against Humanity in International Criminal Law* (1992).

It will no doubt take a long time for the Tribunal to bring to justice many of the individuals charged by it with the serious violations of humanitarian law over which it has jurisdiction, and some might for one reason or another escape punishment. The very fact, however, that the Tribunal has been established is an important development in the evolution of international humanitarian law and in giving it "teeth." The caselaw that will emerge from it is likely to clarify many contested issues of humanitarian law and thus strengthen the normative framework of this branch of international human rights law. *See generally* Bassiouni, "The United Nations Commission of Experts Established Pursuant to Security Council Resolution 780 (1992)," 88 Am. J. Int'l L. 784, 790–94 (1994); Meron, "War Crimes in Yugoslavia and the Development of International Law," 88 Am. J. Int'l L. 78 (1994). *But see* D'Amato, "Peace vs. Accountability in Bosnia," 88 Am. J. Int'l L. 500 (1994).

CHAPTER 7

THE U.S. AND INTERNATIONAL HUMAN RIGHTS

I. INTRODUCTION

This chapter examines the governmental policies of the United States as they relate to the development and enforcement of international human rights law. It deals with questions relating to U.S. ratification of human rights treaties, with Congressional legislation designed to promote human rights abroad, and with the application of international human rights law by U.S. courts.

The position of the U.S. with regard to international human rights has been full of contradictions. For decades it refused to ratify any major international human rights treaties and, although it has adhered to some of them in recent years, it still lags behind most Western democracies. At the same time, the U.S. has strongly supported UN efforts to promote human rights and is among the first nations of the world to adopt a substantial body of domestic law designed to bolster the enforcement of internationally guaranteed human rights. That law serves as the legal foundation of the human rights foreign policy of the U.S. Other nations have also looked to it as a model for shaping their own legislation on the subject. *See* J. Egeland, *Impotent Superpower—Potent Small States* (1988).

The U.S. entered the Second World War as one of the strongest advocates of a treaty-based international system for the protection of human rights. J. Green, *The United Nations and Human Rights* 13–15 (1956); A. Holcombe, *Human Rights in the Modern World* 4–5 (1948). On the important role the U.S. played drafting the human rights provisions of the U.N. Charter, see L. Sohn & T. Buergenthal, *International Protection of Human Rights* 506–9 (1973). By the late 1950's, however, its official policy on the subject was complete nonparticipation. This policy was formally reversed in the 1960's. Buergenthal, "International Human Rights: U.S. Policy and Priorities," 14 Va. J. Int'l L. 611 (1974). The years 1973–74 mark the revival of U.S. interest in and commitment to an effective international human rights system. During that period, the U.S. Congress began to address the subject and laid the legislative foundation for America's current human rights policy. Committee on Foreign Affairs, *Human Rights in the World Community: A Call For U.S. Leadership* (U.S. House of Representatives, 1974). The Carter Administration made human rights the centerpiece of its foreign policy. Although the Reagan Administration initially showed little enthusiasm for the subject, it gradually recognized that it was in the interest of the U.S. to maintain the promotion of human rights as an important item on its foreign policy agenda. Its human rights policy was amplified by President

Reagan's Democracy Initiative, which focused on support for democratic institutions and elections. This approach was strengthened in the Bush Administration and has been continued and amplified by the Clinton Administration. The latter expanded the policy to include, in addition to the promotion of human rights, efforts to bolster the rule of law and democracy, and the strengthening of the rights of labor.

Despite the fact that these Administrations all acknowledged the need for infusing human rights concerns into the foreign policy agenda of the United States and did just that, none of them has escaped justified criticism for the manner in which they at times implemented or failed to implement that policy. *See generally* A. G. Mower, *Human Rights and American Foreign Policy: The Carter and Reagan Experience* (1987); "Symposium on Human Rights: An Agenda for the New Administration," 28 Va. J. Int'l L. 827–917 (1988); Schifter, "Building Firm Foundations: The Institutionalization of United States Human Rights Policy in the Reagan Years," 2 Harv. Hum. Rts. Y.B. 3 (1989); Shestack, "An Unsteady Focus: The Vulnerability of the Reagan Administration's Human Rights Policy," 2 Harv. Hum. Rts. Y.B. (1989); Leslie, " 'The Human Spirit Cannot be Locked Up Forever:' An Analysis of the New Agenda on Human Rights from the Bush Administration," 6 Fla. J. Int'l L. 119 (Fall 1990); Burkhalter, "Bargaining Away Human Rights: The Bush Administration's Policy Towards Iraq and China," 4 Harv. Hum. Rts. J. 105 (1991);

Carothers, "Democracy and Human Rights: Policy Allies or Rivals?," 17 Wash. Q. 106 (1994). *See also* Orentlicher, "The Power of an Idea: The Impact of United States Human Rights Policy," 1 Transnat'l L. & Contemp. Probs. 43 (1991).

II. THE U.S. AND HUMAN RIGHTS TREATIES

§ 7–1. Introduction

Until 1988, the United States had not ratified any major international human rights treaty. That year the Senate gave its advice and consent to the ratification of the Genocide Convention; President Reagan ratified it shortly thereafter. The Genocide Convention was first submitted to the U.S. Senate by President Truman in 1949 and resubmitted by President Nixon more than two decades later. (A series of other treaties whose ratification President Carter had asked the Senate to authorize fared no better.)

The Senate's 1988 action on the Genocide Convention marked a turning point in U.S. policy towards human rights treaties. In 1992, the United States ratified the International Covenant on Civil and Political Rights. Stewart, "U.S. Ratification of the Covenant on Civil and Political Rights: The Significance of the Reservations, Understandings and Declarations," 14 Hum. Rts. L.J. 77 (1993). Two years later it ratified the International Convention on the Elimination of All Forms of Racial Discrimination and the Convention Against Torture and Other Cruel, Inhuman or Degrading Treatment or Punishment. *See* Stewart, "The Torture Convention and the Reception of International Criminal Law Within the United States," 15 Nova. L. Rev. 449 (1991). Of course, as a member of the United Nations and the Organization of American States, the U.S. had earlier assumed various treaty-based human rights obligations enunciated in their Charters. The U.S. is also a party to the 1949 Geneva Convention on humanitarian law, but not to their 1977 Additional Protocols. Some of the treaties the U.S. has thus far failed to ratify include the International Covenant on Economic, Social and Cultural Rights; the Convention on the Elimination of All Forms of Discrimination Against Women; the Convention on the Rights of the Child; and the American Convention on Human Rights. The U.S. has also not adhered to the Optional Protocol to the Covenant on Civil and Political Rights.

Although it is very likely that the U.S. will in the future become a party to additional human rights treaties, its pre–1988 position regarding these instruments and its practice of attaching a variety of reservations to those it ratifies require explanation. The following sections will put the issues relevant here in their historical, constitutional and political context.

§ 7–2. Treaties and the U.S. Constitution

Article VI of the U.S. Constitution provides, *inter alia,* that "this Constitution, and the Laws of the

United States which shall be made in Pursuance
thereof; and all Treaties made, or which shall be
made, under the Authority of the United States,
shall be the supreme Law of the Land." This
provision has been interpreted to mean that federal
statutes and the treaties to which the U.S. is a
party have the same normative rank under the
Constitution. In the case of conflict between a
federal statute and a self-executing treaty provision
(a treaty provision that does not require additional
implementing legislation), the later in time prevails
as far as the domestic law of the U.S. is concerned.
Whitney v. Robertson, 124 U.S. 190 (1888); *Diggs v.
Shultz,* 470 F.2d 461 (D.C.Cir.1972), *cert. den.* 411
U.S. 931 (1973); *Restatement (Third)* § 115. It is
also no longer disputed today that a treaty provision
may not be given effect as U.S. domestic law if it
conflicts with the Constitution. Reid v. Covert, 354
U.S. 1 (1957); *Restatement (Third)* § 302. As federal law, treaties supersede all state laws and, unless they contain provisions to the contrary, they
also federalize a subject that may heretofore have
been governed by state law. *Missouri v. Holland,*
252 U.S. 416 (1920); *United States v. Pink,* 315
U.S. 203 (1942).

As will be seen, § 7–3, *infra*, this legal regime,
that is, the place treaties have in U.S. law and the
consequences flowing from it, have in the past
played a major role in determining the willingness
of the U.S. Senate to approve the ratification of
human rights treaties.

§ 7–3. The U.S. Senate and Human Rights Treaties

When World War II ended in 1945 and the United Nations was established, racial discrimination and a variety of other forms of discrimination were either legally mandated or not unlawful in the U.S. Much of the law codifying *de jure* racial discrimination was state law, most of it in the South, but certainly not all: racially segregated schools, anti-miscegenation statutes, poll taxes, segregated public services and accommodations, etc. A coalition of Southern Democrats and Conservative Republicans in the U.S. Congress made change by federal legislation extremely difficult.

The political groups interested in doing away with *de jure* racial discrimination and other forms of discrimination recognized that the human rights provision of the UN Charter and the UN treaties then being drafted might be used to strike down the laws that Congress was unwilling to repeal or nullify. Among the first judicial suggestions that the UN Charter, being a duly ratified treaty of the U.S., was a federal law that outlawed racial discrimination, were the concurring opinions of Justices Black and Murphy in *Oyama v. California,* 332 U.S. 633, at 649–50 and 673 (1948). They relied on Articles 55 and 56 of the UN Charter, which impose on the Organization and its Member States the obligation to "promote ... universal respect for, and observance of, human rights and fundamental freedoms for all without distinction as to race, sex, language or religion." The domestic legal effect of this obli-

gation was faced squarely in *Sei Fujii v. California,*
38 Cal.2d 718, 242 P.2d 617 (Cal. Dist. Ct.App.
1952). Here an intermediate California court held
that California's Alien Land Law, by discriminating
against aliens of Asian origin, was unenforceable
because it violated the human rights provisions of
the UN Charter. The court reasoned that the
Charter, being a treaty of the United States, was
equal in rank to a federal statute and thus superseded any inconsistent state legislation. The Supreme Court of California rejected this view. It
ruled that the human rights provisions of the UN
Charter were non-self-executing and, as such, could
not supersede state law unless and until they were
implemented by Congressional legislation. Sei Fujii
v. California, 38 Cal.2d 718, 242 P.2d 617 (1952).
(The Court also held, however, that the challenged
state law violated the Fourteenth Amendment of
the U.S. Constitution.) Since no appeal was taken
from this ruling, the holding that the human rights
provisions of the Charter were non-self-executing
was not challenged in the U.S. Supreme Court. For
literature on this case, see L. Sohn & T. Buergenthal, *International Protection of Human Rights* 944
(1973). *See generally* Paust "Self–Executing Treaties," 82 Am. J. Int'l L. 760 (1988); Buergenthal,
"Self–Executing and Non–Self–Executing Treaties
in National and International Law," 235 Recueil
des Cours 303, 368 (1992).

The *Sei Fujii* holding did not, however, allay the
fears of those who saw UN human rights treaty
provisions as a threat to discriminatory state legis-

lation, which had heretofore withstood constitutional challenge. The clearest warning was sounded by Senator John W. Bricker of Ohio, who spelled out the danger to his conservative colleagues in the following terms: "if the Fujii case [lower court's opinion] should eventually be affirmed by the United States Supreme Court, or if the principle announced therein should be sustained, literally thousands of Federal and State laws will automatically become invalid." To avert this danger, "something must be done to prevent treaties from having such far-reaching and unintended consequences." 98 Cong. Rec. 911 (1952). What needed to be done, according to Senator Bricker, was the adoption of an amendment to the U.S. Constitution that would limit the treaty-making power. *See* D. Tananbaum, *The Bricker Amendment Controversy: A Test of Eisenhower's Political Leadership* (1988); Kaufman & Whiteman, "Opposition to Human Rights Treaties in the United States Senate: The Legacy of the Bricker Amendment," 10 Hum. Rts. Q. 309 (1988).

Although different versions of the so-called "Bricker Amendment" were introduced in the U.S. Senate between 1952 and 1957, they all had three basic aims. The different versions are reproduced in "Report on the 1957 Bricker Amendment," 12 Rec. Bar Assoc. N.Y. 320, at 343–46 (1957). The three aims were: first, to make all international agreements non-self-executing under U.S. law, which means that they would require implementing legislation before they could be enforced in U.S. courts; second, to reverse *Missouri v. Holland*, 252

U.S. 416 (1920), which held that the Tenth Amendment did not limit the treaty-making power of the Federal Government since that power was expressly delegated to the United States, permitting treaties to federalize subjects within the jurisdiction of the states; and third, to provide expressly what had always been implicit, namely, that under U.S. law, international agreements are subject to those restraints of the Constitution that limit all powers of the federal government. *Compare De Geofroy v. Riggs*, 133 U.S. 258 (1890) *with Reid v. Covert*, 354 U.S. 1 (1957). *See generally* L. Henkin, *Foreign Affairs and the Constitution* 129–67 (2d ed. 1975).

The major targets of Senator Bricker's attack were the human rights treaties the United Nations had already adopted and the proposed human rights covenants, which seemed to be nearing completion at the time. *See* Senator Bricker's testimony, *Hearings on S.J. Res. 1 and S.J. Res. 43 Before a Subcomm. of the Senate Comm. on the Judiciary,* 83d Cong., 1st Sess. 10–11 (1953). In the negotiations that eventually resulted in the defeat of the Bricker Amendment, Secretary of State John Foster Dulles had to make a policy commitment on behalf of the Eisenhower Administration that the U.S. Government did "not intend to become a party to any such covenant [on human rights] or present it as a treaty for consideration by the Senate." *Id.*, at 825. This policy statement was officially communicated to the United Nations. 13 M. Whiteman, *Digest of International Law* 667–69 (1968).

The United States adhered to this policy until 1963. In that year, President John F. Kennedy transmitted three human rights treaties to the Senate for its advice and consent. They consisted of the Supplementary Convention on the Abolition of Slavery and the Slave Trade, the Convention on the Abolition of Forced Labor, and the Convention on the Political Rights of Women. *See* 49 Dept. State Bull. 23 (1963). It took four years for the Senate to schedule hearings on this request. *Hearings on Executive J, K, and L,* 88 Cong., 1st Sess., 90th Cong., 1st Sess. (Feb. 23 and March 8, 1967); *id.,* Part 2 (Sept. 13, 1967). These hearings produced consent to the ratification by the U.S. of only the Slavery Convention. Thereafter, in 1976, the United States was finally able to ratify the Convention on the Political Rights of Women. U.S. adherence to the Protocol Relating to the Status of Refugees was easily authorized by the Senate in 1968, but it was not presented as a human rights treaty.

To demonstrate his Administration's strong commitment to human rights, President Jimmy Carter, in an unusual act for a head of state, personally signed three major human rights treaties during his first year in office. He signed the two International Covenants of Human Rights at UN Headquarters in New York and the American Convention on Human Rights at the seat of the Organization of American States in Washington, D.C. A year later, in 1978, President Carter transmitted these instruments, together with the International Convention on the Elimination of All Forms of Racial Discrimination, to the Senate for its advice and consent to ratification. *Message from the President of the United States Transmitting Four Treaties Pertaining to Human Rights,* Senate Ex. C, D, E, and F, 95th Congress, 2d.Sess. (Feb. 23, 1978). In 1979, the Senate Foreign Relations Committee held extensive hearings on this request. *Hearings before the [Senate] Committee on Foreign Relations on Ex. C, D, E, and F, 95–2—Four Treaties Relating to Human Rights,* Nov. 14–16 and 19, 1979 (1980).

As previously noted, no further action was taken on these treaties until 1992 and 1994 respectively, when the Senate gave its consent to the ratification of the Covenant on Civil and Political Rights and the Racial Convention. The big breakthrough came earlier, in 1988, with the U.S. ratification of the Genocide Convention.

§ 7–4. Legal and Policy Considerations Affecting Ratification

In analyzing the views of those who have over the years opposed U.S. ratification of human rights treaties, it is not always easy to distinguish the legal from the policy arguments. *See, e.g., Hearing before the Subcommittee on the Constitution of the Senate Committee on the Judiciary on the Constitutional Implications of the Proposed Genocide Convention,* 99th Cong., 1st Sess., Feb. 26, 1985 (1985); L. J. Le Blanc, *The United States and the Genocide Convention* (1991). Basically, three legal arguments have been advanced at different times by opponents of U.S. adherence to these treaties.

The first argument is that human rights are a matter of domestic jurisdiction and that the U.S. Constitution does not permit the use of the treaty-making power to regulate a matter that is not a proper subject for international negotiations. The problem with this contention is that, even assuming that the treaty-making power applies only to matters that are of international concern, it cannot be seriously contended that human rights fail to meet this test. The huge number of international human rights agreements in force today, which have been ratified by a substantial majority of the international community of states, attests to the internationalization of the human rights concern. *See, e.g., Filartiga v. Peña–Irala*, 630 F.2d 876 (2d Cir.1980); *Restatement (Third)* § 302, Comment (c). *See also* United Nations, *Human Rights: A Compilation of International Instruments*, Vol. 1 (First Part) (1993). In short, the constitutional standard about what is or is not a matter of international concern, assuming there is in fact such a requirement, cannot be divorced from contemporary international realities and diplomatic practice.

The second argument against U.S. adherence to human rights treaties is that many of the rights these instruments protect are at present regulated in the U.S. by state rather than federal law. Their ratification by the U.S., it is contended, would improperly federalize these subjects. It is not all that clear, given the manner in which this argument is often put, whether its proponents believe that this federalization would be unconstitutional or merely unwise. For example, in testifying in 1981 against U.S. ratification of the Genocide Convention, Senator Strom Thurmond, then Chairman of the Senate Judiciary Committee, declared:

Matters concerning fundamental criminal conduct involving murder or conspiracy to commit murder should be primarily a matter of State domestic jurisdiction—I repeat, State domestic jurisdiction. The use of the treatymaking power in this area is inappropriate. In effect, the [Genocide] Convention would continue the policy made possible by the Supreme Court in its decision in *Missouri v. Holland,* 252 U.S. 416 [1920], in which the Court held that State powers could be transferred to the Federal Government through the treatymaking process as a de facto method of amending the Constitution. *Hearing before the [Senate] Committee on Foreign Relations on the Genocide Convention,* 97 Cong., 1st Sess., Dec. 3, 1981, at 9 (1982).

In *Missouri v. Holland,* the Supreme Court held that the Tenth Amendment, which provides that "the powers not delegated to the United States by the Constitution, nor prohibited by it to the States, are reserved to the States respectively, or to the people," does not limit the treaty-making power of the U.S. since it was expressly delegated to the U.S. On this subject generally, see Henkin, "The Constitution, Treaties and International Human Rights," U. Pa. L. Rev. 1012 (1968).

Finally, it has been argued that some human rights treaties contain provisions that are in conflict with the U.S. Constitution. This is true of a very small number of these provisions. One such clause, for example, is Article 20(1) of the Covenant on Civil and Political Rights, which requires that "any advocacy of national, racial or religious hatred that constitutes incitement to discrimination ... shall be prohibited by law." Here and in similar cases appropriate reservations must be made upon ratification to ensure that the U.S. does not assume international obligations which it would be unable to discharge on the domestic plane because they violate the Constitution. *See generally* R. Lillich (ed.), *U.S. Ratification of the Human Rights Treaties: With or Without Reservations?* (1981); Stewart, "U.S. Ratification of the Covenant on Civil and Political Rights: The Significance of the Reservations, Understanding and Declarations," 14 Hum. Rts. L.J. 77, 79–81 (1993).

Some opponents of U.S adherence to human rights treaties have argued that the Supreme Court might at some future time hold that treaties in general were not subject to any of the limitations the Constitution imposes on the exercise of all governmental power. If that were to happen, so the argument goes, Americans might be deprived of their constitutional rights by human rights treaties. Representatives of the Liberty Lobby advanced this proposition in the following terms in their 1981 testimony before the Senate Foreign Relations Committee:

Genocide Convention supporters usually cite the 1957 Supreme Court case of *Reid vs. Covert* in which the Court ruled that treaties did not over-rule the Constitution. However, at various times in history, different rulings have been made on this issue—and nothing prevents the Supreme Court from making a new ruling in the future that would again make treaties supreme over the Constitution. *l981 Genocide Convention Hearings, supra,* at 85.

As the Liberty Lobby itself acknowledged, the Supreme Court expressly rejected this interpretation in *Reid v. Covert. See also Restatement (Third)* § 302(2), which declares that "no provision of an [international] agreement may contravene any of the prohibitions or limitations of the Constitution applicable to any exercise of authority by the United States." Moreover, various human rights treaties contain a clause similar to that of Article 5(2) of the Covenant on Civil and Political Rights, which declares that

There shall be no restriction upon or derogation from any of the fundamental human rights recognized or existing in any States Party to the present Covenant pursuant to law, conventions, regulations or custom on the pretext that the present Covenant does not recognize such rights or that it recognizes them to a lesser extent. *See also* American Convention on Human Rights, art. 29(b).

In giving its advice and consent to the ratification of the Genocide Convention, the Senate attached a reservation, providing "that nothing in the Convention requires or authorizes legislation or other action by the United States of America prohibited by the Constitution of the United States as interpreted by the United States." For the full text of the resolution of ratification, see 132 Cong. Rec. S1377–78 (daily ed., Feb. 19, 1986). The Senate Foreign Relations Committee explained this reservation by pointing out that it had no doubt whatsoever that "no treaty can override or conflict with the Constitution. The Constitution is paramount. Reid v. Covert, 354 U.S. 1 (1957)." *Report of the [Senate] Committee on Foreign Relations on the International Convention on the Prevention and Punishment of the Crime of Genocide, Exec.O., 81st Cong., 1st Sess.,* Exec. Rep. 99–2, 99th Cong., 1st Sess., at 20 (1985). The Committee emphasized instead that the purpose of the reservation was to anticipate the possibility that the International Court of Justice might at some future time interpret the Genocide Convention to require the U.S. to adopt measures that would be unconstitutional. *Id.,* at 20–21. Some members of the Senate Foreign Relations Committee opposed this reservation and argued that it was both unnecessary and unwise. They were unsuccessful in urging the full Senate to vote against it. *Id.,* at 30–31. Similar language has been adopted by the Senate in giving its advice and consent to other treaties subsequently ratified by the U.S., but no longer in the form of a reservation.

Instead, it is now formulated as a "proviso, which shall not be included in the instrument of ratification deposited by the President...." *See, e.g.*, Report of the Senate Foreign Relations Committee on the International Covenant on Civil and Political Rights, March 24, 1992, Exec. Rep. 102–23, at 24; approved by full Senate, 102 Cong. Rec. S4781–4784 (daily ed. April 2, 1992).

§ 7–5. The New Policy: Ratification With Reservations, Understandings and Declarations

Over the past decades, the attitude of the United States to human rights treaties has changed dramatically from a policy of total non-participation to one, reflected in the actions of the Reagan, Bush and Clinton Administrations, that proceeds on a treaty-by-treaty basis in deciding whether or not to ratify a particular instrument. This latter decision is made by taking account of various factors, including the national interest in U.S. participation and the likelihood that the Senate will give its advice and consent to ratification. Recent Administrations have gradually reached the conclusion that, in general, it is in the U.S. national interest to join such treaties and that, in principle, there are no compelling constitutional objections to their ratification. There is general agreement, moreover, that almost all such treaties present some constitutional problems, but that these can be overcome by appropriate reservations.

To obtain the requisite political support of the Senate, which has to give its advice and consent to the ratification of these treaties by a two-thirds majority, the Executive Branch has evolved a practice of addressing all real and potential objections relating to a particular treaty provision by proposing numerous reservations, understandings and declarations—so-called RUDs—designed to overcome these objections. The practice began in the Carter Administration and has continued since then through the Reagan, Bush and Clinton Administrations. Driven by a combination of constitutional imperatives, legal considerations and political expediency, the practice has now become a tradition insisted upon by the Senate and fully supported by the Executive Branch regardless of its political affiliation.

Before addressing the implementation of this practice, it is worth elaborating the nature and legal effect of RUDs. A reservation is designed to modify the terms of the treaty as between the reserving state and the states accepting the reservation to the extent of the reservation. As such, a reservation changes the international obligation of these states *inter se*. Understandings and declarations are traditionally thought of as unilateral statements by a state regarding its interpretation or position with regard to a given provision of a treaty. They will not as a rule modify a state's international obligations. But whether they will or will not have any international legal consequences is not always clear because the label a state attaches to these statements is not determinative as a matter of international law. *See* Vienna Convention on the Law of Treaties, art. 2(1)(d). Hence, on the international law plane a statement denominated as an "understanding" might be treated as a reservation if it appears that its purpose was to modify the international obligations assumed by a state. Under U.S. constitutional law, however, when the Senate conditions its consent to ratification on certain reservations, understandings or declarations, and the President ratifies the treaty subject to them, they are binding on U.S. courts as a matter of domestic law, provided they are within the Constitutional power of the Senate to adopt. *See generally Restatement (Third)* § 313 and 314.

Certain categories of RUDs are now uniformly attached to all human rights treaties ratified by the U.S. First, there are the reservations which the U.S. will attach to any treaty provisions that might be deemed to conflict with the U.S. Constitution. This problem arises most often in the context of First Amendment rights. Typical is the following reservation the U.S. made when it ratified the Racial Convention:

> The Constitution and laws of the United States contain extensive protections of individual freedom of speech, expression and association. Accordingly, the United States does not accept any obligations under this Convention, in particular under Articles 4 and 7, to restrict those rights, through the adoption of legislation or any other

measures, to the extent that they are protected by the Constitution and laws of the United States.

The U.S. made a similar reservation when it ratified the Covenant on Civil and Political Rights. That reservation, made with regard to Article 20 of the Covenant, which deals with war propaganda and advocacy of national, racial, religious hatred, provides "that Article 20 does not authorize or require legislation or any other action by the United States that would restrict the right of free speech and association protected by the Constitution and laws of the United States." Note that the reservation applies not only to the Constitution but also to U.S. laws, which may go further than is constitutionally required.

Second, the U.S. will as a rule also attach reservations (or understandings) to any provision of a human rights treaty that is in conflict with existing U.S. law or that would require the U.S. to conform its law to the treaty standard. Thus, the U.S. made the following reservation with regard to the Torture Convention:

The United States considers itself bound by the obligation under Article 16 to prevent "cruel, inhuman or degrading treatment or punishment," only insofar as the term "cruel, inhuman or degrading treatment or punishment" means the cruel, unusual, and inhuman treatment or punishment prohibited by the Fifth, Eighth and/or Fourteenth Amendments to the Constitution of the United States.

The U.S. attached a similar reservation to its ratification of the Covenant. Here it also made a reservation relating to the application of the death penalty to persons under the age of 18. Another example of this type of reservation is one attached to the Covenant, which provides "that because U.S. law generally applies to an offender the penalty in force at the time the offense was committed, the United States does not adhere to the third clause of paragraph 1 of Article 15." The applicable provision of the Covenant requires the States Parties to give the offender the benefit of a lighter penalty if one is adopted subsequent to the commission of the offense. This type of reservation is designed to ensure that the treaty will not be deemed to have superseded existing domestic law in conflict with it.

Third, it has now become the practice of the U.S. to attach an understanding containing a so-called "federalism" clause to any human rights treaty to be ratified by this country. The language of these understandings has been refined over the past few years. The most recent one, attached to the Racial Convention, reads as follows:

That the United States understands that this Convention shall be implemented by the Federal Government to the extent that it exercises jurisdiction over the matters covered therein, and otherwise by the state and local governments. To the extent that state and local governments exercise jurisdiction over such matters, the Federal Government shall, as necessary, take appropriate measures to ensure the fulfillment of this Convention.

The purpose of this understanding is to ensure that U.S. ratification will not have the effect of federalizing those subjects regulated by the treaty over which the states and local governments have heretofore exercised jurisdiction. In other words, this understanding seeks to prevent the application of or to override the rule enunciated in *Missouri v. Holland, supra*, at § 7–4, which would deprive states of jurisdiction over matters dealt with in a treaty. Unlike the traditional federal-state clauses, however, this understanding is not designed to limit the international obligations of the United States. It is intended to make clear that the ratification of the treaty does not produce a federal preemption of all matters to which the treaty applies while recognizing the international obligation of the U.S. to "take appropriate measures to ensure the fulfillment of this Convention."

Fourth, it has now also become the practice for the United States to ratify human rights treaties with a declaration to the effect that the United States considers their substantive provisions to be non-self-executing. This declaration is designed to ensure that the particular treaty not be deemed to create rights directly enforceable in U.S. courts. *See* Damrosch, "The Role of the United States Senate Concerning 'Self–Executing' and 'Non–Self–Executing' Treaties," 67 Chi.-Kent. L. Rev. 515 (1991).

Finally, the Senate now also attaches a statement or "proviso" to its resolution giving advice and consent to the ratification of a human rights treaty, which provides that "Nothing in this Convention requires or authorizes legislation, or other action, by the United States of America prohibited by the Constitution of the United States as interpreted by the United States." The proviso is not, however, to be included in the U.S. instrument of ratification.

It is thus readily apparent that when the United States ratifies a human rights treaty today, it attempts through its reservation practice to ensure that it has assumed no international human rights obligations not already guaranteed by U.S. law. Moreover, by making the treaty non-self-executing, it seeks to prevent individuals from relying in U.S. courts on provisions of the treaty, and by resorting to the federalism clause, it avoids federal preemption of applicable state laws. It is ironic that this approach for all practical purposes accomplishes the goals which the proponents of the Bricker Amendment sought to achieve with respect to human rights treaties. *See* § 7–3, *supra*. *See also* Kaufman & Whiteman, "Opposition to Human Rights in the United States Senate: The Legacy of the Bricker Amendment," 10 Hum. Rts. Q. 309 (1988).

It is clear, of course, that the United States cannot ratify a treaty which, without an appropriate reservation, would violate the U.S. Constitution. It does have the constitutional power, however, to ratify a human rights treaty that conflicts with other domestic laws. Under the later-in-time rule, the treaty would then supersede the incompatible domestic law. The decision of the Senate to insist on reservations whereby the U.S. assumes no international obligations requiring a change in its domestic law is a policy decision not compelled by any constitutional mandate. The Constitution authorizes the President with the consent of the Senate to ratify treaties that become law and, if they are self-executing, that will supersede conflicting provisions of prior domestic law. The argument of the proponents of the Bricker Amendment and their contemporary disciples that this result can only be achieved by legislation passed by both Houses of Congress has no basis in the Constitution when applied to human rights treaties. The same can be said about the need for the non-self-executing declaration and the federal-state clause. These are all policy decisions with which one may or may not agree, but they certainly are not compelled by the Constitution. For arguments for and against these policies, see *Hearing before the Senate Foreign Relations Committee on the International Covenant on Civil and Political Rights, November 21, 1991, S.Hrg. 102–478 (1992); Hearing before the Senate Foreign Relations Committee on the International Convention on the Elimination of All Forms of Racial Discrimination, May 11, 1994, S.Hrg. 103–659 (1994). See also* Stewart, "U.S. Ratification of the Covenant on Civil and Political Rights: The Significance of the Reservations, Understandings and Declarations," 14 Hum. Rts. L. J. 77 (1993); Lawyers Committee for Human Rights, "Statements on U.S.

Ratification of the CCPR," *id.*, at 125; "Symposium: The Ratification of the International Covenant on Civil and Political Rights," 42 De Paul L. Rev. 1167–1412 (1993).

Here it should also be noted that a number of western European states, including the Netherlands, Germany, France, Italy, Belgium, and various Scandinavian countries, formally objected to some U.S. reservations to the Covenant on Civil and Political Rights as being incompatible with the object and purpose of the treaty and therefore invalid. These objections were addressed to the reservations of the U.S. relating to the death penalty and to cruel and usual treatment and punishment. The views of these states are echoed by an interpretative declaration made by the U.N. Human Rights Committee with regard to reservations in general. *See* General Comment No.24 (52) on Issues Relating to Reservations, U.N. Doc. CCPR/C/21/Rev.1/Add.6 (1994).

III. HUMAN RIGHTS LEGISLATION

§ 7–6. Introduction

In the early 1970's, the Congress of the United States began a thorough assessment of international human rights issues and their foreign policy implications. The person principally responsible for initiating this process was Congressman Donald M. Fraser of Minnesota, who at that time chaired the Subcommittee on International Organizations and Movements of the House Committee on Foreign

Affairs. In 1973, Congressman Fraser's subcommittee held extensive hearings on the subject. Subcommittee on International Organizations and Movements of the House Committee on Foreign Affairs, *Hearings on International Protection of Human Rights,* 93d Cong., 1st Sess., Aug. 1—Dec. 7, 1973. A year later, the subcommittee presented a comprehensive set of recommendations calling for legislation and other action to ensure that human rights considerations would receive serious consideration in the formulation and execution of U.S. foreign policy. Subcommittee on International Organizations and Movements of the House Committee on Foreign Affairs, *Human Rights in the World Community: A Call for Leadership,* 93d Cong., 2d Sess., 1974.

The legislative and bureaucratic underpinnings of contemporary U.S. human rights foreign policy have their origin in the efforts of the Fraser committee and the policies of President Jimmy Carter, who was elected in 1976. The latter enthusiastically espoused many of Congressman Fraser's recommendations and made the promotion of human rights the cornerstone of his Administration's foreign policy. *See* Weissbrodt, "Human Rights Legislation and U.S. Foreign Policy," 7 Ga. J. Int'l & Comp. L. 231 (1977); Schneider, "A New Administration's New Policy: The Rise to Power of Human Rights," *in* P. Brown & D. MacLean (eds.), *Human Rights and U.S. Foreign Policy* 3 (1979). *See also* Subcommittee on International Organization of the House Committee on International Relations, *Hu-*

man Rights in the International Community and in U.S. Foreign Policy, 1945–76 (Congressional Research Service, 1977).

The legislation and other measures that the initial Fraser committee hearings produced have been significantly transformed and amplified since then. Today there exists a substantial body of law on the subject. The subsequent sections examine the major provisions of that law.

§ 7–7. Military and Economic Aid Cut–Off: Laws of General Applicability

The cornerstone of U.S. human rights legislation consists of two laws of general applicability. This legislation ties the grant of military and economic assistance to the human rights policies of the recipient governments. The relevant laws are § 502B of the Foreign Assistance Act of 1961, as amended (22 U.S.C.A. § 2304), and § 116 of the same Act (22 U.S.C.A. 2151 n). Their underlying policy is well articulated in § 502B(a)(1), which reads as follows:

The United States shall, in accordance with its international obligations as set forth in the Charter of the United Nations and in keeping with the constitutional heritage and traditions of the United States, promote and encourage increased respect for human rights and fundamental freedoms throughout the world without distinction as to race, sex, language, or religion. Accordingly, a principal goal of the foreign policy of the United States shall be to promote the increased observance of internationally recognized human rights by all countries.

The reference to the human rights obligations of the U.S. under the UN Charter gives expression to Congress' view that the Charter legitimates the use of foreign aid as an instrument to promote human rights and that such action, consequently, does not constitute illegal intervention in the domestic affairs of the recipient states. This same concern is reflected in Congress' decision to invoke the concept of "internationally recognized human rights" as the standard that is to be promoted and observed.

Although § 502B deals with military or security assistance and § 116 applies to economic aid and development assistance, both laws have the same purpose: to deny such assistance to countries which engage in activities that reveal "a consistent pattern of gross violations of internationally recognized human rights." *See* §§ 116(a) and 502B(a)(2). The concept of "gross violation of internationally recognized human rights" is defined in § 502B(d)(1) as "including" violations such as

torture or cruel, inhuman, or degrading treatment or punishment, prolonged detention without charges and trial, causing the disappearance of persons by the abduction and clandestine detention of those persons, and other flagrant denial of the right to life, liberty, or the security of person.

Section 116(a) uses almost identical language. The use of the word "including" indicates that Congress recognized that other human rights may also qualify as being "internationally recognized." Although one commentator, S. Cohen, "Conditioning U.S. Security Assistance on Human Rights Practices," 76 Am. J. Int'l L. 246, 267 (1982), finds no support for this view in the legislative history of the act, the language used speaks for itself.

In looking at the language of this legislation, it is important to note that the phrase "consistent pattern of gross violations," mirrors the language of UN Economic and Social Council Resolution 1503 of 1970. That resolution is at the heart of the UN Charter-based system for dealing with human rights complaints and reflects the view that a state guilty of such violations is in breach of its obligations under the Charter. *See* § 2–24, *supra.* Resort by the U.S. Congress to the UN language is no accident and indicates a desire to ensure that these laws not be considered as constituting illegal intervention in the domestic affairs of other countries. The language also suggests that the Congress wished to penalize only governments which systematically engaged in or tolerated massive violations of human rights. Isolated instances of even serious violations would presumably not be covered by the statute, particularly if they revealed that these acts were not the result of a governmental policy. For an analysis of the manner in which the U.S. State Department has applied this test, see Cohen, *supra,* at 267–68. *See also* Forsythe, "Congress and Human Rights in U.S. Foreign Policy: The Fate of General Legislation," 9 Hum. Rts. Q. 382 (1987).

For a critical analysis of the application of these laws, see Lawyers Committee for Human Rights, *Human Rights and U.S. Foreign Policy* 6 (1992).

Section 116 establishes an elaborate reporting requirement under which the Department of State must provide a human rights status report for all states receiving aid and now also, for all UN Member States. Similar obligations are imposed by § 502B. These reports have become a valuable source of information about world-wide human rights conditions and violations. In compiling these reports, the State Department relies on information provided by U.S. embassies as well as on findings of inter-governmental and non-governmental human rights organizations. *See, e.g.,* Department of State, *Country Reports on Human Rights for 1994* (Report Submitted ... in Accordance with Sections 116(d) and 502B(b) of the Foreign Assistance Act of 1961, as amended, Feb. 1995).

Here it is important to note that the legislation requires the State Department, in determining whether a state is a gross violator of human rights, to take into account, among other considerations, "the relevant findings of appropriate international organizations, including nongovernmental organizations, such as the International Committee of the Red Cross...." § 502B(b)(1). Similar language is found in § 116(c)(1). Both laws also attach considerable weight to the extent to which the particular country cooperates with and permits such organizations "an unimpeded investigation of alleged violations of internationally recognized human rights."

§ 116(c)(1) and § 502B(b)(2). These requirements cannot but strengthen the effectiveness of public and private human rights institutions that investigate and judge violations. Hence, findings—for example, by U.N. or regional human rights bodies such as the U.N. Human Rights Committee or the Inter-American Court or Commission on Human Rights—that a government has engaged in large-scale violations of human rights, should be taken into account by the State Department in preparing its reports and in deciding on the action to be taken in application of § 116 or § 502B.

Each law contains various exceptions. Thus, economic aid does not have to be terminated if "such assistance will directly benefit the needy people in such country." § 116(a). Moreover, the President may continue security assistance to a gross violator if he certifies to the Congress "that extraordinary circumstances exist warranting provision of such assistance." § 502B(a)(2). These and other provisions give the Executive Branch considerable latitude in administering the law with more or less vigor. On this subject, see, Americas Watch *et al., Critique: Review of the Department of State's Country Reports on Human Rights Practices,* published periodically. Ultimately, of course, the question of whether a government is a human rights violator within the meaning of this legislation is a matter of judgment. For one thing, it is not always easy to determine whether conditions have improved in a country to justify resumption of aid. Much also depends upon the political will of the Executive

Branch in implementing a strong or weak human rights policy. *See* Forsythe, "Congress and Human Rights in U.S. Foreign Policy: The Fate of General Legislation," 9 Hum. Rts. Q. 382 (1987); Carleton & Stohl, "The Foreign Policy of Human Rights: Rhetoric and Reality from Jimmy Carter to Ronald Reagan," 7 Hum. Rts. Q. 205 (1985); Cohen, *supra,* at 256. Efforts to force the Executive's hand by resort to the courts have not been successful due to the application of the political question doctrine. *Crockett v. Reagan*, 720 F.2d 1355 (D.C.Cir.1983), *cert. denied* 467 U.S. 1251 (1984); *Clark v. United States* 609 F.Supp. 1249 (D.Md.1985). *See* Gibney, "Judicial Failure to Enforce Human Rights Legislation: An Alternative Analysis of Crockett v. Reagan," 4 N.Y. L. Sch. Hum. Rts. Ann. 115 (1985); Griffin, "Constitutional Impediment to Enforcing Human Rights Legislation: The Case of El Salvador," 33 Am. U. L. Rev. 163 (1983).

§ 7–8. Country–Specific Legislation

In addition to the legislation of general applicability described in the preceding section, the Congress has from time to time enacted so-called country-specific human rights laws. *See* D. Newsom (ed.), *The Diplomacy of Human Rights* 229 (1986). One purpose of this legislation is to force the Executive Branch to cut off aid to a particular country to which the laws of general applicability, in the Congress' view, are not being applied as strictly as they should be. Another purpose is to focus attention on especially serious human rights violations in a given country. *See* Cohen, *supra,* at 254. Among the states thus singled out at one time or another have been Argentina, Chile, Haiti, Salvador, and so on. This legislation usually has a one-year duration, and may be renewed or extended depending upon the actions of the target government. Country-specific legislation can be very useful in complementing the laws of general applicability by providing the Congress with a more powerful instrument to compel action by an uncooperative or timid Executive Branch. Sometimes the Congress will also simply refuse the Administration's request for security assistance to a country it considers to be a gross violator of human rights. *See* Lawyers Committee for Human Rights, *Human Rights and U.S. Foreign Policy* 15 (1992).

§ 7–9. International Financial Institutions (IFI's)

The U.S. channels substantial amounts of economic aid to needy countries through international financial institutions, the so-called IFI's. These include the World Bank, the International Finance Corporation, the International Development Association, and various regional development banks. Although in most of these institutions the U.S. lacks the power to veto loans or grants to a specific country, it is a major contributor and as such has very substantial influence on the decision-making process of the IFI's. This fact explains why, once Congress began to use economic and technical aid as a lever in seeking to reduce human rights violations, it also started to look at the role the U.S. Government could play in the IFI's in promoting that same policy. See Harkin, "Human Rights and Foreign Aid: Forging an Unbreakable Link," in Brown & MacLean, *op.cit. supra,* at 15. (Congressman, now Senator, Tom Harkin was the leading advocate of the policy that introduced human rights considerations into the decision-making process of the IFI's and the principal sponsor of the legislation on the subject.)

This legislation requires the U.S. Government and U.S. representatives to the IFI's to advance the cause of human rights by using their "voice and vote" to prevent development aid from going to countries whose governments engage in gross violations of human rights. *See* 22 U.S.C.A. § 262d (1988). The test for determining what types of violations of human rights are covered by this law and how they are to be assessed mirrors the criteria contained in the legislation that has been described in § 7–7, *supra.* The same is true, as a general proposition, of the certification requirements and escape clauses. For a report on how the Executive Branch complies with these provisions of the law, see *Oversight of State Department Country Reports on Human Rights Practices for 1992 and U.S. Human Rights Policy (Hearing before the Subcommittee on International Security, International Organizations, and Human Rights, 103rd Cong., 1st Sess., March 4, 1993),* which also contains testimony by various human rights organizations criticizing the Executive Branch's performance in specific cases.

§ 7–10. The Bureau for Democracy, Human Rights and Labor

The U.S. Department of State is divided into so-called functional and geographic bureaus through which it carries on its work. Each of these divisions is headed by an assistant secretary of state (and in a few instances by an undersecretary of state). Until the mid–1970's, human rights subjects were handled by relatively low-level State Department officials working in different bureaus. As a result, human rights policy questions rarely received high-level attention within the Department and were poorly coordinated. For examples, see Buergenthal, "International Human Rights: U.S. Policy and Priorities," 14 Va. J. Int'l L. 611, 614–17 (1974).

In 1976, the Congress took the first steps to deal with this problem. It mandated the establishment of an office of Coordinator for Human Rights and Humanitarian Affairs. A year later, the Congress adopted legislation changing the Coordinator's rank to that of an Assistant Secretary of State, who would head the Bureau on Human Rights and Humanitarian Affairs. Public Law 95–105, 91 Stat. 846. By taking this action, the Congress wished to demonstrate that human rights concerns should have a bureaucratic status within the Department of State comparable to that enjoyed by other major foreign policy subjects. In the Clinton Administration this office was renamed the Bureau for Democracy, Human Rights and Labor. Public Law 103–236, § 161, 108 Stat. 402 (April 30, 1994).

The powers and functions of the Assistant Secretary of State for Democracy, Human Rights and Labor are now set out in Public Law 103–236, § 161, 108 Stat. 402. This legislation requires the Assistant Secretary to report through the Under Secretary for Global Affairs to the Secretary of State on matters relating to the formulation and implementation of U.S. human rights foreign policy. He/she is also responsible for the preparation of the human rights country reports, prescribed by § 116 and § 502B, as well as the reports mandated by other applicable legislation. The Bureau for Democracy, Human Rights and Labor has a sizeable specialized staff, which plays an important role in administering and coordinating U.S. laws and policies relating to the promotion of human rights, democracy and labor rights.

The effectiveness of the Bureau depends on the commitment to human rights of the particular Assistant Secretary, his/her bureaucratic skill and clout and, above all, the political will of the President and Secretary of State to have a strong U.S. human rights foreign policy. The attitude of the Executive Branch towards international human rights in general also influences the manner in which U.S. legislation on that subject is applied as well as the foreign policy initiatives the U.S. is likely to take. For different views on this subject, see Young, "Human Rights Policies of the Carter and Reagan Administrations: An Overview," 7 Whittier L. Rev. 689 (1985); Thyden, "An Inside View of United States Foreign Policy under the

Reagan Administration," *Id.,* at 705. *See also* Poe *et al.,* "Human Rights and U.S. Foreign Aid Revisited: The Latin American Region," 16 Hum. Rts. Q. 539, 543–44 (1994).

IV. INTERNATIONAL HUMAN RIGHTS LAW IN U.S. COURTS

§ 7–11. Introduction

As a general proposition, treaties and customary international law are the principal sources of international human rights law. To understand how American courts deal with international human rights law, it is consequently necessary to review the place treaties and customary international law have in U.S. law. U.S. constitutional law accords treaties the same normative rank as federal statutes and equates customary international law to federal common law. *Edye v. Robertson,* 112 U.S. 580 (1884); *Diggs v. Shultz,* 470 F.2d 461 (D.C.Cir. 1972) *cert. denied.,* 411 U.S. 931 (1973); *Banco Nacional de Cuba v. Sabbatino,* 376 U.S. 398, 425 (1964). *See generally* Restatement (*Third*) § 131. A treaty provision will supersede an earlier federal statute in conflict with it or any inconsistent state legislation only if it is self-executing. *Foster v. Neilson,* 27 U.S. (2 Pet.) 253 (1829). Restatement (*Third*) § 111(3). A federal statute will take precedence over an earlier treaty provision and any customary international law rule in conflict with it. Wherever possible, however, U.S. courts will attempt to reconcile U.S. law with the country's international obligations to avoid unintended conflicts. _See generally_ Steinhardt, "The Role of International Law as a Canon of Domestic Constitutional Construction," 43 Vand. L. Rev. 1103 (1990).

In sum, when an international human rights norm has become binding on the U.S. either as treaty or customary international law, it has the status of U.S. law. How that law will be applied by American courts and what legal effect it will be accorded depends on whether it has been superseded by a federal statute and whether, in the case of a treaty, it can be applied without implementing legislation; that is, whether it is self-executing. The sections that follow will look at the manner in which U.S. courts have applied international human rights law. _See generally_ Lillich, "The Role of Domestic Courts in Enforcing International Human Rights Law," _in_ H. Hannum (ed.), _Guide to International Human Rights Practice_ 228 (2d ed. 1992); Bayefsky & Fitzpatrick, "International Human Rights in United States Courts: A Comparative Perspective," 14 Mich. J. Int'l L. 1 (1992). _See also_ Lillich, "The United States Constitution and International Human Rights Law," 3 Harv. Hum. Rts. J. 53 (1990).

§ 7–12. Human Rights Treaties

Since the United States had not until recently ratified any major human rights treaty, U.S. courts have had little opportunity to consider their domestic legal effect. This situation may well change in the next few years now that the U.S. has become a party to the Genocide, Torture and Racial Conventions and to the Covenant on Civil and Political Rights. It remains to be seen, however, whether these treaties will have a significant effect in U.S. courts considering that the U.S. Senate has attached "non-self-executing" declarations to them. The answer to this question will depend on the extent to which the courts will hold that they are bound by these declarations, which is an issue that remains to be resolved and is by no means clear. *See* Riesenfeld & Abbott, "The Scope of U.S. Senate Control over the Conclusion and Operation of Treaties," Chi.-Kent L. Rev. 571 (1991). Thus far, much of the litigation in U.S. courts involving treaty-based human rights norms has focused on the application of the UN Charter.

The human rights provisions of the UN Charter have been invoked in U.S. courts on a number of occasions. The most important case on the subject is *Sei Fujii v. California*, 38 Cal.2d 718, 242 P.2d 617 (1952). Here a lower California court, relying on Articles 55 and 56 of the UN Charter, invalidated the discriminatory provisions of the California Alien Land Law. *Id.*, 217 P.2d 481 (Cal. Dist. Ct.App.1950). Although the California Supreme Court struck down the law as being in violation of the Fourteenth Amendment of the U.S. Constitution, it declared that the human rights provisions of the UN Charter were non-self-executing and that, consequently, they lacked the necessary domestic legal force to invalidate the challenged California law. For the vast literature challenging the soundness of the holding that these Charter provisions are non-self-executing, see L. Sohn & T. Buergenthal, *International Protection of Human Rights* 946–47 (1973). Although this holding might also have been challenged on the ground that a non-self-executing treaty provision reflects federal policy on the subject and that a state law in conflict with that policy must yield to it, see Zschernig v. Miller, 389 U.S. 429 (1968), U.S. courts have generally followed the *Sei Fujii* view. *See, e.g., Hitai v. Immigration and Naturalization Service*, 343 F.2d 466 (2d Cir. 1965); *Spiess v. C. Itoh & Co.*, Inc., 643 F.2d 353 (5th Cir.1981). For other cases, see Sohn & Buergenthal, *supra*, at 944–45; Lillich, "The United States Constitution and International Human Rights Law," 3 Harv. Hum. Rts. J. 53, at 62–69 (1990). See also, *Frolova v. Union of Soviet Socialist Republics,* 761 F.2d 370 (7th Cir.1985), where the court ruled as follows:

The provisions of the United Nations Charter on which plaintiff relies are Articles 55 and 56. We have found no case holding that the U.N. Charter is self-executing nor has plaintiff provided us with one. There are, however, quite a few decisions stating that the Charter is not self-executing. Indeed, a significant number of decisions have rejected the precise argument made here with respect to Articles 55 and 56. We agree with those rulings: Articles 55 and 56 do not create rights enforceable by private litigants in American courts. *Id.,* at 373–74.

Various other international agreements that might be characterized as human rights treaties have from time to time been invoked in U.S. courts. The courts have either held them to be non-self-executing or sidestepped the issue. *See, e.g., Huynh Thi Anh v. Levi*, 586 F.2d. 625 (6th Cir.1978) (finding the Geneva Convention Relative to the Protection of Civilian Persons in Time of War not self-executing); *Tel-Oren v. Libyan Arab Republic,* 726 F.2d. 774 (D.C.Cir.1984) (J. Bork, concurring) (holding that the Hague Convention on the Laws and Customs of War on Land, the Geneva Convention Relative to the Treatment of Prisoners of War, and the OAS Convention to Prevent and Punish the Acts of Terrorism Taking the Form of Crimes Against Persons and Related Extortion That Are of International Significance are not self-executing); *Linder v. Portocarrero*, 963 F.2d 332, 337 (11th Cir.1992) (declining to address the district court's finding that Common Article 3 of the Geneva Convention is not self-executing); *Doe v. Plyler*, 628 F.2d 448, 453 (5th Cir.1980) (dictum that the Protocol of Buenos Aires, amending the OAS Charter, "has never been considered self-executing"); *In re Alien Children Educ. Litig.*, 501 F.Supp. 544 (S.D.Tex.1980) (holding that article 47(a) of the Protocol of Buenos Aires was non-self-executing); *Manybeads v. United States,* 730 F.Supp. 1515 (D.Ariz.1989) (dictum that the Genocide Convention is not self-executing). *But see United States v. Noriega*, 746 F.Supp. 1506, 1525 (S.D.Fla.1990) (holding that the prisoner of war provisions of the Third Geneva Convention of 1949 were self-executing). For the indirect impact on U.S. Law of the Protocol Relating to the Status of Refugees, which incorporates by reference the principal provisions of Convention on the Status of Refugees, see Lillich, "The United States Constitution and International Human Rights Law," 3 Harv. Hum. Rts. J. 53, 64–66 (1990). *But see Sale v. Haitian Centers Council, Inc.*, 113 S.Ct. 2549 (1993) for a questionable reading of the Protocol. For a compelling criticism of this case, see Bederman, "Revivalist Canons and Treaty Interpretation," 41 UCLA L. Rev. 953, 987–96 (1994). *See also* Meron, "Extraterritoriality of Human Rights Treaties," 89 Am. J. Int'l L. 78, 81–82 (1995).

§ 7–13. Customary International Law

There is a growing body of international human rights law that can be characterized as customary international law. *Restatement (Third)* § 702. Much of that law has evolved from norms proclaimed in international human rights instruments, which have their basis in the Charter of the UN and other treaties of a universal character. *See* Chapter 2, *supra*. U.S. courts have from time to time relied on this law to grant judicial relief. The most interesting case falling into this category is *Filartiga v. Peña–Irala,* 630 F.2d 876 (2d Cir.1980), which held that the right to be free from torture "has become part of customary international law, as evidenced and defined by the Universal Declaration of Human Rights...." *Id.,* at 882. To substantiate its conclusion, the court traced the evolution of this rule from the UN Charter, the Universal Declaration and other major international human rights instruments. *See* Blum & Steinhardt, "Federal Jurisdiction Over International Human Rights Claims: The Alien Tort Claims Act after Filartiga v. Peña–Irala," 22 Harv.Int'l L.J. 53 (1981); Lillich, "Damages for Gross Violations of International Human Rights Awarded by U.S. Courts," 15 Hum. Rts. Q. 207 (1993). A similar methodological approach was adopted in *Fernandez v. Wilkinson,* 505 F.Supp. 787 (D.Kan.1980), aff'd, 654 F.2d 1382 (10th Cir.1981) (arbitrary detention). *See also Von Dardel v. Union of Soviet Socialist Republics,* 623 F.Supp. 246 (D.D.C.1985). For an interesting analysis of the attitudes of U.S. courts towards the use of international human rights law, see Christenson, "Using Human Rights Law to Inform Due Process and Equal Protection Analysis," 52 U. Cinc. L. Rev. 3 (1983). *See generally* T. Franck & M. Glennon, *Foreign Relations and National Security Law* 150 (2d ed. 1993). *See also* Bazyler, "Litigating the International Law of Human Rights: A 'How To' Approach," 7 Whittier L. Rev. 713 (1985). Subsequent judicial developments suggest, however, that the approach adopted in the Filartiga case will not lead to a wholesale application of customary international human rights law by U.S. courts. *See Fernandez–Roque v. Smith,* 622 F.Supp. 887 (N.D.Ga.1985), *aff'd sub. nom. Garcia–Mir v. Meese,* 788 F.2d 1446 (11th Cir.1986). *See generally* Bayefsky & Fitzpatrick, "International Human Rights Law in United States Courts: A Comparative Perspective," 14 Mich. J. Int'l L. 1, 18–21 (1992); Hoffman & Strossen, "Enforcing International Human Rights in the United States," *in* L. Henkin & J.L. Hargrove, *Human Rights: An Agenda for the Next Century* 477 (1994). For an interesting historical study, see Paust, "On Human Rights: The Use of Human Rights Precepts in U.S. History and the Right to an Effective Remedy in Domestic Courts," 10 Mich. J. Int'l 543 (1989).

It may well be that the recent ratification by the U.S. of a number of major human rights treaties may in time make U.S. courts less reluctant to apply customary international human rights norms. For even if the courts give effect to the Senate's declarations determining these treaties to be non-self-executing, see § 7–5, *supra*, this would not prevent them from concluding that at least some of these treaty provisions are declaratory of customary international law and applying them as such. They should now be more willing to do so than in the past because the doubts the courts might have had before concerning the specific content of a customary rule could be resolved by reference to the text of the particular treaty provision. The fact that the U.S. ratified these treaties and was bound by them internationally should make it easier for U.S. courts to adopt this approach with regard to treaty provisions that can be shown to be declaratory of customary international law. Of course, while customary international law will not supersede a federal statute, it is federal law and as such takes precedence over all state law in conflict with it. *See Banco Nacional de Cuba v. Sabbatino*, 376 U.S. 398, 425 (1964).

CHAPTER 8

NON–GOVERNMENTAL HUMAN RIGHTS ORGANIZATIONS

I. INTRODUCTION

The development of international norms, institutions and procedures for the protection of human rights has gone hand in hand with the proliferation of non-governmental international organizations (NGO's) working in the human rights fields. On this subject generally, see H. Steiner, *Diverse Partners: Non–Governmental Organizations in the Human Rights Movement* (1991). As a matter of fact, as with the chicken and the egg, it is difficult to say which came first. Some NGO's played an important role in San Francisco during the drafting of the UN Charter. There they lobbied for the inclusion of human rights provisions in the Charter and for a system that would give NGO's formal institutional affiliation with and standing before UN organs. The result was Article 71 of the UN Charter, which provides that "the Economic and Social Council may make suitable arrangements for consultation with non-governmental organizations which are concerned with matters within its competence."

Article 71 was implemented in due course by ECOSOC. The subject is currently regulated by

ECOSOC Resolution 1296 (XLIV) of May 23, 1968. It establishes a formal system that enables qualified NGO's to obtain one of three types of consultative status with the Organization. *See* Center for Human Rights, *United Nations Action in the Field of Human Rights* 31–32 (1994). The existence of this system has encouraged the creation of more NGO's, the adoption of similar consultative systems by other international and regional organizations, all of which has produced more NGO's. Today, as a result, there exist a myriad of these groups throughout the world. Some specialize in only one subject, such as human rights, health, or environmental matters; others focus either on more general interests and agendas or on particular issues of a given specialty.

Whether or not they have a formal affiliation with an intergovernmental organization, the NGO's resemble domestic pressure groups or lobbies. Human rights NGO's have played a particularly important role in the evolution of the international system for the protection of human rights and in trying to make it work. Governments which violate human rights are always eager to make sure that the applicable international human rights norms, institutions, and procedures remain weak and ineffective. The human rights NGO's provide a needed counterpoint to these governmental attitudes and deserve much of the credit for the progress that has been made in recent decades. *See* Wiseberg, "Protecting Human Rights Activists and NGOs: What More Can Be Done? " 13 Hum. Rts. Q. 525 (1991).

II. INTERNATIONAL ACTIVITIES

§ 8–1. Introduction

The functions human rights NGO's perform differ depending upon the purpose for which they were established, their resources, the geographic regions in which they operate and the nature of their membership. There are NGO's which are interested in the world-wide promotion of human rights. Others limit their activities to human rights problems in specific regions or sub-regions (for example, Central America, Africa, Asia) or to specific countries or issues. Amnesty International, the Lawyers Committee for Human Rights, the International League for Human Rights, the International Commission of Jurists, the Watch Committees, to cite but a few well-known NGO's, have world-wide interests. The Andean Commission of Jurists and the Washington Office for Latin America (WOLA), for example, are organizations with regional and sub-regional agendas.

The methods NGO's employ in the pursuit of their goals also differ from group to group. Some choose to resort to only one or a limited number of techniques or activities, be it the preparation of reports, the filing of complaints with international organizations, the promotion of international legislation, lobbying before national and international bodies, and so on. Others use all of these tools depending upon the circumstances. Some NGO's limit themselves to the protection of specific groups or to specific concerns. This is true of the Anti–

Slavery Society, the Minority Rights Group, or the International Committee of the Red Cross. Others have much broader concerns. *See generally* Weissbrodt, "The Contribution of International Non-governmental Organizations to the Protection of Human Rights," *in* T. Meron (ed.), *Human Rights in International Law: Legal and Policy Issues* 403 (1984); Wiseberg, *supra. See also* Cotler, "Human Rights Advocacy and the NGO Agenda," in I. Cotler & F.P. Eliades (eds.), *International Human Rights Law: Theory and Practice* 63 (1992).

§ 8–2. The NGO's as International Lobbyists

All major human rights NGO's have consultative status of one form or another with the UN, the Council of Europe, the Organization of American States, UNESCO and other regional or specialized intergovernmental organizations. This status permits their representatives, subject to certain conditions and restrictions, to present reports to these organizations, to be heard by their committees and commissions and, in certain cases, to affect the agendas of these bodies. *See generally* Rechenberg, "Non–Governmental Organizations," *in* R. Bernhardt (ed.), *Encyclopedia of Public International Law,* Instalment 9, at 276 (1986).

Many contemporary human rights instruments can be traced to proposals and/or drafts prepared by NGO's. *See, e.g.,* Leary, "A New Role for Non–Governmental Organizations in Human Rights: A Case Study of Non–Governmental Participation in the Development of International Norms on Torture," *in* A. Cassese (ed.), *UN Law/Fundamental Rights: Two Topics in International Law* 197 (1979); Wiseberg & Scoble, "The International League for Human Rights: The Strategy of a Human Rights NGO," 7 Ga. J. Int'l & Comp. L. 289, 294–95 (1977). The NGO's have on various occasions succeeded in getting the UN Commission on Human Rights, its Sub–Commission for the Prevention of Discrimination and Protection of Minorities and other UN bodies to focus on specific human rights violations, which they would otherwise not have done. The NGO's also deserve a great deal of credit for the creation by the UN and its Specialized Agencies of institutions and procedures for dealing with human rights violations. This has been accomplished by NGO's through their written and oral interventions in the proceedings of these bodies and by lobbying key representatives and delegations. *See, e.g.,* Clark, "The International League for Human Rights and South West Africa, 1947–1957: The Human Rights NGO as Catalyst in the International Legal Process," 3 Hum. Rts. Q. 101 (1981); Steiner, *supra*, at 62. For the important role played by one such NGO, see H.B. Tolley, Jr., *The International Commission of Jurists: Global Advocates for Human Rights* (1994).

In recent years, some NGO's have also contributed significantly to the strengthening of the reporting systems that have been established under various human rights treaties. Thus, for example, the International Covenants on Human Rights and the International Convention on the Elimination of all

Forms of Racial Discrimination require the States Parties to file periodic reports indicating what action they have taken to comply with their obligations under these treaties. These reports are examined by special committees which these conventions created. See, Chapter II, *supra*. As a rule, these committees lack the power to investigate the veracity of the claims made in the reports which the states submit. They are usually also not empowered to hear witnesses or to request information from sources other than the state representatives, who are heard when their country's report is discussed by the committee. On that occasion committee members are permitted to ask the state representatives questions about the contents of their reports. The restraints under which these committees operate make reliable fact-finding difficult. This has prompted a number of NGO's to prepare their own country reports. Their findings are then passed on to any interested committee members prior to its meetings with the representatives of the reporting state. The information supplied by the NGO's enables the members to probe the veracity of the state reports and to get material into the record that does not appear in the state reports. *See generally* Coliver, "International Reporting Procedures," *in* H. Hannum (ed.), *Guide to International Human Rights Practice* 173 (2d ed. 1992); Posner, "The Establishment of the Right of Nongovernmental Human Rights Groups to Operate," *in* L. Henkin & J.L. Hargrove (eds.), *Human Rights: An Agenda for the Next Century* 405 (1994).

§ 8–3.   The NGO's and International Judicial and Quasi-judicial Proceedings

Over the past five decades, many intergovernmental organizations have established legal mechanisms that permit individuals, groups and non-governmental organizations to file human rights complaints.   On this subject generally, *see* Shelton, "The Participation of Nongovernmental Organizations in International Judicial Proceedings," 88 Am. J. Int'l L. 611 (1994).   NGO's have invoked these procedures and filed numerous complaints, particularly in cases involving allegations of massive violations of human rights.   Here NGO's are often in a much better position than individuals to gather reliable information and to prepare the necessary legal documentation.

NGO's have filed many complaints with the Inter–American Commission on Human Rights, both under the American Convention and under the OAS Charter-based petition system.   Thus, for example, a decision by the Inter–American Commission on Human Rights holding that the U.S. had violated the right to life by permitting the execution of minors originated from a complaint filed by the American Civil Liberties Union and the International Human Rights Law Group.   Case No. 9647 (United States), Resolution No. 3/87, *Annual Report of the Inter–American Commission on Human Rights 1986–1987*, OEA/Ser.L/V/II.71, doc.9, rev.1, at 147 (1987).   This is also true of various cases that have reached the Inter–American Court of Human Rights either in the form of requests for advisory opinions or contentious cases. The Court has permitted NGO's to file *amicus curiae* briefs in advisory proceedings, and a number of them have done so regularly. *See, e.g.,* Advisory Opinion on Restrictions to the Death Penalty, OC–3/83 of Sept. 8, 1983, Inter–American Court of Human Rights, Series A: Judgments and Opinions, No. 3, para.5 (1983). *See also* Shelton, *supra,* at 638–39.

In three contentious cases that were referred to the Inter–American Court by the Inter–American Commission in 1986, the latter invited the lawyers of the NGO's which had originally filed the cases to join its legal team before the Court. *Annual Report of the Inter–American Commission on Human Rights 1986–1987,* OAS/Ser.L/V/II.71, doc.9, rev.1, at 25–26 (1987). These cases are interesting for yet another reason: they demonstrate how national and international NGO's can cooperate in certain circumstances. Here a national NGO—the Honduran Human Rights Commission—first brought the cases to the attention of the Commission. Thereafter the Honduran group asked an international NGO with offices in Washington—Americas Watch—to assist it. The latter's lawyers then stepped in to handle the cases before the Commission. When the Commission referred the cases to the Court, the Commission asked the NGO lawyers to join its legal team, which they did. *Id.,* at 26. On the role these lawyers performed in these cases, see Grossman, "Disappearances in Honduras: The Need for Direct Victim Representation in Human Rights Litigation," 15 Hastings L. Int'l & Comp. L.

Rev. 363, 378–82 (1992). The Commission now routinely resorts to this practice.

Human rights NGO's have also pioneered the practice of using distinguished foreign lawyers or judges as observers at trials of individuals who have been charged with or appear to be tried for political offenses. Amnesty International and the International Commission of Jurists try to make frequent use of trial observers in order to ensure due process of law for the accused. See, for example, the annual reports of Amnesty International. The mere presence at such trials of foreign lawyers acting as trial observers has tended to prevent some abuses; at times it has even produced acquittals.

A related practice, utilized with considerable success—particularly by the International Committee of the Red Cross—consists of inspections of prisons and detention centers for political prisoners. *See* § 6–7, *supra*. The ICRC attempts to ensure that those in detention are treated humanely and that they are provided with medical services and other basic necessities. Other NGO's have carried out important *in loco* investigations of human rights violations for use by intergovernmental human rights organizations and international tribunals. *See, e.g,* International Human Rights Law Group, *No Justice, No Peace: Accountability for Rape and Gender–Based Violence in the Former Yugoslavia* (1993).

III. NATIONAL ACTIVITIES

§ 8–4. Introduction

The policies governments adopt in confronting specific violations of human rights being committed in other countries are made on the national level. The same is true of the policies that determine what powers governments are willing to confer on international organizations to enable them to deal with such violations. National political consider- ations also affect governmental decisions whether to ratify human rights treaties or what methods, na- tional or international, should be employed to pro- mote respect for human rights abroad. All of these and related issues must be addressed by a country's human rights foreign policy. *See* Chapter 7, *supra*. Decisions affecting the formulation and execution of these policies are as much subject to various forms of lobbying as are other foreign policy decisions.

§ 8–5. Influencing Human Rights Foreign Policy

Human rights NGO's devote a great deal of time and resources to activities designed to influence the human rights policies and diplomacy of various countries. In the United States, for example, hu- man rights NGO's are very active in promoting U.S. ratification of international human rights instru- ments. *See, e.g.,* Hearing before the Senate Foreign Relations Committee, S. Hrg. 102–478, November 21, 1991 (1992) (containing the various submissions favoring U.S. ratification of the International Cove- nant on Civil and Political Rights). They advocate legislation to deny U.S. economic and military assistance to governments that engage in large-scale violations of human rights. They also monitor compliance with that legislation by the Executive Branch. To this end, they present evidence to Congressional committees, publish reports critical of Executive action, launch public information campaigns and institute legal proceedings. *See, e.g.,* Lawyers Committee for Human Rights, *Human Rights and U.S. Foreign Policy* (1992); Lawyers Committee for Human Rights, *Critique: Review of the Department of State's Country Reports on Human Rights Practices* (published annually) (analyzing the human rights country reports Congress requires the State Department to prepare).

The following description of the activities of one human rights NGO operating in the U.S. provides a good example of the different functions such groups perform:

Amnesty International U.S.A. has developed an organization of legal workers, lawyers, and law students. . . .

The Legal Support Network's activities include: litigation, public education, outreach, work for lawyers who are victims of human rights abuses, research and work for the ratification of human rights treaties.

Hoffman, "The Legal Support Network," 1 Amnesty International U.S.A. (Legal Support Newsletter 1, June, 1984). Similar activities focusing on legal actions are carried out by other human rights

NGO's including, among others, the Lawyers Committee for Human Rights and the International Human Rights Law Group.

Informal coalitions and relations between these groups allows them to speak with one voice on important human rights issues when that appears indicated, which gives them considerable political strength.   At times they also coordinate their research and lobbying activities to avoid unnecessary duplication and to preserve scarce financial and human resources.   Most of these organizations derive their funding from private foundations, membership dues, and fundraising campaigns.   To preserve their political independence and impartiality, which are their strongest assets, a majority of these groups refuse contributions from governmental entities or from sources that might have a political or ideological interest.

*

AUTHOR INDEX

References are to Pages

331

References are to Pages

*

SUBJECT INDEX

References are to Pages

†